America's Fatal Leap

America's Fatal Leap

1991–2016

Paul W. Schroeder

VERSO
London • New York

First published by Verso 2025
Collection © Paul W. Schroeder 2025
Introduction © Perry Anderson 2025

"The New World Order: A Historical Perspective" reprinted by permission of Taylor & Francis Ltd, tandfonline.com. "International Order and Its Current Enemies": doi.org/10.5840/jsce200424211. "From Hegemony to Empire: The Fatal Leap" © 2009 Lynne Rienner Publishers, Inc. Used with permission of the publisher. "Europe's Progress and America's Success, 1760–1850" used with permission of the publisher.

All rights reserved

The moral rights of the authors have been asserted

1 3 5 7 9 10 8 6 4 2

Verso
UK: 6 Meard Street, London W1F 0EG
US: 207 East 32nd Street, New York, NY 10016
versobooks.com

Verso is the imprint of New Left Books

ISBN-13: 978-1-80429-576-2
ISBN-13: 978-1-80429-577-9 (UK EBK)
ISBN-13: 978-1-80429-578-6 (US EBK)

British Library Cataloguing in Publication Data
A catalogue record for this book is available from the British Library

Library of Congress Cataloging-in-Publication Data

Names: Schroeder, Paul W., author.
Title: America's fatal leap : 1991-2016 / Paul W. Schroeder.
Description: London ; New York : Verso, [2024] | Includes bibliographical references and index.
Identifiers: LCCN 2024023925 (print) | LCCN 2024023926 (ebook) | ISBN 9781804295762 (hardback) | ISBN 9781804295786 (ebook)
Subjects: LCSH: United States—Foreign relations—1989- | Geopolitics—United States—History—21st century. | World politics—1989-
Classification: LCC E895 .S37 2024 (print) | LCC E895 (ebook) | DDC 327.73009/05—dc23/eng/20240603
LC record available at https://lccn.loc.gov/2024023925
LC ebook record available at https://lccn.loc.gov/2024023926

Typeset in Sabon by Biblichor Ltd, Scotland
Printed and bound by CPI Group (UK) Ltd, Croydon CR0 4YY

Contents

Introduction
Perry Anderson vii

PART I

1. A Just, Unnecessary War 3
2. The New World Order: A Historical Perspective 21

PART II

3. The Risks of Victory: An Historian's Provocation 51
4. The Case against Preemptive War 74
5. A Papier-Maché Fortress 97
6. International Order and Its Current Enemies 109
7. For Shame 120
8. Misreading the 9/11 Report 125
9. The War Bin Laden Wanted 132
10. Liberating Ourselves 145
11. Mirror, Mirror on the War 164
12. Open Fire 183

13. Leave or Lose 207
14. From Hegemony to Empire: The Fatal Leap 212

PART III

15. Europe's Progress and America's Success 249
16. An Organized Hypocrisy 280

Sources 297
Index 299

Introduction

Perry Anderson

US foreign policy in the Middle East has never lacked domestic critics. But the wars launched in the region by the administration of the younger Bush saw a notable increase in their number and vehemence. The literature attacking, for one reason or another, the invasion and occupation of Afghanistan and Iraq grew over time with public disaffection from them. Reporters and commentators multiplied critical accounts of each. Intellectually, the criticism of greatest weight came from thinkers and scholars in the universities of the country, typically concerned with the direction of its grand strategy in the world at large. Much of this arose from specialists in international relations, formed by or working in political science departments, a few with ready access to the press, radio, or television. Among significant figures in this company can be numbered Robert Art, Andrew Bacevich, Richard Betts, David Hendrickson, Christopher Layne, John Mearsheimer, Barry Posen, Robert Tucker, Stephen Walt—all still active today.[1]

In the landscape of distinguished opposition to America's conduct abroad, as the country entered the twenty-first century, Paul Schroeder formed an exception. He did so by reason of professional background, specialism within it, and personal conviction. He was not a political scientist, unlike all but one of those

---

1 Authors of, among other works, Robert Art, *America's Grand Strategy and World Politics* (New York, 2009); Andrew Bacevich, *American Empire* (Cambridge, MA, 2002); Richard Betts, *American Force* (New York, 2012); David Hendrickson, *Republic in Peril* (Oxford, 2017); Christopher Layne, *The Peace of Illusions* (Ithaca, NY, 2007); John Mearsheimer, *The Great Delusion* (New Haven, CT, 2018); Barry Posen, *Restraint* (Ithaca, NY, 2014); Robert Tucker and David Hendrickson, *The Imperial Temptation* (New York, 1992); Stephen Walt, *The Hell of Good Intentions* (New York, 2018).

just mentioned, but a historian. Bacevich is that, too, while Hendrickson and Tucker could be accounted—as they would reckon themselves—such as well. These, however, are historians of the United States. Schroeder differed. As a scholar he was a Europeanist, not an Americanist, whose temporal range was much longer, extending back beyond the Enlightenment that produced the US to the time of the Reformation. He was a historian *pur sang* of a more classical kind. He was also a rarity of another sort in the gallery of contemporary critics of American foreign policy, as a self-declared conservative, of Christian belief. He came late to any intervention in current politics, at the age of sixty-five. But when he did, he brought a depth and breadth of historical reflection on them like no other. The result was an arresting originality of standpoint, argument, and proposal, expressed with great eloquence and from the outset singular clairvoyance. His thinking about American foreign policy, and eventually the society that produced it, was not static, however. The writing collected here traces his response to changes in these across two decades.

The book that follows is divided into three chronological sections. Part I comprises two essays written in the 1990s, when the Cold War was over and optimism about the era succeeding it was at its height. Part II consists of twelve texts published between 2001 and 2009, opening with an analysis of the attack of September 11 on the World Trade Center and the Pentagon, composed in the immediate aftermath of the American response to it, and closing with an essay on the conceptual and historical lessons of the still ongoing wars in Afghanistan and Iraq. Part III is composed of two subsequent essays, dating from 2012 and 2016, the first reflecting on the international conditions of America's uniquely smooth and sweeping path of success as a power in the world, the second on the domestic transformation of the Republican Party since the era of the Reagan presidency, and its consequences for the American political system. All these texts were punctual interventions tied to events or developments of the time, with the exception of the penultimate essay, which ends with remarks on the present but is concerned with the eighteenth and first half of the nineteenth century. The venues in which they appeared—with the same exception and two others, the first and second pieces here—were publications reflecting Schroeder's political temperament: the *National Interest*, *American Conservative*, and *American Interest*.[2]

Schroeder drafted his first political intervention, he reports, on the morning of January 15, 1991; the paradox of its title, "A Just, Unnecessary War: The Flawed American Strategy in the Persian Gulf," gives a foretaste of his ability to confound expectations of standard positions on world affairs. Two days later, January 17, Operation Desert Storm was unleashed on Iraqi forces in Kuwait, ending with their expulsion and rout by January 22. On that day Schroeder wrote to Oxford University Press, announcing completion of the work for which he was under contract that would become his signature achievement as a historian when it was published as *The Transformation of European Politics*. In March, his text on the Gulf War was released with minor revisions as an "occasional paper" by the program concerned with such topics at his university in Illinois. It attracted little attention. Schroeder opened it by explaining why a private citizen like himself, with "no responsibility for any decision, no particular forum for which to write, and no special audience to address," should feel impelled to write on the war about to be waged. If the answer was partly "as catharsis, an acquittal of conscience, a symbolic gesture," it was mainly because "largely missing from the debate was the perspective of history"—not analogies between Saddam Hussein and Hitler, or Munich or Vietnam, but serious analysis of the crisis set within "the broad history of international politics."[3] There, three great changes were ripening in our time. The first was that the success of states was coming to depend more and more on economic proficiency rather than military prowess. The

---

2 The *National Interest* was founded in 1985 and edited by Owen Harries and Robert Tucker as an open-minded conservative journal, intellectually of realist outlook. In 2005, when it was acquired by a think tank founded by Nixon a decade earlier, though retrospectively was very critical of the Iraq War, its editorial board split. Contending it was now insufficiently committed to democracy promotion, Francis Fukuyama, Samuel Huntington, and others departed, setting up the *American Interest*, a glossier periodical that ceased publication in 2020. The *American Conservative*, a more activist journal created by Pat Buchanan and Scott McConnell in 2002, was resolutely opposed to the Iraq War from the start.

3 See p. 3 of this volume.

second was that war, which in the past had yielded great gains to the victors, had become so destructive that it had ceased to be profitable in the same way. The third was the increasing reliance on consensus and law, rather than force, in the resolution of differences between states. These were very positive changes, offering the best chance of a more stable, peaceful, and just international order to come.

Saddam's invasion of Kuwait was a clear-cut act of aggression, defying these developments, which could not be allowed to stand. But the right way to do so was not a military onslaught to expel the Iraqi army from the territory it had occupied, but to blockade Iraq with sanctions cutting it off from all economic contact with the surrounding world, until it was obliged to withdraw on pain of internal collapse, since no modern state could survive in complete sequestration. That alternative would take longer than a military blitz to oust the occupier, requiring patience. Did the American people, who typically wanted quick results, really have that? If they did not, was his reply, it would mean that "as a nation we are unfit for world leadership. No people so immature and no political leaders so incapable of educating it or leading it, can be entrusted with the position and power the United States now enjoys." Fortunately, it was not so. Without attributing over-much sophistication to the American public, Schroeder expressed confidence that "forty-five years of American presence in Europe, forty in Korea, thirty or more in support of Israel, demonstrate its ability"—sensibly instructed—"to understand the central realities of international politics, gird itself for the long term, and wait patiently for results." The course he had proposed was not neo-isolationist. Avoidance of a war that was just, but unnecessary, was the best way to uphold the welcome international changes in the world of recent years. To urge it was the task of "a disenchanted loyalty, a disillusioned patriotism."[4]

Three years later, Schroeder returned to the charge with an essay dealing directly with "The New World Order: A Historical Perspective," this time in the journal of the country's foreign policy establishment, *Washington Quarterly*. The catchphrase of a new world order, used by not a few previous occupants of the

---

4   See pp. 16–18.

White House, had been broadcast by Bush Sr. at the end of the Cold War and after the Gulf War. But by 1994 indiscriminate use of the slogan by functionaries and journalists had lowered its credit, and Schroeder sought to put it on a sounder, more scholarly basis. Properly defined, it was "an international system in which the United States and like-minded friends and allies act together, preferably under the aegis of the United Nations, to preserve or establish peace by upholding international law and order against aggressors, lawbreakers, and oppressors."[5] Gratifying to American officialdom, this was clearly a formulation owing a good deal to Bush's propagation of the notion, since it assumed that the world, no longer divided by the Cold War, had become de facto unipolar. Yet Schroeder did not confine to it to the early nineties, arguing that the emergence of a New World Order (NWO) could be traced back to 1945. For since then former Axis foes had become prosperous, peaceful allies; Western Europe been integrated; Great Power wars averted; the United Nations expanded. Decolonization had proceeded and democracy had spread. This was an international order in many ways superior to the Vienna system of the previous century, whose merits his forthcoming *Transformation* would show. It emerged after World War II from a consensus among a number of states, which gradually extended beyond them, that previous forms of the power politics and recourse to violence rife in international relations in the first half of the century needed to be replaced by a new principle of interstate relations, not the couplet of compellence-deterrence but of inclusion-exclusion—that is, associations whose benefits to members made joining them naturally attractive to others, while failure to satisfy the criteria of membership incurred the sanction of exclusion from them.

Collective learning was required for a nation to understand and come to practice the rules necessary for inclusion in such associations. But this was just what Germany and Japan had done after their defeat in World War II, becoming the peaceful, prosperous democracies they are today. It was the lesson Britain and France learnt after the fiasco of the Suez expedition, when each gave up their colonies and accepted integration into the European

---

5 See p. 22.

community. It was the story of Soviet perestroika and abandonment of its socioeconomic system. Not coercion and pressure, but the gains of inclusion and costs of exclusion wrought these decisive changes. Might not the impasse of violent solutions and attraction of a durable settlement be moving Israelis and Palestinians in a similar direction? Was not the UN, too, no longer just a talking-shop but a valuable component of the NWO? True, compellence could not be just a thing of the past. There were evils so urgent they required the use of force to eliminate them, and others too deeply rooted to be undone. Gentz's adage had not lost its sharp edge—"All historic rights are wrongs, sanctioned by time"—to which the sanest response was often Metternich's advice to "outlive the evil." The current conflict in Yugoslavia was a case in point: in Bosnia, both Serbia and Croatia were ethnic cleansers, but using force against them was not the best way to bring them to their senses. Exclusion from the UN, and specially the European Community, until they gave concrete evidence of having changed their conduct toward other nationalities around them, was likely to be much more effective. Such learning took time. Some would say such a conception of the NWO did not fit the US character or political system, but Schroeder was not sure that so radical a verdict on them was warranted. Americans needed to take part in a collective learning as much as any other people, perhaps more.

Written during the early Clinton administration, at the height of Western euphoria over the dissolution of the USSR and Soviet control of Eastern Europe, when the US had never been on better terms with Russia and China, American society basked in apparent unity and prosperity, and "globalization" was the watchword of the hour, Schroeder's "New World Order" projected its optimism into an extended and improved version of the pacification it described, with the mechanisms of inclusion-exclusion now rendering resort to force in international affairs increasingly an anachronism. Retrospectively, the Gulf War could look like a fortunately brief anomaly. Seven years later, 9/11 blew this post–Cold War constellation apart. Schroeder reacted to the attentat with extraordinary balance and clairvoyance. Comparison of the assaults on the World Trade Center and the Pentagon with Pearl Harbor, events of a different order, were completely misplaced. If a historical analogy were wanted, the assassinations in Sarajevo were the obvious one. In both cases, terrorist plots by small groups of conspirators were calculated to provoke the great power they targeted into war, through which the region from which they came could achieve liberation. Austria-Hungary reacted by declaring war on Serbia, unleashing World War I; the United States by declaring War on Terror, a futile overreaction. Though, of course, neither in situation nor structure nor strength was there any similarity between the two powers: Austria-Hungary was isolated in the Balkans, ethnically divided and militarily weak; the United States was internally united, surrounded by friends and allies in a generally peaceful world, in command of an enormously strong economy and armed forces without equal.

Yet both states suffered from grievous blind spots. In the case of Austria-Hungary, besides its own myopia in not foreseeing just what a European war would do to it, the Habsburg monarchy was the victim of a general inability or indifference of the other Great Powers to see what the consequences of the forcible deletion of one of the members of their company would mean for all of them, and for the continent. In the case of the United States, the myopia was more purely national: its inability to envisage the problems it would confront if it removed the Taliban regime by force, as it clearly intended to do, and the consequences of unleashing an invasion of Afghanistan for the international system as a whole. Blind to either, it failed to foresee the probable impossibility of stabilizing any substitute government in Afghanistan, or to grasp the damage its imminent blitz on the country would do to American hegemony in the New World Order it had proclaimed—in other words, the "risks of victory," not defeat, in the Middle East. For why had al-Qaeda struck symbolic buildings in New York and DC? The answer was plain and simple. "The terrorists attacked us *here* because we are *there*"—where America was popularly regarded throughout the Arab region as the overlord of widely hated local regimes, and guardian of Israel.[6]

For a hegemony in the true sense of the word to be stable, Schroeder insisted, it had to be perceived by those over whom it

---

6 See p. 69.

was exercised as natural, invulnerable, and tolerable. None of those conditions obtained in the Middle East, where its power was felt by many as "alien, oppressive, and corrupting." It was an intrusion: "The obvious truth is that we do not belong there in the same way as we belong in the Western Hemisphere, the Atlantic, central and eastern Europe, and the Pacific." Would the campaign in preparation alter that? It would do the opposite: "*Victory in this war against terrorism will unfailingly commit us to an even more direct and intrusive hegemony than before.*"[7] What preferable course did Schroeder then propose? The scale of the blow on 9/11 should not be exaggerated. "It was not a *national* tragedy, much less a national disaster or catastrophe," but rather "a sneak punch that caught us surprisingly unprepared." The best response would be to "declare victory at the earliest possible moment and go part way home," reducing rather than expanding the US footprint in the region. Schroeder was no enemy of American hegemony as such, which needed to be saved and prolonged—where it was seen as tolerable and benign, not otherwise. Such an argument ran counter to the public mood of the moment, with its "self-pity over our loss, self-congratulation over our virtues, and calls for dissenters to shut up."[8] But it would be good sense. Americans had less to fear from the patent fanaticism of their enemies than their own latent variety of it.

Arguably the most penetrating and powerful single judgment ever delivered in what would become a torrent of commentary on the "forever" wars launched in the Middle East by the United States over the next decade, this was also the earliest, before a single missile had hit Kabul, and the most prescient. It was followed a year later by another article in the *National Interest* of a very different sort, an intellectual demolition of a much-lauded attempt at its own kind of international history, *The Shield of Achilles*, by Philip Bobbitt. The essay confined itself strictly to the book under review: whether Schroeder was aware of the background of its author, nephew of Lyndon Johnson, adviser to Tony Blair, consultant to the CIA, and leading theorist of the "War on Terror"—his sequel, *Terror and Consent*, would appear a few

---

7 See p. 70.
8 See pp. 71–2.

years later—or decided to ignore it, we do not know. If the former, the review was serendipity. It was his last contribution to the journal, most of his writing about the next American operation in the Middle East appearing in the *American Conservative*.

The US assault on Iraq started in March 2003, but that it would be launched was plain by the autumn of 2002, and in October, six months before "Shock and Awe" struck Baghdad, Schroeder published his view of it. This was an assault on a country supposedly in league with al-Qaeda, on the pretext of a preemptive war to destroy the weapons of mass destruction it harbored. In reality no one knew if it held such weapons, and the administration had produced no proof of them. The true aim of the war was regime change—to overthrow Saddam Hussein. This was not the right American way for dealing with a threat to US interests, which was the path of deterrence through sanctions and exclusion from accepted society. What should it be called? It was imperialism. He went on:

> I know full well how slippery, ill-defined, and emotionally loaded this term usually is, and how often and easily it is abused. Let me, at the risk of personalizing the discussion, state quickly the standpoint from which I make this claim. I consider myself by every standard save that of the current one-sided American political spectrum a conservative, especially in political outlook and general world view. I have no sympathy with the view that America has been historically an imperialist power. There are major imperialist chapters and aspects in its history, of course, and it was a full participant with others in the great wave of late nineteenth- and early twentieth-century European imperialism, but its founding ideology was and remains anti-imperialist, it has passed up more tempting opportunities for imperialist gain than it seized, and its overall record is more anti-imperialist than imperialist down to this day. Nor do I share the left-wing denunciation of American hegemony as per se a great menace today. It has its dangers and negative aspects, but on balance American leadership has done much more good than harm in the decades since World War II, and I want it in general to continue. It is precisely from this conservative, pro-American stance that I claim that this would be an imperialist war.[9]

---

9 See p. 92.

There was no defensible label of imperialism—which might be defined as "simply and centrally the exercise of final authority and decision-making power by one government over another government or community foreign to itself"—that would not apply to the projected attack on Iraq. It would be "an unjust, aggressive imperialist war." Nor was there any foundation for the claim that it was preemption to suppress terror before it struck. "Trying to eliminate all the possible nests and sources of terrorism through military action is like trying to kill fleas with a hammer: it does more damage to oneself and the environment than to the fleas."[10] Many nineteenth-century governments had been obliged to deal with worse terrorism than the United States now faced, and none had been so foolish as to declare war on it, which could only be a charade. What the war, once it was under way, actually meant was that of the four major dangers now threatening the NWO—terrorism, failed states, massive "global inequities and deformities," and the current international policies and actions of the US government, reflecting the outlook of a large segment of American society—while in the long run the most serious was the third, the most urgent was the last, amounting to a "frontal assault" on the New World Order. By invading Iraq, the United States had given Osama Bin Laden the war he wanted. For his aim in attacking it had been to provoke an American retaliation in the Middle East so brutal and destructive that it would undermine his real targets, the corrupt regimes in the region that did Washington's bidding and were dependent on it. What, too, did it say about so many Americans, if they failed to express any shame at the sickening abuses inflicted on captives of the US Army in the prison of Abu Ghraib, part of a Gulag Archipelago of detention and interrogation centers extending far and wide?

In his revulsion at the war in Iraq, Schroeder felt at first that however painful for him this was, he must hope that his country would fail in it, though moderately enough to allow it to change course. By 2006, he had reached a more general conclusion. In matters of foreign policy, acknowledgment of failure had often been the path to success of an unexpected kind. During the Cold

---

10   See pp. 92, 76, 94.

War, in at least four major conflicts where America could not achieve victory, acceptance of what seemed defeat had turned into ultimate success. The drive to the Yalu in Korea, refusal to recognize Red China, defense of South Vietnam, maintenance of nuclear superiority over the Soviet Union—in each case, US goals were not achieved, and compromise solutions of one kind of another, whose price was often paid by allies rather than itself, had to be reached. In each, enemies were perceived as more united and powerful than they proved to be, and once the conflicts were over, the arena and rules of the contest between the two sides changed into one where America was well placed to prevail, as the side whose political, social, and economic system was better at peaceful coexistence. In Iraq the road to such an outcome required renunciation of the professed goals of the American attack on it—regime change, democratization, delivery of Western values to the Middle East—and convocation, not by Washington but concerned states at large, of an international conference to discuss how to manage US withdrawal and civil strife in Iraq. That would be a way to put disimperialism into practical effect and convert the defeat of America's original goals into potential gains for itself and the region. Realistically, however, it had to be admitted that there was an insuperable, structural obstacle to such an outcome: the "elephant in the room" of Israel, and the forfeiting of American freedom of action in the Middle East to it. No US administration was going to challenge that.

In 2007 Washington announced a "surge"—of more troops and armor—that would put an end to Iraqi resistance once and for all. In Schroeder's view no panacea could be expected from it. Given the huge disparity between the two sides in arms and resources, success might be achieved: historically, most insurgencies petered out on their own, or were crushed with a mailed fist. But success in that sense would not mean victory for the US in the Middle East. It would simply tie the United States down further in the region, as a target for Arab anger it could not palliate and would have to be contained—during which time local troops trained to help America suppress such resistance might defect or melt away. While there was now much talk in the US of an exit from Iraq when the job was done, it was mostly—schemes of redeploying bases nearby and the like—a pretense of leaving while staying, which was to be found in both parties: witness Senators Clinton and Biden. Americans were not yet aware of how disconnected they were from the Middle East as the products of a hugely wealthy and powerful Western society, Christian and capitalist, materialist and individualist, and to boot pro-Israeli. They were not going to change that and no doubt were right not to want to do so. But all such traits disqualified them from trying to transform the Middle East in their image, not least in seeking to convert its peoples virtually overnight to a democracy it had taken the West a millennium to achieve. Looking back, in the last spring of the Bush administration, at the record of Operation Iraqi Freedom, what was the balance sheet? "Five years of scandal, crime, humiliation, and destruction": it was disheartening to repeat a verdict pronounced so many times before, knowing that it would be of no more effect to do so. Schroeder's final judgment? "One senses a ghastly inevitability about this American adventure—half tragedy, half farce and all folly."[11]

This was not quite his last word on the experience. In many ways that came in an earlier essay written for the *American Interest* prior to the surge, that would be his most striking historical reflection on the Iraq War. It took the form of an analogy between Operation Iraqi Freedom and the Dreyfus Affair in France. In the scale of events and consequences, linking the two might seem incongruous, he wrote. But in one crucial respect they were similar: each was significant for what it revealed about the human qualities of the actors involved in them, and the society in which they lived. They said something about the "essence" of each. The Dreyfus Affair, contrary to its reputation, did not endanger the French Republic. It began with a judicial error, the conviction of Dreyfus for treason, followed by a military cover-up which, when threatened with exposure, senior officers compounded with deliberately criminal actions to protect the honor of the army—bribery, intimidation, false witness, and illegal arrest of the accuser. The Republic itself was never at risk from the controversy aroused by the case. Yet what it demonstrated was a grave deficit in the moral and political integrity of the officer caste and those who rallied to it. So, too, the Iraq War

---

11 See p. 211.

was a less earth-shaking crisis than it seemed. America was in no danger from the insurgency it confronted, whose scale was restricted. The invasion that set off the insurgency was also, like the miscarriage of justice in France, a blunder rather than a crime. But the cover-ups that followed were worse than those in France, and the crimes they sought to justify or conceal were accepted by most Americans, who preferring their lies to uncomfortable truths in their self-deception became complicit with them. The US had long depended on the rule of law, and though not always respecting it, had not systematically violated it. In Iraq, however, it had not just broken but trampled on the law, thereby exposing a grave moral deficit too.

But, Schroeder went on, a deficit is not bankruptcy. Dreyfus was cleared and released, and the United States loomed anyway too large in the international order to be bankrupted. Historically, it had enjoyed an extraordinary margin of error in its foreign policy, and could no doubt do so again with a decent withdrawal from Iraq. Would that thereby close the matter? Fin-de-siècle France, the most democratic country in Europe, had survived the crisis over Dreyfus intact. But its ideals? They had found temporary relief, but exhausted by World War I, when World War II came the Republic collapsed into the moral-political disgrace of the Vichy regime, of whose leaders de Gaulle said, over-generously but accurately, that they had thought too much about the French and not enough about France—"that is, what it really stood for." Would the same prove true of America too? It might escape relatively unscathed from what it had done in Iraq, but what in the longer run of the other deficits it was running up at home—could they resemble the delayed legacy of the Dreyfus Affair? Adapting the question of Christ reported by Luke: "What will an America that took this route when the wood was green (and never rejected it as wrong) do when the wood is dry? And what will we do thereby to what America stands for?"[12]

Addressing head-on the basic conceptual and historical questions underlying all that he had written about the Iraq War, Schroeder ended his sequence of interventions on it in an essay first published in 2004, doubled in length under Obama in 2009,

---

12   See p. 182.

revolving around the difference between empire and hegemony. Empire was exercise of political control over another community, with the power to impose its decisions on it, whereas hegemony was leadership in a community not under a single authority, whose responsibility was to ensure that common decisions were reached. Empires ruled the areas they controlled; hegemons managed them. Imperial power could not be shared; hegemonic power could. The dichotomy was not airtight, but a distinction of degree—"like warm, hot, and boiling water." Hegemonies often tended to develop into empires, and empires could resile toward hegemonies. But as contrasting principles of international politics, the two were essentially incompatible.

Empires bred wars between them, and resistance to them, typically ending in failure, whereas hegemonies could achieve a type of power that was stable and secure, a kind of order that was peaceful. In the history of Europe there was a clear-cut contrast between their performance. Failed empires extended from Charles V, Philip II, and Ferdinand II to Louis XIV and Charles XII, to Napoleon, Hitler, and Stalin. Hegemons were Ferdinand I and Matthias in the Holy Roman Empire, Richelieu and Mazarin in the next century, Walpole/Fleury and Leopold II in the eighteenth century, Bismarck in the nineteenth, the United States in the Cold War. The absence of such hegemons could lead to chaos and war, like empires. In Iraq, America had opted for empire. Did it ever have a chance of success in its bid for one? If it wanted a recipe for success, all it had to do was look at Britain's imperial control of Egypt, which lasted from 1885 onward for some forty to sixty years, and recreate the same in Iraq. But by 2003 the world had changed completely: none of the conditions that had allowed the British empire to hold down Egypt without undue difficulty existed any longer. In the twenty-first century a re-edition of the same experience was not just impossible, it was unthinkable.

What then was to be done with the American forces in Iraq? The solution was to recover US hegemony by changing the goal of American power from either military victory or just quitting. The example it should learn from was Britain's alteration of course in the fight against Napoleon, from building out its empire overseas while France won one victory after another in Europe, to leading a coalition of powers capable of defeating France and securing a durable peace till midcentury. If the US could listen to the allies who had been right in warning it at the UN of where an invasion of Iraq would lead, it had a chance of becoming a responsible hegemon of the West again. There could be no certainty such a change of direction would succeed. In his more pessimistic moments, Schroeder feared the country's potential for constructive international initiatives had been compromised beyond repair; at others he still hoped that over time it could be recovered. But for that to occur, it would first have to make a clean breast of its derelictions.

On that ambivalent, somber note, Schroeder closed the register of his analysis of American foreign policy in the first decade of the twentieth century. It had been grounded throughout in an overall vision of the trajectory of international relations since the eighteenth century that saw it as a movement toward a more orderly, cooperative, and peaceful world that had just received a sudden severe shock from the US. Over the course of a decade the tenor of his judgment of American society and its public had altered. His initial confidence in the patience and good sense of his fellow citizens declined; his opinion of their leaders darkened. What did not change was the originality of his mind in thinking about events as they unfolded, or the sources of his distinctive conception of international politics, which combined a cool, hard realism with an implicit—never advertised or expounded—idealism informed by his religious background. His sensibility was a far cry from that of the chaplains of the Cold War.

The coda to his body of writing on the politics of his own time came with the historical essay he subsequently published on "Europe's Progress and America's Success, 1760–1850," setting out an argument as strikingly critical and original as anything he ever wrote, in a field to which—as he explained—he was a relative newcomer. The United States, he began, was incontrovertibly a success story—"all rise and no fall." It could be said that after Britain had cleared the way for it by defeating France and its Indian allies in the Seven Years' War, no other nation ever had such a smooth path to independence, expansion, and greatness—a record unique in scope, continuity, value of acquisitions, and absence of obstacles, all of which were won with only modest military exertions and generally mediocre military performance.

Since independence, the country had undergone no major invasion and suffered no occupation. Nor had it ever fought a major external enemy without a powerful ally, save Japan in the Pacific War—a state with half its population, a tenth of its industry, and less than that in national territory. For a century after 1815, the relatively minor and limited wars (by the standards of the continent) in Europe had each involved more fighting than all American wars from 1815 to 1917.

There were many—above all geographical—reasons for this remarkable good fortune: the two great ocean moats around the US, and the shift in British imperial strategy after 1776 toward free trade and naval control of the world's sea lanes, not to speak of the abundant natural resources in North America and unprecedented flow of immigrant labor into it. But there was also a key exogenous factor, too often overlooked, not so much a condition as a catalyst of American success. That was the emergence in Europe in the course of the eighteenth century of a new international order regulating relations between states, and promoting at the Congress of Vienna in the nineteenth century peace and cooperation among them, that afforded the United States a quasi-legal community it could join and a global environment in which it could rise without hindrance. This did not mean the success of America reproduced the pattern of progress in Europe. Violence does not necessarily have to take the form of interstate war, and there America excelled. In a period in which European powers abstained from territorial aggrandizement and organized violence, the United States—so Schroeder—exploited virtually every opportunity it had for them. Facing no foreign threat, America "carried out an unprecedently rapid and extensive course of territorial expansion marked by aggressive war, treaty violations, ethnic cleansing, coercive diplomacy, and widespread organized and spontaneous violence."[13]

It could thus be said that, internationally speaking, the US was historically "a rentier state." That is, a consumer without being a producer of progress in international order: a beneficiary of, without being a contributor to, advances under way in Europe. Understandably, it had no compunction about such a role,

---

13 See p. 273.

confident that it earned its good fortune by making what it considered its contribution to the general welfare of the time, the gift of its values and ideas to humanity at large. But if these were among conditions enabling its success, they could not last forever. Today, the tide that carried the United States so irresistibly forward to success was over. The nation was no longer exceptional, in this as in other respects.

Before he died, Schroeder spoke of one of these as the election of 2016 loomed. Domestically, a deterioration in the political life of the country had occurred with the drastic change in the GOP since the Reagan "revolution" of the '80s, which had plunged the party system into crisis. Republicans were not alone responsible for neoliberal globalization, and the rapid growth in inequality accompanying it—the Rubin-Summers wing of the Democratic Party had been the major architects of that. But Republicans had refused to do anything about it, at first ignoring the social and economic ills that ensued, then failing to propose any remedies for them, simiply insisting on the magic of unregulated markets and the dangers to property and liberty of any government interference with them. Under Obama they had instead resorted to systematic obstruction of the executive, and sabotage of normal functions of an opposition in Congress. Mitch McConnell's refusal to allow the nomination of Merrick Garland to the Supreme Court to be even considered by the Senate, supposedly in the name of not preempting the will of the electorate, was symptomatic of the "organized hypocrisy"—as Liberals had once described Conservatives in Britain—that the Republican Party had become.

The result was a general deadlock and dysfunction of the party system. Looming over it was the dire candidacy of Donald Trump as the Republican contender for the presidency, a rabble-rouser for whom "demagogue" would be too mild a term. The most urgent priority was to defeat him in November. But there were many deeper problems in American society—crises of financialized capitalism, climate change, education, child care, and more—that Republicans dismissed and for which Democrats had yet to propose any convincing answer. A healthy two-party system was a condition of addressing them, and for that to exist there had to be a normal Republican Party again, as in the past.

The essential first step forward for the country was the reform of its party and its electoral system.

The American occupation of Iraq was formally wound up at the end of 2011, in the last month of Bush Jr.'s presidency, but US troops were promptly on hand again in 2014, and still retain bases and operatives in the country ten years later, as Washington continues to exercise a measure of control, if now shared with Tehran, over the regime in Baghdad. In Afghanistan, the American occupation suffered a straightforward defeat by the Taliban, ending in ignominious scenes of flight from Kabul. But far from this exit presaging the kind of prudent—conditional and cooperative—US withdrawal from the Middle East advocated by Schroeder, the last months of Biden's presidency saw a steep escalation of American intervention in the region, this time to help Israel crush its enemies in Gaza, Lebanon, and Yemen, with the provision of weapons, bombs, missiles, even troops, in campaigns to obliterate them, and to keep Iran at bay from aiding them. Nor has the United States been less active in the European war in Ukraine, supplying Kiev with training, weapons, armor, intelligence, and oversight of military operations against Russia.

In both geopolitical theaters, America has hewed to the strategic principles adopted by the Obama administration in the light of the outcome of the invasion of Iraq. As already evident by 2013, these comprised three rules. In any conflict, reduce American casualties to a minimum—optimally zero—by use of advanced technology and airpower to destroy the enemy from afar, without risking battlefield contact; where ground combat is unavoidable, rely on proxy forces wherever possible; secure allied support in the First World to ensure international legitimacy for actions taken.[14] The novelty of the wars in Gaza and the Donbas is simply to have shown that the repertoire is strengthened if allies themselves can act as proxies, not in their own eyes, but in those concerned with strategic calculations in Washington, for whom there is no prowess like that of high-tech warriors fighting in

---

14 See Perry Anderson, *American Foreign Policy and Its Thinkers* (New York, 2015), 149–50.

defense of their country. The casualties of warfare along the Mediterranean or by the Black Sea are, humanly if not quite economically, cost-free for the population of America.

Schroeder would not have made his peace with that. It is not difficult to imagine what he might have written about the war in Gaza: he knew the hold of Israel over American policies in the Middle East. Nor about the war in Ukraine: he had warned against the expansion of NATO to the borders of Russia.[15] Not that he would have been alone in his opposition to them. Intellectually if not politically speaking, there has been plenty of each in America since the last wars started. But very little that has had the historical depth or passion of Schroeder's writing on the questions they pose.[16] America's fatal leap is not over yet.

---

15   He linked the two in the same breath—"expanding NATO to the borders of a shrunken, chaotic and humiliated Russia, or the decision to invade Iraq"; see Paul W. Schroeder, "The Vienna System," in *Stealing Horses to Great Applause: The Origins of the First World War Reconsidered* (New York, 2025), 353.

16   Compare, as striking cases of the myopia afflicting even repentant critics of US policies in the Middle East, two accounts by former officials at the highest levels of the Obama administration, each quite willing to admit their own participation in actions they now repudiate, neither with any hint of awareness of the longer-term, systemic logic behind them: Philip H. Gordon, *Losing the Long Game: The False Promise of Regime Change in the Middle East* (New York, 2020), and Stephen Simon, *Grand Delusion: The Rise and Fall of America's Ambition in the Middle East* (New York, 2023). As a critique of successive US attempts at regime change, from Iran in 1953 to Syria in 2011, Gordon's book is more radical than Simon's; as a portrayal of US policy in the region, much less so. Simon's balance-sheet begins: "Since the end of the Second World War, America's overriding purpose has been to secure two states, Israel and Saudi Arabia. Like the warp and weft of a tapestry, they weave in and out of the wider story, sometimes invisible, always indispensable." The word "Israel" does not even appear in Gordon's index, as befits a tactful national security adviser to Kamala Harris.

PART I

A Just, Unnecessary War: The Flawed American Strategy in the Persian Gulf

1991

This essay was first written on the morning of January 15, 1991, and it has undergone only minor changes since. Why should anyone write another analysis of American policy in the Persian Gulf after all the decisions had been taken, every viewpoint had been aired, Congress had debated and voted, diplomacy had failed, and war was just about to begin? Why, especially a private citizen, with no responsibility for any decision, no particular forum for which to write, and no special audience to address?

Partly as catharsis, an acquittal of conscience, a symbolic gesture. But also, and mainly, out of a feeling that not everything had been said and considered, and that what was omitted needed saying, especially during the war. One thing largely missing from the debate was the perspective of history. Not, of course, some kinds and pieces of history. On the immediate history of this crisis there was plenty, plenty also, probably too much, of historical analogies between Saddam and Hitler, or the present situation and Munich or Vietnam, but very little serious analysis of this crisis in terms of the broad history of international politics in recent decades and centuries. In the debate over the immediate question "What should we do right now?" other questions were drowned out. "Where do we and the world stand now in the light of history, recent and remote? What kind of turning point is this? What are its historic dangers and possibilities? If history is any guide, where will the decisions and actions we take now be likely to lead in ten or twenty years' time?"

These questions are not only of interest to historians of international politics like myself. They, and the possible answers to them, are relevant and important even after the decision for war is made and while war is going on. For one thing, they concern its conduct and the character of the peace to follow. For another (here I express a conviction impossible to demonstrate to skeptics, but one which long study of the history of international politics impresses on me), its history is not simply one of constant struggle for power and advantage, punctuated by frequent wars. Along with that, it is also a record of a long, painful, costly, and uneven process of learning—learning how to combine peace with reasonable security and some measure of justice, how to conceive of a viable international system, and how to define and build a tolerable world order. Whatever the root causes of war may be, one major problem of dealing with war is clearly one of know-how: how to manage international politics under the structural conditions of the existence of many actors with conflicting, sometimes incompatible, purposes, rights, claims, and needs. Constructing a viable international system is extremely difficult work, the hardest political task the nations of the world face. Each generation faces it anew, with some accumulated wisdom and technique, and even more accumulated ignorance and prejudice, and must somehow build on the one and overcome the other. The learning process always works imperfectly, and sometimes breaks down disastrously, but it must and does go on.

This essay has a purpose, therefore, even though it can make no difference in immediate events. If the conduct of international politics finally involves collective learning, then someone who has reason to believe that he or she sees where a wrong turn is being taken has a kind of duty to say so. If that person is wrong, no great harm will be done except to his/her reputation, and if right, it will contribute to the learning process.

Where History Has Brought Us

There are three great changes in international politics, the culminations of decades or centuries of development, that one can detect ripening in our age.[1] The first is the rise of the trading state.[2] This

---

[1] This essay contains many broad assertions like this with which other scholars may well disagree. I regret that both space and the nature of the essay forbid an attempt to back them up with evidence.

[2] Richard Rosecrance, *The Rise of the Trading State* (New York, 1986).

means not merely the increasing preeminence of economic factors in international politics, but the fact that the long-term existence and success of states comes to depend more and more upon their efficiency in promoting commerce rather than their prowess and success in waging war. In the seventeenth and eighteenth centuries, especially in Europe where our current international system originated, states were literally made by and for war. Only by acquiring the permanent means for war, above all reliable revenues and a strong standing army or navy or both, could a state hope to survive and prosper, and the best way to acquire revenues and develop a military establishment was to wage war successfully. In the late twentieth century, states are increasingly made by and for trade. Without abandoning their power and security functions, they depend increasingly upon the promotion and protection of commerce for their internal stability and external influence. Many examples could be cited—as successes, Japan, West Germany, Western Europe, many newly industrializing countries, and as relative failures, the Soviet Union, Eastern Europe, Vietnam, and others.

The second is closely connected the decline in the utility of military victory. One might suppose that war has always been a bloody, costly, senseless business. In a moral or religious sense, no doubt, but not in a supposedly "realistic" power-political one. Until recent times, in European history till approximately the end of the nineteenth century, successful war usually paid off. The winner could turn a handsome profit, not merely in honor, prestige, and territory, but often in terms of hard cash. Many examples could be cited, the most recent in European history being the Franco-Prussian war of 1870–71, though some colonial wars were highly profitable well after that. More than that, military victory in war could usually be thought of as genuinely solving problems, or at least solving them as much as international politics allowed a solution at all. The only remedy available for countering aggression, gaming security, fulfilling vital interests, or achieving national self-determination was a successful war.

In our time, as a consequence of many familiar developments (the exponential development of the costs and destructiveness of warfare, the increasing complexity and fragility of modern economic activity, the politization of the masses everywhere, the organization of the whole world into nominally independent states, the speed and pervasiveness of modern communications), war and military victory can no longer, in most cases, be seen as profitable, or, in themselves, an answer to problems. This does not mean, of course, that military power and its use in war have become useless and absurd, an obsolete relic in history.[3] Military power is still indispensable in international politics and inseparable from it, wars may still be necessary and justified, and military victory may still be required as a foundation for solving a critical problem. Military victory was necessary to end both World Wars and try to solve the problems that had caused them. But military victory in itself did not pay off and did not solve those underlying problems—the history of both postwar eras testifies to that—and often, military victory can weaken the victor and make the underlying problems worse (witness Britain and France in the aftermath of World War I).

The third change is harder to define and demonstrate, yet important and closely connected with the first two. It is the rise in integration and community and the increasing reliance on consensus and law in international politics. Along with the rise of the trading state and the decline of the utility of military victory, has gone a growing awareness that many major international problems cannot even be approached save on a broad international, even global level. We have become increasingly aware that individual states, regardless of their power, cannot solve these alone—the environment, the law of the sea, international trade, famine and underdevelopment, and most of the really critical problems of peacekeeping, including those of the Middle East. The world has grown and is growing together in other ways, including the pervasive penetration of modern communications, the dominance of capitalism, and the increasing acceptance of democratic elections as a form of political legitimation for governments. We see evidence for this trend in the integration of Western Europe, the eagerness of Eastern Europe to join it, the increasing usefulness of the United Nations and

---

[3] This represents, much oversimplified, the thrust of John Mueller's *Retreat from Doomsday* (New York, 1989), a valuable if one-sided book.

its agencies, and the proliferation of transnational actors in international politics.

These three changes are, in the main, very positive. They represent our best chance, not merely of survival in the nuclear age, but of a more stable, peaceful, and just international order.

Where Do We Stand Now?

Perhaps the question should be, where does all this get us? What do these assertions, some of them commonplace, some subject to serious challenge, have to do with the crisis and war in the Persian Gulf?

Quite a bit, actually. Saddam Hussein represents, as clearly as any leader can, a defiant challenge to all these changes. We should not demonize him. He is only a particularly nasty specimen of the kind of power politician common in European politics of previous centuries and far from unknown in our own.[4] What needs emphasis is not his ambition, lack of scruples, and reliance on force; these are obvious. It is the fact that, in his way, he relies on these changes in international politics, uses them for his own purposes. Like many power politicians, he despises others' scruples and inhibitions as weakness and exploits them as his opportunity. The fact that other states and peoples, especially in the West, increasingly rely on the undisturbed course of world commerce, no longer desire or believe in military solutions, and want to act in community and by consensus, is what originally made him think he could get away with his seizure of Kuwait, just as he earlier expected to take advantage of Iran's revolutionary chaos to get away with his aggression there.

Therefore, Saddam needs to be stopped and eventually evicted from Kuwait and made less dangerous. Even more is at stake here than those who have advocated the use of force against him usually recognize. We need to worry not only about his dangerous example of successful aggression, his potential leadership in

---

4 If one wants an analogy, Hitler is not the best; Saddam cannot compare with him in the scope of his ambition, the power he wielded, and the monstrosity of his ideals. But Saddam does make a pretty good Arab Mussolini.

a critically unstable region with vital oil supplies and strategic waterways, and his likely development over time of nuclear, bacteriological, and chemical weapons. We also should be concerned about the continuation, rather than the reversal, of the favorable developments of recent decades in international politics.

If, then, the common argument were true, that the only choices in our dealings with Saddam were negotiation or force, one would have reluctantly to accept the necessity of force. One would also have to face its costs squarely: not only an uncertain but perhaps high price in lives, destruction, and economic and political chaos, but also a threat to the still shaky fabric of an emerging, better and more peaceful world order. Like it or not, we necessarily run the risk in making war on Iraq of destroying the new emerging international system in order to save it.

Was that our only choice—to let Saddam undermine these hopeful advances, or to risk ruining them ourselves, and being unwillingly dragged down closer to his level, by resorting to a military solution. Or was there another way to ruin Saddam, or let him ruin himself?

What We Could Have Done

The question is this: Did the very changes in international politics already mentioned—the preeminence of economics, the nonutility of military victory, and the increased importance of international integration, shared values and notions of political legitimacy, and law—offer us a way simultaneously to defeat Saddam and to demonstrate the effectiveness of these principles in action? I think so. In fact, we started out doing it, and the great tragedy, as so often happens in history, is that our very success in doing one thing caused us to overreach, trying for something different, allegedly better but really not as good.

First, some comments on two ideas or slogans constantly used in this crisis: victory, and the use of force. By any sane definition, "victory" in international politics means not the destruction of the opponent's capacity to resist, but the achievement of one's own purposes, sensibly conceived, at a minimal cost to oneself, the general environment, the world, and even one's opponent. It was said in the eighteenth century that the goal of international politics was to do as much good as possible to one's neighbor in time of peace and as little harm as necessary in time of war. Of course, this idealistic conception was seldom, if ever, followed in practice, but now it has become a practical requirement for survival in our tight little nuclear world.

Even by such a definition, victory over Saddam would require some use of force. The claim that negotiations failed and alone were bound to fail is correct. But a great deal depends on how one conceives of the use of force in international politics. The administration has seemed fixed for some time on a concept of direct confrontation, force against force. The picture evoked by President Bush's language (a line drawn in the desert) is that of a gunfight in the American West. The whole procedure followed since November—massive reinforcements, warnings, and an ultimatum followed by the overwhelming application of force—confirms this image.

There is a better model for the use of force where it is necessary in international politics: judo. In judo, the goal is not to exert the maximum force possible directly against the opponent, but to let his own use of force throw him off balance, and then to add just enough force of one's own to bring him down and disarm him.

No one has ever presented his opponents with a better opportunity for the successful use of political judo than Saddam did last August 2. He invaded Kuwait and met a world reaction for which he was wholly unprepared. I do not suppose for a moment that the United States government lured him into a trap by having its ambassador express its disinterest in his dispute with Kuwait, but had we wanted to lure him into one, we could not have done it better. Everything he did thereafter was clearly improvised, an attempt to find some way to extricate himself with a victory, or at least without a defeat fatal to a dictator like himself.

That scramble could have told us something. Our goal from the beginning, at least our immediate one, should not have been to force Saddam out of Kuwait, but to pin him down there and make him stay, and by staying in Kuwait, gradually to undermine his armed forces, his economy, his position in the Middle East and the Arab world, and ultimately his rule. Saddam's aggression presented us with a great opportunity to prove the preeminence of economics, the uselessness of military victory, and the effectiveness of world consensus and international law, in the process of ruining him.

This was not simply a possible opening for American policy, it seemed for a short while to be the actual policy, and one pursued with skill and success. Leave aside the very interesting but essentially irrelevant question of earlier American policy toward Iraq and Saddam and the extent to which it may have helped build up Saddam as a menace and contributed to the crisis. The main point is, as even George Bush's critics admit, that everything he did for the first two months was sensible and effective—putting a defensive force in the Gulf to prevent further Iraqi aggression, mobilizing a remarkable coalition of world opinion behind the American stand against Iraq, helping make the United Nations an effective instrument of sanctions as well as diplomacy, and above all putting together by far the most airtight and powerful system of economic sanctions the world has ever seen.

At that point Saddam was not merely stopped but trapped. There was nothing he could do. Everything he attempted did him no good or made his situation worse—peace with Iran at the sacrifice of the meager gains of eight years of war, futile appeals to other Arabs, self-defeating propaganda, empty threats and demonstrations, even more self-defeating seizures of hostages, followed by their piecemeal release in a manner that gained Iraq nothing and made Saddam look ridiculous.

By the same token, the United States and its allies need have done nothing more against Saddam. We could have said with good conscience that much as we sympathized with the Kuwaiti regime and its people and condemned what Iraq had done and was doing, once the crime was done we could not liberate Kuwait except at a cost in death and destruction far greater than the suffering Kuwait had already endured. Our goal was, therefore, to ensure that Iraq would not profit from its aggression, export Kuwait's oil, import weapons and supplies, or do any of the things a would-be modem economy and military machine in a developing country must do to keep going. The first objective of the United Nations, we could have said, was not to force Iraq out of Kuwait, whether by force, negotiations, or sanctions. The first objective was to uphold the new emerging standards of international politics by exacting a suitable cost for aggression from a naked aggressor, proving to Iraq that so long as it clung to stolen goods, it could not sell either those goods or its own or buy anyone else's. What Iraq chose to do about this situation was for Iraq itself to decide. If it wished the sanctions to stop, Iraq itself would have to change the mind of the world community, convince it that Iraq deserved to come back into that community and share in its trade. The first condition of that readmission, of course, would be that Iraq evacuate Kuwait.

This would have been diplomatic and military judo. Militarily, by mobilizing a small fraction of our forces, we would have pinned down the greater part of Saddam's, and robbed him of all the sources of modern technology and weapons while we and our allies continued to develop our own. Fiscally, a minor expenditure of our own collective resources would have forced the Iraqis constantly to drain theirs. Economically, the rest of the world would have had, as it has now, plenty of oil without Iraq's, and Iraq would have had no revenues without the trade of the rest of the world. Politically, we would not have placed ourselves in the position of having to force Saddam to retreat, thereby risking making him a hero to much of the Arab world because he had the courage to defy us. We would have put him instead into the position, humiliating and dangerous to a military dictator, of having blundered into a trap not knowing how to get out.

Why This Would Have Worked Better than War

The first reason is that it would have been cheaper, simpler, more economical in resources, and more calculable. War not only brings bloodshed, destruction, and waste, but incalculable side effects. No one can tell, of course, what Saddam might have done in response to such a strategy, but we would have known what we and our allies had to do—essentially, maintain our position and wait—and we would have known that whatever violent act he might try in reply would not help him. Of course it would have taken time for the effects of this economic blockade to cripple Iraq—perhaps a year, perhaps longer. But the longer it took, the more compelling the lesson would be.

Second, Saddam would, in the end, be driven out and quite possibly overthrown, not through force applied by a superpower, making him a hero to resentful Arabs for generations to come (which by many accounts is precisely what he wants and what may well be happening in the Arab world), but by his own doing. The worst thing that could happen to him was that he be made to appear a fool before his own people. This strategy would also have had the best chance of achieving his overthrow by the Iraqis themselves. Economies cannot survive forever without key imports. War, even Cold War, cannot be waged indefinitely without revenues, modern armies and air forces cannot sustain themselves without new weapons and parts. It is notorious that Iraq's power was built up by first-world arms and technology, including some from the United States. This would cut it off. An army is more likely to follow its leader and fight in a lost cause than to let itself die on the vine in a futile one.

Third, this would achieve exactly what we want for the international system—to demonstrate the preeminence of economics, the futility of Saddam's military victory, the effectiveness of international consensus and law.

Finally, this would have left the political initiative and freedom of maneuver in the hands of the United States and its allies, while robbing Saddam of it. Any political or military response of his could have been met with further judo tactics on our part. Take, for example, the most effective political argument he has had: his claim to want justice for the Palestinians, and offers to evacuate Kuwait in exchange for an Israeli withdrawal from occupied territories or an international conference on the Palestinian question. Our answer to this transparently hypocritical ploy has been a justified but clumsy and rigid rejection of linkage and insistence on unconditional withdrawal. This has given Saddam a propaganda advantage in regard to questions where, as we must recognize, world opinion is as decisively against us as it is behind us on Kuwait.

Diplomatic judo would have avoided this. We could have replied to all Saddam's offers of a withdrawal from Kuwait, on his conditions, by repeating that our objective was not to persuade Saddam to leave Kuwait, but to establish that his aggression was unprofitable. Any bribe or payment of any kind to Iraq for leaving Kuwait was therefore unacceptable, incompatible with the objective of the United Nations. As for a conference on the Palestinian problem, we could have replied that we had long favored this in principle and under the right circumstances, and were willing to try to persuade the various parties, including Israel, to agree to one, though we could not force it on them. Iraq's actions, however, had made one thing crystal clear, so long as Saddam ruled Iraq, Iraq could not be permitted into any Middle Eastern conference, on the Palestinian question or any other. Not only had he spawned the current threat of war by another aggression and added more atrocities to his earlier ones, but also during this crisis he had repeatedly and solemnly promised, if war broke out, to attack Israel, a bystander in this quarrel. Such a deliberate profession of terrorism, such a total disregard of international law and humane standards of conduct, must disqualify Saddam himself, and Iraq, so long as he rules it, from any peace conference anywhere. A stand of this sort, pledging American support, in principle, for a conference on the Palestinian question, on the strict condition that Saddam Hussein and Iraq be excluded, would have turned Saddam's ploy to our advantage, isolating him further and making Palestinians and other Arabs see (insofar as they are accessible to evidence) that he could only hurt the Palestinian cause and damage those who associated with him.

Why (Supposedly) This Could Not Have Worked

Advocates of the use of force against Saddam naturally reject all this as wishful thinking. The objections are worth considering, but when one does, the case for judo rather than a gunfight, sanctions as positively better and more effective than military force, only gets stronger.

1. Sanctions did not work. They did not materially weaken Iraq's warmaking capacity in five months, and could not have been expected to force Iraq out of Kuwait within any acceptable time frame. Reply: of course they did not achieve the final desired effect in five months, and could not be expected to. This is like

saying that a siege failed because the fortress being starved out could still fight after three weeks. The aim of this policy would have been to wear Iraq down slowly over time; in that sense, the longer it would have taken, the better it would have worked. The object lesson would have been not that sanctions could throw Iraq out of Kuwait, but that sanctions could make the price for staying in Kuwait intolerably high.

2. Sanctions and diplomacy would not have changed Saddam's mind; he only understands force. Reply: true—and this is precisely why repeated threats of force failed to move him, and were bound to. There has always been something strange about the administration's insistence that Saddam is a ruthless, power-hungry dictator, and that therefore only the threat of force or force itself could move him. Since he is a ruthless power-hungry dictator, he knows that yielding to threats of force, especially from a foe he and his people regard as Satan, would destroy him. These threats, followed by the actual use of force, particularly by the United States, have, in a certain sense, played into his hands, enabling him to make innocent people suffer the havoc his crimes have instigated, while preserving his image as a fearless defender of the Arab and Muslim world against the infidel. We should never have wanted to change Saddam's mind, we should have wanted to change the mind of the Iraqis and Arabs about Saddam, by showing him up as a fool and a failure, a leader who committed a folly and then made his own people pay for it.

3. Sanctions could not have been sustained long enough to do the job; before they could bite, the coalition would have broken up, trade with Iraq would have been renewed, and the West would have suffered an immense political defeat. Reply: this is constantly asserted, but somewhere those who claim this ought to give some evidence. The sanctions remained to the end incomparably the most complete, effective, and universal set ever imposed. The only perceptible strains on the coalition (in France, Germany, and some Arab states) emerged at the prospect that the economic sanctions and blockade would be turned into open war. Besides, if the United States really had well-grounded fears of defection from the coalition, there were very effective measures it could have taken to maintain it, without harming or threatening any of our partners. It could, for example, have

officially declared war on Iraq, announcing at the same time that it would undertake no offensive action unless Iraq did, but merely intended to exercise its belligerent rights on the sea and in the air in order to maintain the blockade imposed by the United Nations more effectively. This would put anyone proposing to trade with Iraq on notice that by doing so it might incur the direct enmity of the United States—a sobering prospect.

4. The imposition of sanctions always implied the use of force if sanctions did not obtain results quickly. If the United States and its allies had in effect backed down by failing to follow them up quickly with force, Saddam would have emerged triumphant from this test of strength between the two sides. All the weak and vacillating regimes of the region would have leaned toward him, the coalition and its sanctions would gradually have collapsed, and the whole world would have been increasingly threatened by the leadership of this ruthless, power-hungry dictator over an area critical for the world's economy and political order. Reply: this is a strange argument. One would have difficulty taking it seriously were it not advanced by serious commentators (e.g., Geoffrey Kemp of the Carnegie Endowment for International Peace) and journals (e.g., the *Economist* of London in several issues in December and January 1990–91). What the argument does is to describe fairly accurately the unfortunate results of the massive reinforcement of American forces in the Gulf region since November, and of subsequent American policy down to January 15. These moves transformed the question by making it into a *mano a mano* test of strength between George Bush and Saddam Hussein, so that Bush as well as Saddam came to face unacceptable political losses if he backed down without a clear victory. By committing itself to forcing Iraq out of Kuwait within a short period of time, the American government committed a critical blunder, laid a trap for itself and fell into it. Sanctions neither implied further force nor required it. They implied and required patience, the simple recognition that the longer Iraq stayed in Kuwait, the worse its situation and the better that of the United Nations would be.

5. The American public could not have waited long enough for such a policy to work. The American forces deployed in the Gulf had to produce results within a fairly short period of time,

or public pressure would have demanded that the boys be brought home. Besides, an administration that tried to wait Iraq out by sanctions would soon have appeared indecisive and weak at home, like Jimmy Carter's in the Iranian crisis, and like his, would soon have been discredited and swept aside. Reply: I suspect, without any sure knowledge or basis for it, that this was an important reason for administration policy since November. Moreover, the political calculation involved could conceivably be correct, i.e., it is possible that the American people in this instance would not have been willing to wait for results, but would have demanded that its government either go in and get the job done quickly, or pull out. If one accepts that this calculation was a major reason for the current policy, and that it was backed by the best evidence available, then one has to say that this argument, as a justification of the administration's policy, is at once unworthy and unanswerable. Unworthy in that the impatience and ignorance of the American public, and the unwillingness of national leaders to guide and educate it, constitute no defensible ground for engaging in war ourselves, much less pulling others into it with us, unanswerable in that one cannot expect politicians to jump over their own shadow, to risk political suicide. (To be sure, one might wish for a willingness, over a great national and world issue, at least to risk losing the next election.)

But more must be said if this was a real factor behind American policy, even if only one among several. We need to face squarely what this means. It means first that as a nation we are unfit for world leadership. No people so immature, and no political leaders so incapable of educating or leading it, can be entrusted with the position and power the United States now enjoys. Second, we ought to understand what we are really saying when we give such a reason or excuse for American policy. We say something like this: "It is true that the United States is following a stupid and counterproductive policy, but you must understand the reason for this. The reason, in the final analysis, is that we really are stupid and unreliable, and we don't want to learn or change."

I do not believe this. Without holding a sanguine view of the American public's political sophistication, I think that the forty-five years of America's presence in Europe, forty in Korea, thirty or more in support of Israel, demonstrate the public's ability, sensibly led and instructed, to understand the central realities of international politics, gird itself for the long term, and wait patiently for results.

The Uses of Disenchanted Loyalty

Is this not all water under the bridge? Is it not time to close ranks behind the President and our armed forces after a policy has been decided by the democratic process and we have fully exercised our constitutional liberties to protest and to try to influence the decision? Must not this kind of argument sow disunity and discouragement, and make the situation worse?

First, an observation that while this argument has been made during many wars, I can think of none where it was good advice in the long run. The best statesmen and citizens during a number of wars—World War I, the Crimean War, the War of 1812, most of the Napoleonic wars, and more—seem to me to have been those in various countries who were ready to say, "We may have made a mistake in getting into this war, and even if we must fight it now, we must think of how to limit and repair the damage."

True, recognizing the mistake does not enable one to undo it. The citizen who believes neither, with some, that this war is just and necessary, nor, with others, that it is unnecessary, unjust, and imperialist, is in an awkward position. He may regard it, as I do, as something common enough in history—a war more or less justified but unnecessary.[5] One who sees his country stumble into such a war is not allowed even the psychic satisfaction of blaming it on particular villains in the White House, the Pentagon, Wall Street, or wherever, and believing that things would be better if these scoundrels were thrown out. Nor is there comfort in the reflection that the bad consequences of a just, unnecessary war, even a victorious one, will be the same as if it were unjust,

---

5 I mean just in the sense of being waged for a justifiable end, to remedy a genuine evil and prevent worse evils. Whether the war will also be just in respect to the proportionality of means to ends and the avoidance of unnecessary harm to innocent parties is another question.

merely because it was unnecessary. It is a sound maxim in international politics, above all in war, that nothing is more expensive than what is superfluous.

Yet I remain convinced that there is a special value to a disenchanted loyalty, a disillusioned patriotism, precisely in times like this. First of all, it should heighten the willingness and capacity of citizens to learn from the war, to figure out how to be smarter at international politics from here on. Neither a jingoistic celebration of American power, nor a denunciation of American arrogance and war crimes are any good for that. Second, and even more important, a disenchanted patriotism should help Americans do what is always most important with any war, which is not to celebrate its victory or denounce its stupidity and brutality or even learn how to avoid the next one, but to see as clearly as we can, the real consequences of this one and try to deal seriously with them.

Whether the war is brief and glorious or prolonged and grinding, two things can be assumed: the United States and its allies will win the war, which is far better than losing or allowing Saddam to win, and it will cause collateral damage, both economic and political, in the Middle East and elsewhere. No one can predict what the consequences will be, but they may include the discovery that we, as well as Saddam, have a price to pay for ignoring some of the new realities of international politics.

This country is likely to learn anew the long-term preeminence of economics over politics. We already owe a high bill for having pursued power politics while largely ignoring our mounting deficits, failing educational systems, lagging competitiveness, and crumbling infrastructure. A war in which we have continued that pursuit while others have continued to attend to trade will make that bill higher still.

We will further discover, in various ways, the declining utility, even the disutility, of military victory as a real solution to long-range problems. We are likely to experience what the leaders of successful military coalitions often do that those who have been rescued prove notably ungrateful, and those who have helped in the coalition expect the hegemonic leader to pay them for their services in various kinds of coin. A heavy bill for Israel's restraint has already been presented, and more will be coming. It is impossible to see how the war can make the central problem of the region, the Palestinian question and the Arab-Israeli conflict, any more soluble on terms the United States could endorse. It has deepened the chasm between Palestinians and Israeli, discouraged if not destroyed any inclination by even moderate Israel to trade land for peace, and discredited Yasir Arafat and the PLO as spokesmen for the Palestinians without raising any substitute in their place. The entry into the Israeli cabinet during the war of the small Moledet party, whose only platform is the expulsion of Arabs from the occupied territories, is an ominous sign. At the same time the war has raised popular Arab passions on the issue to new heights, imperiled moderate Arab governments, and focused Arab hatreds and frustrations more directly on the United States instead of Israel, further weakening and discrediting our government as the leader in a negotiated peace. We may remember the war as the triumph of American and United Nations arms over despotism and aggression. Most Arabs will remember it as one in which the superpower and its powerful allies destroyed a small Arab country and people trying to stand up for Arab rights, and many others may come to share that view more than ours. We deal here not with questions of right or wrong, but the fact of selective perception.

Finally, we may come to see more clearly our own need, as well as the world's, for international consensus and cooperation in meeting common problems. The original coalition in favor of economic sanctions was a remarkable example of how cooperation can be based on an agreement on a common goal and a common legitimation for action. It has thus far held up well, even in war, because a consensus on the use of force was obtained in advance and its limited goal, the liberation of Kuwait, so far, observed in practice. But no such consensus exists for what to do after that goal is achieved, and that is when the need for it will be painfully apparent. Opponents of the war sometimes claim that in Panama the United States committed an aggression as bad as Saddam's seizure of Kuwait or worse. This is a good example of the equation of unequals, and of missing the point. The lesson of Panama is not the evil of American imperialism, but the nonutility of military victory as a solution to political and economic chaos and upheaval, and the need for a wide consensus among all the main participants in a military-political action as to what the final outcome should be. More than a year after American forces easily occupied a small nearby country with which the United States had long had close ties and was familiar, most of whose citizens welcomed the Americans as liberators, the United States still has not been able to erect a stable regime and pull out. This was because there was no agreement between us and the Panamanians, other Central Americans, or anyone else on the actual goal and outcome of intervention. Iraq and the Middle East will be much worse. Not only will we find it vastly more difficult to forge a coalition and create a consensus for peace than we have for war, we will also find even close allies questioning why we are so selective in our use of force to punish aggression and end illegal occupations, and wondering how often we propose to draw the sword to save peace and build a new international order.

This is in no way an argument for neo-isolationism, neither is it Monday-morning quarterbacking or blaming America first. It simply urges that Americans recognize now that the war we are engaging in, whether or not it was a mistake, will have serious consequences, that like it or not it has been a setback for some hopeful trends in international politics, ones we and others need for peace in the Middle East and elsewhere. If we can face that possibility and talk about it soberly now, we may be better able after the war, without useless recrimination or gloating, to pick up the pieces and repair the damage, go back to promoting the rise of the trading state, the decline in the search for military solutions, and the quest for international consensus, legitimation, and legality.

2

The New World Order: A Historical Perspective

1994

The New World Order (NWO) is a term that burst onto the scene with the outrage accompanying Iraq's annexation of Kuwait and seems to have passed as rapidly from the scene as its creator, George Bush.* As a rallying cry it certainly has fallen from favor, but as a kind of conceptual shorthand it continues to engage anyone interested in the character of the post–Cold War world.

Most of the writing about the NWO has been done by policy specialists, but the rest of us should not allow them to coopt entirely the discussion of post–Cold War order. After all, they are usually preoccupied with the present, looking little beyond the immediate task of defending or criticizing specific policy initiatives by the United States on the world scene. Questions of order and disorder in the international system cannot be brought into focus in this fashion. Here the historian has something unique to offer, not narrowly in the sense of useful analogies that shed light on specific decisions, but more broadly on how to think about larger questions, issues, and trends.

This historian's perspective on the NWO debate is that the policy pundits have it wrong. A new disorder has not replaced the new world order. The historic moment has not passed. Something important remains in the discussion of the NWO,

---

* The author first wrote this essay as a Jennings Randolph Peace Fellow at the United States Institute of Peace, whose support he gratefully acknowledges. He also wishes to thank Jack Snyder of Columbia University's Institute of War and Peace Studies for his comments. The views expressed in this article are the author's own and do not necessarily reflect the views either of the University of Illinois, or of the United States Institute of Piece.

something that will help the United States and the international community to get their bearings in this period of uncertainty, to chart a course away from the anarchic tendencies of the moment and toward a world more orderly in its affairs.

The most basic questions about the NWO—does one exist? how substantial is it?—cannot in fact be answered without a fairly long historical perspective. Such a perspective is essential for understanding the nature of the contemporary international system by revealing how it developed and how it differs from previous counterparts and thus for understanding where and how to invest the intellectual and political energies of the United States, to say nothing of national blood and treasure.

This article offers one such historical perspective. Admittedly, my task is to paint a big, complex picture inside a very small frame—the short page length of a journal article. By necessity, this means omitting and oversimplifying a great deal and making a few assertions that a lengthier format would permit me to explain and defend. But the point here is to craft a cogent, albeit sketchy line of argument that makes possible some of these other tasks.

The Current Definition

The phrase "new world order" is commonly used without explicit definition, and ideas on it doubtless vary. Yet one can elicit a working definition from the kinds of measures carried out or called for in its name since the end of the Cold War, most of which involve peacemaking actions of various kinds in different world trouble spots—actions intended to preserve or restore law and order; deter, stop, and punish war, aggression, and oppression; relieve civilian suffering; and promote civil and human rights. One therefore could define the NWO as an international system in which the United States and like-minded friends and allies act together, preferably under the aegis of the United Nations (UN), to preserve or establish peace by upholding international law and order against aggressors, lawbreakers, and oppressors. The definition, if the NWO is to survive and work, implies that the international community in some cases will have to proceed beyond persuasion, mediation, and conciliation to deterrence and compellence, that is, the use of force, to make certain actors stop certain actions and perform others. Again, this fits common usage. According to many, including former President Bush, the NWO was founded by the Persian Gulf War, a UN-sanctioned collective war against Iraqi aggression. Actions taken since by the United States and other states in Iraq and Somalia, like those often proposed in regard to Bosnia, involve the use of armed force. Coercive actions against other supposed aggressors and lawbreakers are often urged in the name of the NWO, and the humanitarian and prudential arguments used in favor of such measures assume that there is an NWO that mandates such peacemaking actions by the international community.

Few Americans condemn the idea of such an NWO on principle or oppose all US participation in international efforts to promote peace and humanitarian causes. Disagreement arises, however, over using force (especially US force) to uphold the NWO, namely, to bring supposed aggressors and lawbreakers into line with some law or code of international conduct supposedly set by the international community through compellence and deterrence. Often the concerns are practical (the operation's sustainability, limits, chances of success, costs, risks, precedents, unintended consequences, etc.). But other challenges go to issues of principle. Who is to decide who is right among the parties in conflict, and by what right or principle? What gives UN resolutions the sanctity and force of law? Why should some resolutions be rigorously enforced and others not, some international crimes punished and others ignored?

Thus Americans may agree tacitly on the definition of the NWO, but sharply disagree over its reality, practicability, and desirability. The split can be seen as one between "idealists" and "realists" (by which I do not mean the two schools in international relations theory, but simply those who believe that certain norms, rules, and laws can and should be enforced in international relations, as opposed to those who believe that conflicting state interests and balance of power politics still prevail). Idealists, noting the spread of civil, ethnic, and interstate conflict in the world since the end of the Cold War, argue that a failure now to uphold the rule of law in critical areas will encourage lawlessness and aggression, undermine the NWO, ruin a historic opportunity to promote peace and justice, and promote new violence and conflict throughout the world. Realists, recognizing the same world trends, stress different problems and dangers—the difficulties, risks, and unpredictable consequences of intervention, the limited resources of the United States and its allies and their frequent divergences of views and interests, the shaky juridical basis and controversial nature of claims about international law and justice, and so on. This leads them to an opposite conclusion about the NWO: that it is a mirage, that historical patterns of power politics, national conflict, and great-power rivalry still govern world politics, and that the goals of limiting war and preserving general world peace are better served if US force is used solely for clearly defined and strictly limited US national interests.

Frequently in debates like this, key assumptions are shared by both sides without their being fully aware of it. These assumptions, left unarticulated and unchallenged, distort and stultify the debate. This essay contends that this holds true here, with paradoxical effects. Where the two sides openly disagree, on the likely consequences of acting or failing to act according to the NWO's supposed mandates and requirements, they are both correct; but where they tacitly agree, in how they define and conceive of the NWO, they are both wrong.

How Both Sides Are Right about the NWO

To start with the idealists: they are right to insist that a genuinely new and effective NWO has emerged in the last fifty years, especially the last decade, and further right in believing that this NWO, if not sustained and developed, may break down at great cost and risk to the United States and the whole international community. One need not be an international historian to see that a new era in international relations has emerged since World War II. In fact, the evidence of it is by now so familiar that Americans take it for granted and fail to see how startling it is in historical perspective. The signs include:

- the conversion of Germany and Japan in one generation from militarist, imperialist aggressors to stable, democratic

industrial giants ambitious for trade and prosperity rather than military or political power;
- the economic and political integration and permanent pacification of Western Europe;
- the dismantling of the great European colonial empires, largely peacefully and voluntarily;
- the expansion of the UN to worldwide scope, the recognition of official juridical equality among its members, and its growth in reach and effectiveness for practical peacekeeping;
- the preservation of general peace (i.e., no system-wide wars and no all-out wars between major powers) through four decades of intense ideological and political competition between rival blocs, even while new powers were emerging and dangerous regional conflicts and rivalries constantly flared up;
- the gradual development of restraints on the arms race and the cooling of ideological rivalry even while this competition went on;[1]
- the admission of a host of new or transformed states into the world community; and, finally,
- the end of the Cold War and the (until now, at least) generally peaceful dismantling and transformation of the Soviet empire.

The point is not that this has yielded a brave new world free of war and upheaval. No one claims that; few if any think that such a world will ever come about. The point is rather that accomplishments such as this were unheard of and impossible in previous eras of history. When one adds to these developments others perhaps less spectacular or more disputable but nonetheless hopeful and progressive (e.g., democratization in Spain and Portugal, the end of apartheid in South Africa, progress toward Arab-Israeli peace, the astonishing economic and political development of the western Pacific Rim, and the decline of dictatorships and rise of democracies in Latin America and elsewhere), the case for the existence of the NWO, that is, a genuine new order of international politics, becomes overwhelming.

---

1 Roger Kanet and Edward A. Kolodziej, eds., *The Cold War as Cooperation* (Baltimore, MD, 1991).

The historian's contribution to understanding this remarkable change is not to try to show that the more things have changed, the more they have stayed the same. This is the line some so-called realists take, insisting on the unchanging dominance of power politics and the primacy of the balance of power. The historian should know better. Granted that grave international problems and dangers still exist or will arise, what sensible person would exchange the current problems for those of 10, 50, or 100 years ago, or insist that they are really still the same? The international historian can indeed identify certain roots and antecedents of the NWO in history, can even (in my view) show that it is not solely the product of the last 20 or 50 years, but the climax of a long historical development stretching back to the sixteenth and seventeenth centuries.

Yet the very historical insight that sees the NWO as the fruit of a long evolution highlights the contrast between this era and the past, emphasizing how the NWO now enables statesmen to manage problems and maintain a stable international order in ways that statesmen of previous eras could only dream of. Denying the fundamental differences between the world orders of previous centuries and that of today is like denying the changes in the capitalist system over the same period.[2]

Yet, on the other side, the realist critics are right to claim that current ways of using and sustaining the NWO are not working well, and if pursued much longer may harm both the NWO and world peace. Once again special historical knowledge is not required to see this or understand the reasons; in fact, political and social science, international relations theory, practical experience in international politics, and plain common sense work as well or better. The special contribution of historians is first to point out that the idea of preserving peace and establishing a new international order through collectively enforcing

---

2 In *The Transformation of European Politics, 1763–1848* (Oxford, 1994), I argue that the Congress of Vienna transformed international politics in 1814–15, producing a new international system much more peaceful and stable than any previous one, resembling the current NWO in certain respects. I would argue just as strongly, however, for the superiority of the current NWO over the Vienna system in providing solutions to various problems that the Vienna system only dimly foreshadowed.

international law against violators or imposing certain norms of international conduct on all actors—an old idea that goes back at least to the high Middle Ages and figures in most peace plans developed in the centuries since—has regularly failed in history, proving ineffective and utopian at best and productive of even greater violence and wider war at worst.[3] Second, historians then help show why the reasons for this persistent failure still prevail under the NWO today. The central reason, familiar to all scholars, is that making international politics into a confrontation between alleged lawbreakers and supposed enforcers of the law runs counter to the core of the international system that originated in Europe between the fifteenth and the seventeenth centuries and now embraces the whole world. That system, as the term "international politics" implies, presupposes the coexistence of independent states in juridically coordinate rather than superordinate and subordinate relations with each other, each claiming sovereignty, that is, the sole right to proclaim and enforce the law within its own domains, and demanding recognition of that sovereignty from the others. Carried to its logical conclusion, the concept of the NWO as the collective enforcement of international law against transgressors fundamentally challenges and undermines this order, still the only one available, and therefore must tend to provoke resistance and heighten conflict.

This shows up in international affairs in various ways, obvious and commonplace yet often overlooked. Tactically, this concept of "law enforcement" makes international confrontations and conflicts into something like a gunfight between the sheriff and the outlaws in a movie Western. Yet for purposes of limiting conflict and promoting peace in international affairs, force, if it is unavoidable, should be used as in judo rather than as in a gunfight. The object in judo, to use an aggressor's own force combined with a minimum effort of one's own to overbalance and disarm rather than destroy him, is better not only because

---

3 See, for example, Jacob van Meulen, *Der Gedanke der internationalen Organisation in seiner Entwicklung, 1300–1800* [The idea of international organisation in its development, 1300–1800] (The Hague, 1968 [1917]), or F. H. Hinsley, *Power and the Pursuit of Peace* (Cambridge, UK, 1963).

it results in less violence and destruction, but also because a key assumption in an international system is that all essential actors should be preserved, because even an aggressive opponent, once curbed, has a necessary role to play. Psychologically, when sanctions imposed by the international community are portrayed as enforcing the law against violators, the honor as well as the interests of the accused party are impugned, giving it additional incentives to resist (for a government that cannot defend its honor often quickly loses its power) and effective propaganda to rally domestic support against outsiders. (Precisely this has happened in the former Yugoslavia and Somalia.) Strategically, this outlook pulls the international community into pursuit of a vague, almost undefinable goal (when is the law sufficiently enforced, the lawbreaker adequately punished?). This raises the stakes for the international coalition in terms of its prestige and credibility, while leaving its means of enforcement limited and the concrete interests of its various members in the quarrel divergent—a sure prescription for disunity and defections. Juridically, it encourages challenges to the legitimacy of the action that an aggressor can easily exploit. Practically, it engenders disputes over meeting and sharing the costs and burdens of enforcement, and fears that enforcing the law will result in more suffering and damage than did the original alleged violation.

All this, added to the fundamental reluctance of states to acknowledge an authority higher than themselves and thereby implicitly surrender their right to judge and defend their own cause, makes it clear that the NWO, so long as it is conceived as a collective effort to enforce compliance with international law or the will of the international community, faces grave obstacles.

The conclusion seems to represent an impasse. The NWO is real and vitally important, as its defenders insist, yet the measures it apparently requires are unworkable, counterproductive, and dangerous, as its critics claim. The way out calls for rethinking the NWO.

The NWO: Not Compellence-Deterrence, but Association-Exclusion

This rethinking begins with seeing that the NWO did not basically arise from successful compellence and deterrence, and does not mainly require these means to survive and work today. The account offered here of how the NWO was actually born and has worked is, like the whole essay, brief, oversimplified, and doubtless controversial, but it rests on well-known historical facts. The NWO as it emerged after World War II was principally the product of a durable consensus among a sizable number of major states and smaller powers, mostly West European and well developed politically and economically, that certain kinds of international conduct (direct military aggression and threats, the undermining of foreign governments by subversion, economic practices considered tantamount to economic warfare, and even some forms of civil war or internal oppression) had to be ruled out as incompatible with their general security and welfare. They formed various associations based on this consensus, designed both to deter external actions or threats of this kind and to promote a different kind of international conduct among themselves, namely, to encourage political and economic cooperation and integration, expand trade and communication, resolve conflicts peacefully, and promote broad political participation, civil and human rights, and the economic and social welfare of the member states. The various associations and institutions created for these purposes (the Western European Union, Benelux, the North Atlantic Treaty Organization [NATO], the European Coal and Steel Community, the European Community [EC], the European Free Trade Area, and others) proved over time not only durable, able to withstand external challenges and internal disintegration, but also successful in promoting prosperity, political stability, and democratic freedoms among the members themselves. As a result, these kinds of association promoting these patterns of conduct became a leading model for international politics in the developed world and much of the developing world, tending to pull other states toward it and to undermine associations and practices hostile to it.

The story is familiar; the historian's contribution is again to emphasize how new and unprecedented this development was and remains. A rough rule of thumb on alliances and associations in European international history is this: in the seventeenth century, all alliances worked almost purely as instruments of power politics (i.e., self-defense, war, and territorial expansion), even when ostensibly created for other purposes (e.g., religion or dynastic unions), and all were highly unreliable, no matter how solemnly sworn and guaranteed or expensively purchased with subsidies and bribes—so much so that it was impossible to calculate when or under what circumstances an ally was likely to defect. By the eighteenth century, alliances and associations, although still oriented almost exclusively to power politics, had grown more reliable, but not much more durable. They lasted only so long as they served the special interests of the contracting parties and so long as other more profitable alliances were not available. Thus eighteenth-century statesmen, in concluding alliances, had to try to calculate roughly when and under what circumstances an ally would defect. Nineteenth- and earlier twentieth-century alliances became much more durable, but still normally served the power-political ends of defense against enemies and acquisition of special advantages. Because they primarily served these purposes, their very durability and reliability, and the resultant rigidity of alliance systems, became a prime cause of war, especially World War I. With certain exceptions, it proved impossible in these earlier eras to erect and sustain durable, effective associations to promote the common good and general peace.[4] Only the late twentieth century has

---

4 Even the two most important exceptions really prove the rule. The German Confederation of 1815–66 was originally founded both to provide for the common defense of its members, the various independent German states, and to promote their joint welfare in various ways. Yet its leaders, especially Austria, quickly stultified its potential for advancing the general welfare, for particular Austrian reasons, and after 1848 it could no longer even serve for common defense and for reconciling power-political differences between its members, especially Prussia and Austria. Similarly, the European Concert worked well from 1815 to 1853 to preserve international peace, but mostly failed as a way of promoting a common approach to more general European political and social problems.

seen durable international alliances and associations of a new kind, directed not simply against common dangers, but also for common constructive purposes. These associations control the international conduct of the members themselves and make overt war among them unthinkable. They are also valuable enough that members hardly think any longer of abandoning them, and that outsiders want to join them rather than weaken or break them up. More than anything else, it is this startling change in the structure, purposes, and uses of international alliances and associations that makes the NWO new.

In contrast, the collective action that supposedly gave birth to the NWO, the Persian Gulf War, was not new at all. One can give the Bush administration full marks for skillful diplomacy in forming and sustaining the coalition. Nonetheless, this was normal, old-fashioned power politics, basically no different from other military coalitions against, for example, Louis XIV, Hitler, or Napoleon. Nor was it unique in its success. On Napoleon's return from Elba in 1815, in an era of much slower communications and inferior military technology, the allies formed an even wider coalition still more quickly and won a quicker, more brilliant, more complete, and more durable military success against a more serious foe.

To be sure, compellence and deterrence were not absent from the emergence and the operation of the NWO; some have claimed they were decisive in its creation. According to this view,

- united military action by a huge allied coalition destroyed Nazi and Japanese imperialism in World War II;
- military defeat and occupation plus forced democratization and economic liberalization transformed Germany and Japan;
- the threat of Soviet expansion and subversion compelled Western Europe to integrate, and US leadership, economic aid, and military protection made that integration possible;
- the Western system of political and economic freedom was able to demonstrate its superiority over communism only because NATO held the West together and kept Soviet imperialism at bay; and, finally,
- it was US military and economic superiority that defeated the USSR in the Cold War, causing its internal change of course,

the collapse of its empire, and the downfall of communism itself in rapid succession.

The case looks plausible, but it rests on turning a contributing factor or, at most, a necessary but not sufficient condition in the rise of the NWO into the main cause. Compellence and deterrence may have been indispensable at certain points in the process, but their role was still ancillary. Force cleared away obstacles to positive changes; it did not produce the changes themselves, and carried too far, it could obstruct them. In exaggerating the role played by coercive force in building the NWO, this view obscures the real creative power behind it, which was a broad process of political and cultural learning. This process of collective learning shows most clearly in the defeated enemies of World War II, but it also worked profoundly throughout the Western community, and spread eventually far beyond it.

The process involved absorbing and internalizing two lessons. The first was a widespread recognition of failure, a realization that traditional ways of pursuing vital national and societal goals would not work, had intolerable consequences, and must be abandoned. The second involved devising other kinds of processes and institutions to achieve national goals that went beyond normal power politics, and deciding to try them. In a word, the NWO emerged when a critical mass of the international system's member states and peoples learned to repudiate the old power-political methods of achieving security and welfare and worked out new and different means for doing so.

This formula, although oversimplified, fits all the major post-World War II achievements that prove the NWO a reality—both those changes now permanent and irreversible (in Germany, Japan, Britain, France, other former colonial powers, Western Europe in general, and the western Pacific Rim), those changes under way in Eastern Europe, and those apparently starting in the Middle East, Africa, the People's Republic of China, India and Pakistan, and Central and South America. In every case of such collective learning, even where compellence and deterrence—coercive force—may have played a role, it was never decisive. Germany and Japan were not really forced by armed coercion to become democratic members of a liberal capitalist world system;

rather they were brought by the hard experience of disastrous failure, including military defeat and occupation, to recognize that their former strategies of imperialism, militarism, and autarky could not make them secure, prosperous, and great. Presented with the chance to try an alternative route to security and prosperity, they chose to earn their way back into the international community by it. Many of the forcible measures originally proposed to transform Germany and Japan into safe members of the world community were, fortunately, never carried out—a sweeping partition and total demilitarization of Germany, its permanent deindustrialization, long-term control of German and Japanese education by outsiders, permanent controls on trade, abolition of the imperial office in Japan, abolition of Shintoism as a state religion, and so on.

The same point, that armed force, although needed to defeat their imperialist aggression, was not the main source of their collective learning, holds elsewhere. Great Britain was not compelled by outside force to give up its empire, not even in India. France was not forced out of Algeria—not by the Algerian rebels. France won the military war, and then abandoned the political one. The Soviet Union was not driven by force out of Afghanistan, and still less out of Eastern Europe or the various parts of its former empire, now independent. The United States was not really forced to abandon Vietnam or its military campaigns against Nicaragua and Cuba; not forced to recognize China or end the war in Korea. Change always reflected the same two-sided process of learning (even where it remained incomplete or dangerously reversible): the recognition that an old method, primarily resting on force, would not work or would cost too much or was too dangerous, and that another way was conceivable—and worth a try.

This will sound "soft" to any realist—idealistic in the bad sense, wet, sentimental, willfully ignorant of the realities of power and the need for coercion in international politics. Two comments: first, no one should allow so-called realists to define what is real and genuine in international politics, for nothing is more likely to make one miss what is deeply involved in it, and above all what is changing in it, than their kind of reductionism. Second, the coercion and pressure clearly connected with the

NWO from its beginnings and still involved in its operation are essentially different in kind and operation from power-political compellence and deterrence.

No one claims that these vast changes since World War II came about because governments, leaders, or peoples simply said to themselves, "What we are doing is not working. We need to try another way. Look at what the Americans or the West Europeans or the Japanese are doing; let's try that." Pressure and coercion were needed and frequently exerted, especially at critical points. What counts is the kind of pressure; it did not mean the use or threat of force to compel states to obey international law or deter them from breaking it. Instead, the pressure exerted consisted primarily of the members of the various associations discussed earlier combining the carrot of actual or potential membership with its attendant benefits with the stick of exclusion from the association with the attendant penalties and denial of benefits. The carrot and stick, group association with a promised payoff and exclusion with threatened denial, became the dominant form of sanctions in the development and operation of the NWO.

The psychological and political superiority of this approach over compellence-deterrence is easy to see. The association-exclusion model assumes that states will more readily perform certain desired actions or conform to a desired rule if they are either already members, or have the prospect of becoming members, of an association in which the performance and rules are jointly decided upon and upheld by the group and all share in the group benefits, and in which the main sanction is exclusion from the group and its benefits. There is a major difference between in effect saying to an opponent, or an ally threatening to defect and become an opponent, "Stop what you are doing or threatening to do, and do what we tell you instead, or we will punish you as a lawbreaker," and saying, "What you are now doing or threatening to do is against our group norms; it will eventually fail and hurt you and all of us. If you continue to try it, you will be barred from our group and excluded from its benefits; if you change your policy you can remain in the group, or keep your chance of joining it and promoting your interests within it." It is just as easy to see the tactical, strategic, and economic advantages of this approach.

Clearly this kind of pressure was most effective in promoting the NWO in the past. Germany and Japan were taught to become liberal and democratic not by force (a contradiction in terms in any case), but by the knowledge that this was the price of association with the West and its markets, military security, and respectability. Britain and France were not forced to decolonize by the United States; they were only taught, sometimes with brutal clarity as in the Suez Crisis of 1956, that they would lose the economic and political benefits of association with the United States if they did not. The United Kingdom was not forced into the European Common Market; it was merely compelled to recognize that opposing it was futile and costly, and that it could enter only on Europe's terms, not its own. Superior Western military power did not force the Soviet Union and its former satellites first to revise and then to abandon their social and economic systems. Exclusion from Western technology, markets, and other desirable goods and the knowledge that they were losing the peaceful competition with the West without them was what mainly did it. Examples could be multiplied.

This mode of international sanctions (association with benefits versus exclusion and denial) is not new in the sense of being unthought or untried earlier. The peace plans and dreams conceived in the sixteenth to eighteenth centuries regularly summoned states, rulers, and peoples (at least all the right, qualified states, rulers, and peoples) to unite in a permanent association for peace and share its benefits. The concept is therefore not new; what is new is its present effectiveness, its far greater power to reward and penalize without the overt use of force. Formerly the idea always foundered on the problem of sanctions, among other things: how to maintain the association, enforce its rules, and discipline wayward members or outlaws. Mere exclusion from the association was not enough, but the joint use of armed force against the offender (i.e., war) was impracticable and as harmful as the offense or worse. Only one previous international association, the post-1815 European Concert, succeeded for a time in keeping its great-power members and lesser states in line, not primarily by military force and threats, but by the prospect of exclusion from the Concert and the European family of states with its benefits and privileges.

But this too broke down in time, because some states, like Austria and Russia, ruined the Concert's attractiveness by tying it to their rigid and repressive purposes, while others, like France, Sardinia-Piedmont, and Prussia, developed aims in violation of the association's rules and therefore set out to wreck it, and the leaders of still others, especially Britain's Lord Palmerston, preferred balance of power confrontational tactics to the Concert strategy of grouping and joint pressure for conformity with group norms.[5]

Obviously the NWO today faces analogous dangers of ruin or repudiation. At the same time, the improved effectiveness, broader applicability, and greater durability of these nonforcible mechanisms of association and exclusion make it no longer utopian to hope and work for their indefinite duration and extension. In any case, in one sense the United States can really no longer choose in many instances to use this form of pressure or forcible compellence and deterrence instead. The very success these mechanisms have had, not only in the so-called free world among US friends and allies, but also now in Eastern Europe, the former Soviet Union, much of the Middle East, South Africa, Latin America, and other areas, has effectively deprived Americans of that choice. The fact that one country after another has opted to abandon rivalry with the so-called free world in favor of association with it makes it impossible to revert to Cold War methods, even if the United States wanted to; Americans can only try to help make that choice work for them and themselves. This is really what "the end of the Cold War" means. Even where a confrontation in some form still persists, with Cuba, China, North Korea, and elsewhere, the best hopes for change and means to promote it are those of association-benefits/exclusion-denial. Although the new methods cannot work quickly to end fighting already begun or control parties already locked in mortal combat over irreconcilable positions, as in the

---

5   See Norman Rich, *Why the Crimean War? A Cautionary Tale* (Hanover, NH, 1985); Anselm Doering-Manteuffel, *Vom Wiener Kongress zur Pariser Konferenz* [From the Congress of Vienna to the Conference of Paris] (Göttingen, 1991); Winfried Baumgart, *Der Friede von Paris* [The Peace of Paris] (Munich, 1972); and my own *Austria, Great Britain and the Crimean War* (Ithaca, NY, 1972).

former Yugoslavia and parts of the former Soviet Union, even here they are not useless. Ultimately the only kind of pressure and coercion helpful in producing a durable settlement is one that induces all parties to recognize that violent solutions do not work in the long run, and that another way is open. (Witness the recent signs of a break in the Israeli-Palestinian and Israeli-Arab impasse.) This is what the NWO sanctions of association and exclusion are designed to do; the NWO not only enables the United States to use them, but almost compels it to do so.

Some Implications for Policy

Changing the way Americans think about the NWO and its operation affects their goals, priorities, and expectations in its regard. If the NWO is developed and works, not by enforcing international law and punishing violators, but by forming and maintaining associations that reward those who conform to group norms and exclude those who do not, then the main goal of policy under the NWO should be sustaining this process of association and exclusion. This sounds like a mere truism, but it has specific, important implications. It means that the prime concern in regard to the NWO should not be how it can be used in particular problem areas to advance particular ends, values, and interests, even vital ones like peace, democracy, and human rights, but rather to make sure that the NWO itself is preserved and developed, for its own sake. The NWO, in other words, must finally be seen as an end in itself, the necessary means and condition for other vital ends and values. Americans accept this logic in other contexts. They understand, for example, that even in the hurly-burly of domestic politics they must be concerned to uphold the Constitution and the democratic process, so that politics can remain free. They know that agreements and institutions like the General Agreement on Tariffs and Trade (GATT), the International Monetary Fund (IMF), the World Bank, the Group of Seven, and others are needed not just to promote economic stability and prosperity for themselves and their friends, but to maintain a viable world economic system generally. The same principle applies to international relations. If the NWO's working principle of association-exclusion enables the international community to accomplish important tasks better and more safely than can be done without it, then that system itself deserves support as something of intrinsic and not mere instrumental value. The descriptive analysis must have prescriptive implications.

This applies a fortiori to the associations that produced the NWO and make it effective. The UN, which once could be dismissed as merely a useful talking shop or meeting place handy for certain purposes, has become valuable in its own right as an integral part of the NWO. This is even more true of the narrower associations that in recent decades have succeeded in keeping their members in line and making others wish to join them. The end of the Cold War has made them not less but more important in a practical, immediate way, at the same time presenting them with major challenges of reorientation, consolidation, and expansion. The most vital task in the NWO today is not stamping out conflict and enforcing international law everywhere in the world, but preserving and consolidating gains already made and in danger of being lost—not putting out brush fires in remote areas, but securing and expanding the homestead and the corral as a place of refuge from them. This means keeping the EC cohesive and attractive, NATO intact and functioning as a vehicle of integration and cooperation, the Japanese-American economic and political relationship stable, the progress of the Pacific Rim going, the world system of relatively free world trade working, and the road to freedom and prosperity in eastern Europe and Russia open in the long run.

If one recognizes that the NWO, thus understood, has intrinsic value and is best maintained by preserving and developing the associations and mechanisms that support it, this suggests in turn a simple, practical rule of thumb for policy. Each proposal that the UN, the EC, the United States and its allies, or some other international group should carry out some mission or measure in the name of the NWO must face an initial question: Is this action compatible with the special nature, mission, and methods of the NWO, primarily those of association and exclusion? If so, and if the action is also desirable and practical per se, then it is worth considering; if not, then not. In other words,

Americans must stop expecting and demanding that the NWO perform tasks it was not designed to do, which would wreck it if seriously tried, and then denouncing it or despairing of it when these missions are not undertaken or the effort fails.[6]

---

6 This view rejects, to be sure, the widespread condemnation of the international community for not stopping the current fighting and atrocities in Bosnia. István Deák, a renowned historian at Columbia University, for example, concluded a series of review articles on recent works on the Holocaust in the *New York Review of Books* by remarking that the undertaking had left him with "a sense of hopelessness" at the refusal of states and peoples to learn from the Holocaust—a refusal that the "international failure to act" in the face of ethnic cleansing and other horrors in Bosnia demonstrates. "Holocaust Heroes." *New York Review of Books*, November 5, 1992, 26.
Deák and others are entirely right to remind us that human beings are still capable of bestial conduct, and that many individuals and groups have refused to learn from the Holocaust and other acts of genocide, or learned the wrong things. To ascribe the ongoing tragedy in Bosnia simply to an "international failure to act," however, is a mistake. It misunderstands the nature of the NWO and its methods, as already argued; it underestimates the real, formidable obstacles to any kind of international action capable of preventing or ending this kind of warfare in this region as in many others; and above all it ignores the huge difference between the international response to these particular Balkan horrors and the historic responses to all earlier ones. Central to all previous international responses to internecine Balkan conflicts has been the primary concern of the great powers to safeguard their individual great-power interests, spheres of influence, and positions of power within the region. Even where, as often happened, the great powers did not mainly try to exploit the conflicts for selfish ends but cooperated to regulate and end them, they were always concerned to preserve a favorable balance of power.
The most obvious feature of the current international response is that this long-dominant motive has almost totally disappeared. States that formerly would never have allowed the Balkan balance to shift fundamentally against them—Britain, France, Italy, Germany, Austria, Russia—now would prefer to ignore the struggle entirely and intervene, if at all, primarily for peacekeeping and humanitarian reasons. The frequent argument for forcible intervention in Bosnia is that the conflict should be stopped to prevent it from spreading into a wider Balkan conflict that could trigger another wider war like World War I, touched off precisely in this area. The danger of a Balkan ripple effect is no doubt serious and important; the danger of another 1914 has virtually disappeared, because the general outlook prevalent in 1914 among all the powers, great and small, that the Balkans were vital to the general European and world balances has disappeared. It is one thing to emphasize the tragedy of the current situation for Bosnians and many others on all sides; another to claim that unless the international community under the NWO does something immediately

This happens repeatedly—whenever, in fact, the UN and/or some other international community or authority is called on to intervene in civil wars and ethnic conflicts, restore civil order, alleviate starvation, break illegal blockades, settle territorial disputes, impose armistices, stop governmental oppression and violations of civil rights, establish war-crimes tribunals and judge war criminals, punish countries for defying UN resolutions or supporting terrorism, and so on—all without asking whether the way the NWO actually works makes these tasks necessary or possible. Name any international evil or problem, and it is a safe bet that someone has called on the world community to solve it, and denounced it or proclaimed the demise of the NWO for its failure to do so. Much of the current cynicism and despair about the NWO derives from the inevitable disappointment of unrealistic expectations. Although, as already noted, such proposals are frequently opposed on practical grounds, little attention is given to the danger of ruining the NWO by burdening it with assignments unsuited to its mission and methods.

This perspective also calls for some faith in the NWO, patience with the process of association and exclusion by which it works, and allowing it sufficient time and steady application to work. It is unreasonable to argue, for example, that if there were a real NWO the international community would long since have acted to bring the fighting in Bosnia to an end, stop "ethnic cleansing" and other atrocities, relieve the suffering of civilians, settle the territorial and other disputes there, and establish a viable Bosnian state. Whether one believes that more could have been done earlier to achieve these ends through diplomacy or other means, or believes (as I do) that these goals were largely unattainable from the outset given the circumstances and the attitudes and aims of the various parties involved, and regardless of the inherent desirability or undesirability, feasibility or unfeasibility of these ends, achieving them is not now and never was the kind of task the NWO is designed or suited to carry out, and they must not be made the test of its existence and worth.

---

effective to fix it, the NWO is useless and the world has learned nothing. This very situation, for all its horrors, proves that the international community, especially in Europe, has learned something, changed for the better.

This does not mean that the NWO is useless or irrelevant in situations like Bosnia. It rather means that the real task of the NWO in Bosnia and the Balkans as a whole, and the real test of the efficacy of its principle of association-exclusion, still lie ahead of it, after the current conflict, which Serbia and Croatia have already effectively won, is over. The vital question, once the fighting is ended and some sort of "peace settlement" is patched up, will be whether the international community decides to forget the manner in which the newly independent states of Serbia and Croatia were founded and the integral-nationalist ideologies on which they are based, and receives them back into Europe and the world as full, normal partners. Should this happen, it would constitute weighty evidence that there is no real NWO; for this would represent the old politics pure and simple, even if it were defended as a way to forget the past and promote peace and reconciliation among former enemies. It was characteristic of previous eras that successful aggression usually paid. States could generally expect, once they had made their gains and got them sanctioned in some sort of treaty, to be treated once more as a normal member of the family of states; this is exactly what Serb and Croat nationalist leaders are counting on now. If, however (as could relatively easily be done), the international community chooses to exclude Serbia and Croatia after the "peace settlement," that is, to ban them from full membership and participation in the UN and its constituent agencies and above all from the EC, until and unless these two states give concrete evidence of change in their fundamental outlook toward other states and people, especially Muslims, Albanians, and Macedonians, this would be evidence of the NWO in operation. Moreover, this kind of isolation and confrontation would have every chance of success, given the sorry state of the Croatian economy and the still worse condition of Serbia's—success of course being defined not as the destruction of either state but a realization in both, by leaders and peoples, of what their victory and the policies of aggression and ethnic cleansing used to achieve it has cost them in terms of European and international recognition and status, commerce, technology, academic and cultural exchanges, tourism, foreign investment, international sports, and more. Such long-term pressures of exclusion-denial would have a far better chance of bringing about the needed changes in attitude and political culture in Serbia and Croatia (above all, the realization that prosperity and security in today's Europe and the world cannot be based on aggression, ethnic cleansing, and authoritarian nationalist programs) that using external force for deterrence and compellence could not produce, even in the unlikely case that force was successful in a military sense. This is said merely to illustrate how the NWO could work. Rather than prescribe a policy, it suggests an idea for one, as part of an argument that the NWO makes strategies and outcomes possible now that were futile and utopian even a few decades ago.

Some Objections

There are some likely objections to this view that deserve brief discussion, less to refute them (the answers have mostly already been indicated) than to avoid misunderstandings and correct wrong impressions.

One is that this view of international politics is soft and sentimental, ignores its harsh realities, and relies on reason and moral suasion for peace and stability. Surely, however, a view that gives the maintenance of an impersonal system and process in international politics priority over all other goals, including the promotion of justice, civil and human rights, international law, the relief of innocent suffering, and even the prevention of local wars, is not sentimental. Nor is it soft to call for excluding successful aggressor states from the international community, and making their peoples pay the heavy political and economic price for that exclusion.

Another objection is that this proposal reflects too academic a concept of how human beings learn and the world works. It expects history to teach peoples and states their errors and induce them to change, when in fact people generally learn what they want to from history, mostly the wrong things or nothing at all, and many leaders are totally indifferent to "lessons of history" and the costs of their failures so long as they can keep their state machines and essential followers under control, make the masses pay, and deceive them into blaming the outside world for their sufferings.

This is largely true, but irrelevant. This view of the NWO *does not propose to let* history teach Saddam Hussein or Slobodan Milosevic, or their peoples, that aggression does not pay. True, history left to itself can and does "teach" almost any lessons one wants it to, including the lesson that aggression does pay. This is instead an argument that the NWO enables the current generation, unlike past generations, to control the "lessons" of history in some measure, by affording it means other than external armed force, and better than armed force, to make governments and peoples recognize that certain courses fail and have negative results and that others are unavoidable and more profitable. Certainly peoples often resist learning from history, clinging stubbornly to a familiar version of the past that validates their collective image and self-view and justifies their actions. The historian Lewis B. Namier's comment that Freud's definition of neurosis, to be "dominated by unconscious memory, fixated upon the past, and unable to overcome it," is the regular condition of historical communities, points exactly to a big part of the current problem, especially in the Balkans.[7] But the strategy of exclusion and denial is a good way of helping states and peoples to get over their history, to break out of it. Repeated, long-term experience of failure is a powerful teacher, especially in teaching that one must break with one's past to have a tolerable future.

The most important criticism, however, is the charge of ineffectiveness: that the incentives and sanctions of association-benefits and exclusion-denial are too weak to produce a stable world order. They will be ineffective with dictators like Saddam Hussein or against dedicated or desperate peoples, groups, and organizations of all kinds, and will fail to stop civil wars, settle serious territorial disputes, or curb terrorism. They also act too slowly, and therefore cannot prevent or quickly stop developments too dangerous or horrible to be tolerated—aggressions like the invasion of Kuwait, the acquisition of weapons of mass destruction by rogue governments or terrorist organizations, the spread of aggression, conflict, and ethnic cleansing from one region to another, or genocide and mass starvation. In other

---

7 Lewis B. Namier, "History," in Fritz R. Stern, ed., *Varieties of History: From Voltaire to the Present* (Cleveland, OH, 1956), 375.

words, even if the so-called NWO and its methods may work with reasonably mature, developed, peaceful states, they cannot handle the real problems of a world still violent, hostile, and chaotic. These problems call for either the old instruments of individual state action and power politics, or newer ones in the form of effective forcible sanctions imposed by the international community through the UN, or a combination of the two.

Much of this is true, and has already been admitted; this essay has emphasized that there are tasks the NWO cannot do, and should not be expected or asked to. One can go further: forcible sanctions are still needed in cases where a particular evil or danger so clearly and directly threatens the general peace and the continued existence and operation of the whole international system that it must be averted promptly at almost any cost. But this does not annul the case for the NWO as presented here, or even weaken it. To believe in the reality and efficacy of the NWO does not mean to suppose that everything in international politics is new, that coercive force, including military force, need no longer ever be used, or anything of that sort. Any "new order" in history (even where this much-abused term is legitimate) is never wholly new; the term means only that a corner has been turned, a trend set, a new way of doing things become dominant, and an old one recessive. So, here, the claim made about the NWO means only (but this is a great deal) that the principal hopes and chances for durable, general, relative peace in the world (all the adjectives are important) rest now on a world order operating primarily by association-exclusion rather than deterrence-compellence. This certainly implies that the rewards and sanctions of association-benefits and exclusion-denial must be in general more effective for more of the required purposes of general world order and peace than deterrence-compellence. That claim, however, can be sustained despite exceptions.

To be sure, NWO-style rewards and sanctions will not achieve some desired ends in international politics but neither will armed force. The question of which is more useful under more circumstances for more important goals, moreover, must include an analysis of costs. A historic trend in international politics, rapidly accelerating in this century, has been the steep rise in costs attached to the use of armed force, both absolutely and in ratio to the benefits achieved, and a corresponding diminution in what it can usefully accomplish. To the old familiar escalating costs—possible failure and defeat, blood, lost treasure, diverted resources, ancillary destruction, lasting alienation and bitterness—the emergence of the NWO has added an important opportunity cost: that ends conceivably attainable by association-exclusion become impossible once force is used. Using armed force against an international transgressor like Serbia or Iraq is not a more quick and effective way of teaching it the same lessons about international association and cooperation as are intended by the tactics of association-benefits and exclusion-denial. Instead, trying to "teach" these lessons by armed force obstructs teaching or learning them by the other route at all, as current US experiences in Iraq, Bosnia, and Somalia indicate and many historical examples attest. The more the lesson desired is inflicted by external armed force, the less the experience of defeat and failure is likely to be internalized in a useful way and lead to the kind of durable change desired. Furthermore, every resort to armed force willy-nilly teaches both the participants and the bystanders the retrograde lesson that the NWO and its methods cannot be trusted in critical cases to get the job done—which becomes a self-fulfilling prophecy.

Another major element in the cost-benefit analysis is the consideration that many of the proposed aims in international politics for which NWO methods are admittedly ineffective—enforcing international law, reversing historic wrongs, stopping civil wars, imposing territorial settlements in hotly disputed cases, punishing international crimes and criminals and compensating their victims—are unattainable by any means and incompatible with any working international system.

The truth is that many evils and injustices in the world are too deeply rooted to be undone; that, as the nineteenth-century publicist Friedrich von Gentz said, "All historic rights are wrongs, sanctioned by time"; and that the only sane response to historic wrongs is often, as Prince Metternich of Austria argued, to "outlive the evil." Recognizing and accepting the NWO means, among other things, coming to terms with these commonplace truths, accepting that some goals possibly desirable in themselves cannot be pursued under it and are not worth pursuing at the cost of the system as a whole. At the same time, association and exclusion are not ineffective in achieving the goals most central and important to the NWO, namely, rewarding international cooperation and inducing aggressors and troublemakers to recognize failure and change course. To see this, one need only look at the long list of states that since 1915 have been excluded, or have excluded themselves, from the mainstream of international commerce, industry, technology, communications, travel and tourism, exchange of information, international capital, and so forth. None of these states has found peace and prosperity; most have tried or are trying to escape from that exclusion, often changing the policies the international community objects to in the attempt.

Naturally this learning process required to bring states and peoples into the NWO takes time. Important, durable changes in collective mentality and political culture cannot happen overnight—which means (to reiterate) that some threats may require a different, speedier response, despite the strictures and reservations discussed above. Yet one of the important things making the NWO new is the fact that now such changes can develop much faster and be more predictable, even controllable, than in the past. International history used ironically to illustrate the Old Testament saying that the sins of the fathers are visited upon the children to the third and fourth generation. Generations usually passed before leaders and peoples became aware of the real consequences of past policies, or even recognized past follies and crimes as such. Prussians tasted the full fruits of Frederick the Great's militarism and aggression only in Napoleon's time; only in 1919 and 1935 did the full consequences of Bismarck's founding of the Second Reich in 1871 become clear. This still is often the case, of course; but much learning has now become possible. Germans and East Europeans, for example, have judged and decided between two competing systems in one generation. In the NWO, with history accelerated and the speed and ease of communication enormously increased, it is no longer unreasonable to expect children to see and repudiate the sins of the fathers while the fathers are still around.

There is a further objection to this view of how the NWO works and should be used that, if true, cannot be answered by rational argument. It is that this way of conceiving and managing the NWO does not fit the US character and political system. It requires patience, steady attention to the long view, a willingness to wait for results, and the ability to adjust to changed reality and to accept blurred, complex, uncertain outcomes and live with them if they are the best attainable—all virtues that the US public does not possess and the US political system, focused on domestic concerns, immediate issues, simple solutions, and clear-cut moral dichotomies, neither teaches to citizens nor rewards in politicians.

It is not clear to me that so sweeping an indictment of the US political culture and its effects on international politics is justified. Americans, both leaders and the public, have over the last fifty years or so shown in some instances a striking ability to learn, adjust, stay the course, and adapt to change in the international arena—witness their support of Israel, commitment to NATO, general maintenance of free trade, and acceptance of relative failure and the limits to US power in Korea, Vietnam, and elsewhere. Yet it may be that calling on Americans to accept this version of the NWO and lead it (for who else can?) means calling for a United States different from the existing one—less prone to violence at home and abroad, less shortsighted about its own interests and those of other states, less provincial and ignorant about the rest of the world, and less insistent that in dealing with any crisis it call the shots and that, if it decides to get in, other states must help it get the job done quickly and get out. Clearly the NWO cannot work under this kind of leadership or these conditions. Even more important, this attitude on the part of many Americans is incompatible with the ongoing transformation of international politics through a collective learning process, a change in collective mentalities and political cultures involving whole nations and peoples, enabling them to adjust to each other successfully in a new order. Americans need to be part of this learning process as much as other people, perhaps in some respects more. Americans deny this cardinal need and responsibility whenever they say in effect, "The United States cannot follow this or that policy in international affairs, even though it is necessary and legitimate, because the American people will not support it and the American political system makes it impossible to sell it to them." What they really say by this is that they want to run the NWO and enjoy its benefits, but not belong to it, or change and grow with it—that they are stupid and inconsistent, and prefer to stay that way. A nation that uses that excuse for very long must sooner or later excuse itself into disaster.

PART II

3

The Risks of Victory:
An Historian's Provocation

2001

If it is true, as so many pundits rushed to tell us after the events of September 11, 2001, that everything is different, all is changed, and nothing will ever again be the same, then it follows that the study of history is unlikely to provide any guidance as we navigate our suddenly more uncertain future. But, of course, it is not true. The essential structure of contemporary international politics has not changed, and neither has human nature. That said, there are more and less intelligent ways to engage historical knowledge in service to the present.

The historical analogy most commonly heard after September 11—between the attacks of that sad day and the December 7, 1941, attack on Pearl Harbor—is worse than useless. It is not just superficial but misleading. The attack on Pearl Harbor was a surprise first blow in what the Japanese government knew would be a conventional war about power and territory. It was informed not at all by the strategy of terrorism, a strategy in which the weak attempt to goad their target into counterproductive reaction. The only thing that the attack on Pearl Harbor and the attacks on the World Trade Center and the Pentagon have in common is that both were directed against the United States.

There is another historical analogy, however, of far greater utility, as long as in using it we know the history cited well and, even more important, that we value differences as well as similarities between past and present circumstances. After all, knowledge of history can never tell us exactly what to think or do in a given situation; it only offers a richer reservoir of possibilities to think about. That more useful analogy is to the events of June–July 1914, the beginning of the Great War.

Three lessons emerge from reasoning by historical analogy from the early summer of 1914 to the late summer of 2001. The first is that a great power must avoid giving terrorists the war they want, but that the great power does not want. The second is that a great power must reckon the effects of its actions not only on its immediate circumstances, but with regard to the larger structure of international politics in which it clearly has a significant stake. The third is that a great power must beware the risks of victory as well as the dangers of defeat. If it is not careful and wise, the United States could find itself enmeshed even deeper in the Middle East and Southwest Asia than it is today, and risk generating greater prospective dangers in the process of containing smaller near-term ones.

After sketching the logic of the analogy between July 1914 and September 2001, I will pass lightly over the first two of these lessons but dwell more on the third. Let me say only before pressing on that the analysis presented here is (by temperament, not ideological formulae) a conservative one, and yet it is most likely to challenge—and perhaps even to annoy—those who think of themselves as conservatives. That this is so may bear another kind of lesson for us to ponder.

The Analogy

The easiest way to present the analogy between what happened in June–July 1914 to the events of September 11, 2001, is simply to describe what happened roughly eighty-eight years ago in language germane to what happened about three months ago.

The 1914 crisis and war resulted directly and immediately from a terrorist action: the assassination in Sarajevo, Bosnia (then part of Austria-Hungary), of the heir-apparent to the Austro-Hungarian throne, Archduke Franz Ferdinand, by a group of terrorists—mostly Bosnian students—led by Gavrilo Princip.[1] A widespread network of organizations, agencies and

---

[1] If one objects that assassinating a single political leader and potential head of state is not the same as killing thousands of civilians, the answer is that the goal of both terrorist actions was the same: to sow confusion and division within the enemy state and bring it down. Assassination of monarchs and other

governments was connected directly or indirectly to this conspiracy. In varying degrees of involvement and complicity, these included: secret revolutionary organizations both within the Habsburg Monarchy and in Serbia; the Serbian military intelligence apparatus led by Col. Dragutin Dimitrijević, which trained, supported, and armed these terrorists; the Serbian government headed by Nikola Pasic, who knew something about all this but chose to remain officially ignorant; the nationalist organization in Serbia promoting pan-Serbism and its goal of Greater Serbia, now aimed principally at the destruction of the Habsburg Monarchy and at the Serbian annexation of large tracts of its territories; the Serbian press, parliament, and political public that supported this radical ideology; and the Russian government, which supported Serbia as part of a policy of isolating and paralyzing Austria-Hungary, and whose minister to Serbia actively encouraged anti-Austrian irredentism and subversive revolutionary activity until his death just before the assassination.

The Austro-Hungarian government knew a good deal about this, though not all the details. It considered the assassination the final outrage in a series of Serbian provocations and attacks directed against the monarchy; believed that the heart of the conspiracy lay in Belgrade; was convinced by experience that combating Serbian state-sponsored terrorism and subversion by means other than military force would prove useless because the Serbian government never kept its promises; and therefore concluded that Austria-Hungary's existence as a great power required a direct attack that would, as the phrase went, eliminate Serbia as a political factor in the Balkans.

Yet one cannot simply link the whole terrorist-subversive conspiracy directly to Austria's action and thus to the war. For though several organizations and individuals were complicit to some degree in this terrorist act, the only ones directly responsible for deciding on it and carrying it out were Gavrilo Princip and his small group of co-terrorists. None of the others ordered

---

leaders was the chief method of terrorists in the nineteenth century and the blow this assassination struck to the existence of the Habsburg Monarchy was much greater than the blow struck against the United States on September 11.

it, knew precisely about it, or wanted it to happen. Indeed, though others complicit in the act also hated the Habsburg Monarchy, they opposed making war against it at that particular time. Many anticipated the monarchy's downfall with approval, but a gradual downfall caused by internal dissolution was what most had in mind and were working to promote. Some argued and hoped that such a process would not promote an international war but help prevent one. Princip and his fellow conspirators, however, consciously intended to promote an international war through their deed. Princip said during his wartime imprisonment that he had wanted a war because if Serbia won, then Greater Serbia would be achieved; and if it lost, then Austria-Hungary would annex the Kingdom of Serbia—in which case all the Serbs would be united, even though under hated foreign rule. Princip's act was therefore directed also against his own fellow revolutionaries and sympathizers; it was intended to force them to do what they were as yet unwilling to do—follow the ideology of pan-Serbism and the slogan of "Union or Death"—to its logical, mad conclusion.

Finally, the crowning irony in this ghastly scenario is this: though Princip deliberately tried to start a great war, his terrorist action, which succeeded only by luck, could not in itself produce that war. Only Austria-Hungary could do that by its response, and it did. Yet of all the participants great and small in the 1914 crisis, none more deeply and genuinely feared a great war than the government of Austria-Hungary, or had better reasons to do so. Time and again previously (1904–05, 1908–09, 1912–13) it had considered the war option and rejected it, even when the chances for military victory looked good. One can show that in July 1914, too, though it undoubtedly wanted and aimed for a local war against Serbia, its larger aim was general peace. Its forlorn hope was that Russia would accept a punishment of Serbia for the sake of ending the terrorist-revolutionary threat to all thrones, including Russia's, and that then Austria and Russia could settle their other differences (above all the Ruthenian question) and restore both good relations and the old *Dreikaiserbund* (the "Three Emperors' League") as well.

In other words, the terrorists whose action triggered the great war wanted a war but could not start it by themselves; those who helped them prepare the action did not want the war but were to varying degrees dragged into it; and the terrorists' worst enemy, which had the greatest reasons to avoid war, supplied the war the terrorists wanted.

Anyone can see the parallels suggested here, however imperfect they may be. Bin Laden is Princip, and the countries that abet al-Qaeda's terrorism compose the conspiracy. Only bin Laden and his chief lieutenants plotted and knew about the attacks of September 11 in advance, not the Taliban leadership or the leadership of any other state or sympathetic Muslim group, particularly Pakistan's Inter-Services Intelligence Directorate (ISI). Only bin Laden wanted to touch off a war involving the United States; other fundamentalist groups, the Taliban, the Iraqi, Iranian, Syrian, Sudanese and Libyan governments surely did not. The US government knew plenty about bin Laden and the network of state support for his activities; it had been attacked by bin Laden before, the World Trade Center had been a target, it knew of the existence of al-Qaeda cells in the United States, and airline hijackings have long been part of the terrorist repertoire— and yet it did little to prevent the terrorist act, which led it in turn to fight a war that it would otherwise not have sought.

But if the analogy is easy to follow, at least in its broad stripes, anyone can also see that it is nonsense to imply that the two situations are exactly alike and that the present one could lead to World War III. 1914 and 2001 are entirely different. Austria-Hungary was weak, almost isolated, surrounded by enemies and opponents, internally divided, and therefore prone to commit a suicidal blunder. Europe was then a tinderbox, locked in hostile alliances and bitter rivalries and caught in a spiraling arms race. The United States today is extremely powerful, surrounded by allies and friends, internally united, and in an ideal position to take strong rational action in its own and the world's long-range interests. The world is relatively calm, with no hostile alliances or serious great power crises and enmities. Almost every other important government agrees with the American stand against terrorism and wants to support it. They recognize that international terrorism menaces all decent states and societies, and that the current sophisticated, far-flung, fanatical variety is to the crude, primitive organizations and actions of 1914 what atomic warfare is to tribal banditry. Thus, any notion that the United States might provoke another world conflict by declaring war on terrorism—or rather, by recognizing a war that certain terrorists have declared on it and others—is silly.

Do Not Help Your Enemy

But that is not the point. The point is, if one grants the analogy for the sake of widening our intellectual framework, that there is much to learn about our choice of tactics. Some reflection on this analogy may enable us to see what has happened and what we have done and are doing in response to it in a different light.

So then grant, for argument's sake, that al-Qaeda planned and organized the September 11 attack independently of the wishes and control of the organizations, movements, and governments, including the Taliban and the ISI, which were in some ways complicit with them, and that this terrorist action was intended among other things to drag them into bin Laden's fanatical campaign. Grant that he wanted a war against the United States while they did not, and also that the actions he took, terrible though they were, could not by themselves achieve his goal of war with the United States, because his organization not only could not declare war as a regular state could, but at first dared not even to openly acknowledge the deed. Grant then that he could thus only hope to gain his goal of a great war between the United States and the Muslim world, overthrowing in the process those corrupt governments that supposedly had betrayed Islam by collaborating with the West, if the US government helped by declaring war on him and his cause in response. Grant finally, in the spirit of "know thine enemy," a certain consistency and rationale to this line of reasoning and course of action.

Could this not suggest some questions about the tactics, if not the basic strategy, of the American government's response to this attack from the first moment? That response was to declare immediately that these acts of terrorism were acts of war against the United States, and to answer with a public, solemn, dramatic declaration of war on terrorism, a mobilization for it, a commitment to total victory as the only thinkable outcome, and the demand for total support for this "crusade" (a remarkable, if subsequently retracted, choice of words by President Bush) from every ally, friend, neutral, and even opponent, at the risk of facing the "full wrath" of the United States (Vice President Cheney's phrase) if they declined.

Now, granted that the terrorist action was unquestionably an attack upon the United States as a nation, rather than merely on certain individuals or particular authorities; granted that the deed and its perpetrators deserve the execration universally heaped on them; granted that the American government, for fully understandable and justifiable reasons of domestic politics, international policy and normal human sensibilities, had to respond quickly and strongly to the attack; granted that any appropriate response had to include the use of military force. Yet even granting all this, one should also recognize that this response, even if forced upon us by circumstances, may have given the terrorists just what they wanted but could not achieve on their own: an international stature as a formidable enemy of the United States and the Western world that their actual deeds and power do not deserve, and the open wider war they want. If, as seems clear, they are fanatical ideologues and criminals but not fools or madmen in any clinical sense, and show a high degree of purposive rationality in pursuit of their goal, the safest assumption is that they anticipated and desired this reaction from the United States. Their willingness to make martyrs of themselves for their cause should tell us that they also are ready to make unwilling martyrs of many thousands of their fellow believers and countrymen as well by getting the United States and its allies to come after them with military force. This is a standard tactic for terrorist and guerrilla fighters: provoke an enemy into bloody reprisals so as to destroy the vital center and force everyone to choose between them and the national or religious enemy. It was Gavrilo Princip's calculation, and he was far less clever than these terrorists.

The first reflection to be gained from this parallel and from general historical experience is this: "Try not to give your worst enemies what they want but cannot achieve without your help; or, if you cannot help doing so, at least be aware of the danger and try to limit it." In retrospect, it might have been wiser to treat the attack from the outset as a horrible criminal action (which it also was) that had to be answered by a major international police action against the criminals (which the current operation also is), but without declaring war on terrorism and thereby giving an inflated importance to both the threat and the perpetrators. Many countries have had to combat long-term terrorist threats and campaigns more dangerous to their security than this one is to ours without declaring a general war on terrorism as a phenomenon and on all terrorists in general. This latter, more limited tactic may work better, in any case, on behalf of the goal of separating terrorists from whatever base they may enjoy among the general populace.

To be sure, as the first wave of shock and anger has subsided, so has—somewhat at least—the "all-out war for a total victory over international terrorism" rhetoric. The administration now seems clearly aware of this danger and is working to narrow the target of its operations to specific terrorist organizations, or at least to put its targets in a sober sequential order for a methodical and protracted campaign. Its consistent effort not to make the conflict a war against Islam or against the Arab world is also very commendable, but given the nature of Middle Eastern cultures it may also be futile. In any event, the big questions are, can this narrower and more patient strategy be effectively pursued without expanding inadvertently into a wider war and, even if it can, will the American public understand and accept the limits this must place on both the kinds of operations undertaken and the kind of victory possible? Not everyone will agree with this point of view, but few among us will argue that it is not worth thinking about.

Mind the Structural Impact

A question that has long puzzled historians is why the Austro-Hungarian government in 1914 made the apparently irrational choice it did (as is often said) of committing suicide out of fear of death, trying to survive by risking a war almost certain to kill it. The answer is simple: the monarchy did not commit suicide out of fear of death but out of fear of the hangman.

Throughout its long existence as a great power the Habsburg Monarchy had never been strong and secure enough to meet the many threats confronting it on its own. It had always relied on the support of allies and, increasingly in the nineteenth century, on the international system. That system was composed of the rules, practices, institutions and procedures developed over centuries and culminating in the great power Concert of Europe, and the Habsburg Monarchy used it to help protect its interests and to manage the crises and threats it faced through joint international legal, diplomatic, and military-political measures short of war. By 1914, however, and before the assassination at Sarajevo, Austria-Hungary's leaders had concluded that for purposes of protecting the monarchy's vital interests and existence as a great power, this system was worse than useless—that it was no longer part of the solution but part of the problem. No matter what the monarchy did, the system and its procedures were being used effectively by its many opponents to paralyze and isolate it until it succumbed—so, anyway, the Habsburg elite believed. Hence Austria-Hungary's only option, with the support of its ally Germany, was to break with this system and to act decisively and unilaterally in order to restore its great power position and independence, even at the high risk of a general war. Its hope was that after the monarchy had proved its ability to act decisively, and had regained the respect of Europe, the old system might be restored. This analysis of its situation was, in my view, essentially correct, though it does not necessarily justify the policy Vienna chose in reaction to it.

Obviously, America's situation at the beginning of the terrorist crisis was vastly different in almost every respect. The United States entered the month of September 2001 as easily the most powerful country in the world, united, enjoying unmatched prestige, boasting a vast array of allies and friends, and facing no major threat either internationally or internally except (putatively) that of terrorism—in every way the reverse of Austria-Hungary's position. Nevertheless, in one vital aspect the American government's response to the September 11 attack was like the Austro-Hungarian government's response to Sarajevo—a decision for war that ran against the grain of the expected rules and procedures of the international system.

Austria-Hungary chose war out of despair and the exhaustion of alternatives, convinced that there was nothing else to do because the existing international system was broken, offering it no good alternatives. The United States at the outset chose war out of confidence, but knowing at the same time that trying to handle the crisis through the existing international system in the normal ways (the UN, NATO, other allies, and normal international pressure and coercive diplomacy such as has been applied in the Balkans) might defuse the crisis without solving the real problem. It might, for example, make the Taliban regime expel Osama bin Laden and close some terrorist bases, which, while preserving the general peace, would only alleviate terrorism temporarily without getting at its deeper and wider roots. This would not satisfy the US government or the enraged American public, and would waste an opportunity for a more radical solution to the terrorist problem along American lines. Thus, for different reasons, Austria-Hungary and the United States both saw the business-as-usual parameters of the international system as a hindrance.

Now, many observers would defend US policy precisely on these grounds. But the point to be understood here is that the American choice of war as a first resort does collide with the rules of the reigning international system, which calls for meeting international threats and crises—including those involving revolutionary, subversive, or terrorist attacks by the subjects or citizens of one country on another—not by the old *lex talionis* but through international action. That action, which can include legal, moral, diplomatic, political, and, where necessary, military pressure, is supposed to prevent a crisis from escalating into war and, wherever possible, to bring about a solution acceptable to all parties with legitimate stakes in the dispute.

This is not just a practice developed since the end of the Cold War or since 1945, but a further evolution of practices and rules developed over centuries and already normative in the nineteenth century. A recent book by German scholars, for example, shows that thirty-three instances in which great power conflicts loomed in Europe between 1862 and 1914 were de-escalated and controlled by these means, most often under the aegis of the European Concert.[2] Austria-Hungary's action in 1914, though understandable given its perceptions, unquestionably broke with this tradition.

In our present case, the immediate declaration of war on terrorism may have been more a matter of imprudent rhetoric in the heat of the moment than a carefully calculated decision, and the remarkably successful efforts to build an international coalition in support of American action may constitute in effect an American return to the normal rules. Even the administration's insistence upon reserving its right to act unilaterally does not disprove this interpretation, for that could also be a normal bargaining ploy to recruit allies and keep them up to the mark. (By the same token, the apparently spontaneous rallying to the American cause by so many countries may be in part a normal device to control American action so as to prevent the United States from running amok.) But two points, both easily supported by much history, stand out and need to be taken seriously.

The lesser of these points concerns the integrity of the coalition we are building, which to some degree reflects the integrity and utility of the international system itself. The real struggle going on within the administration and in the press between hawks and moderates is whether the United States—assuming that it succeeds with the help of the international coalition in achieving its more immediate goals of ousting the Taliban regime and destroying the al-Qaeda network—will go beyond these goals, which are widely supported and agreed on by our allies and associates. Clearly, pursuing the punishment or overthrow of other governments such as Iraq, Syria, and Iran in order to get at the supposed roots of international terrorism is a course that even close allies and friends have indicated they would not support, and which may be depended upon to break up the coalition.

Second, and of more direct importance, whichever course the United States follows will affect not just the future of the terrorist threat or American leadership and prestige in the world, but

---

2 Jost Dülffer et al., *Vermiedene Kriege: Deeskalation von Konflikten der Grossmächte zwischen Krimkrieg und Erstem Weltkrieg (1865–1914)* (Munich, 1997).

also the future of the international system. Success in a minimalist campaign against al-Qaeda and the Taliban, even had it required a considerably greater use of military force, would still have strengthened the existing international system, giving it added prestige and a new vital function. Even an indecisive outcome or relative failure would not necessarily have hurt it. On the other hand, even a successful campaign of the maximalist type directed against other supposed terrorist-supporting states could do major damage to the international system by turning it back to unilateralism and the use of preemptive force. A failed campaign would discredit both the United States and the system with it.

Admittedly, it is hard for many people, particularly realists, to get excited over the fate of so abstract and nebulous a thing as the international system, especially under the impact of dramatic events such as those of September 11. And it is true that no international system is foolproof or adequate to meet every challenge; obviously the international system prevented neither World War I nor II. But the present international system is no more abstract, really, than the physical environment or the rules and practices that constitute our civil society, and in its way no less necessary for purposes of international peace and stability. If the comparison between 1914 and 2001 makes us think more deeply about the long-range impact of what we do on the international system and its rules, then so much the better.

Getting What You Wish For

There is one final way in which the 1914/2001 comparison can help us think about the September events. Put colloquially, it is this: "Look for some key element or elements in the whole situation that those involved in the discussion and decisions are *not* thinking or talking about, either because they are genuinely unaware of them or because they choose to ignore them."

In 1914, that ignored element can be identified precisely. European international politics in the decade before 1914 concentrated intensively on a number of interlocking questions—how to avoid a war if possible, but prepare to fight it victoriously if it came; how to shore up the various alliances; how to protect one's own state interests and prestige; how to capitalize on opportunities for gains and relative advantage; and finally, especially in the Balkans, how to prevent local conflicts and wars from erupting into a great power war that would almost certainly become general. These questions were important, but two even more important questions were never seriously discussed, much less taken up and treated—though everyone knew about them. They were, first, how to manage or solve the Austro-Serbian conflict and, second, what to do about the decline and (many thought) the impending collapse of the Austro-Hungarian Empire.

This sounds incredible, I know. From 1908 and the Bosnian Crisis through the Balkan Wars to the outbreak of war in 1914, the Balkans were for most of the time the center and obvious flashpoint of European politics, and Austro-Serbian relations and the general problem of Austria's putative weakness and instability were obviously key elements in them. Yet the statement is nonetheless true. All the Concert diplomacy of that era focused not on doing something to solve or alleviate the basic Austro-Serbian problem (that is, the problem of a small state's repeatedly challenging and provoking a neighboring great power with impunity under the protection of another great power), but only on how to keep the Austro-Serbian conflict from erupting into general war.

The same remarkable myopia prevailed in regard to the oft-predicted demise of the Habsburg Monarchy. Everyone in the chanceries talked about this possibility secretly. Many in the parliaments and press did so openly. But the one thing one cannot find is any serious discussion, much less action, among responsible statesmen to prepare for the inevitable repercussions of such a huge upheaval in the European system. Those officials and diplomats from different countries (there were a few) who warned that Europe needed to pay serious attention to this eventuality and its consequences got nowhere with their own governments. The attitude in St. Petersburg, Rome, Paris, London and (even until early 1914) Berlin, was that this was Vienna's problem.

Historians often fail to sniff out things that are important because they are *not* there but *ought* to be. They are so trained to concentrate on hard evidence that they tend to act by the motto, *Quod non est in actis non est in mundo* ("whatever is not in the documents does not exist in the world"). If the foregoing analysis is right, however, World War I resulted less from what the great powers thought and did than from what they failed to think or do. They failed to address the two problems that, left to fester unattended, were almost bound to lead to war. Historians have debated whether Serbian grievances against Austria-Hungary and vice versa were justified, and devoted even more debate to the question of whether the monarchy in 1914 was staggering toward a deserved demise, or was instead a fairly decent, modernizing state that could have soldiered on indefinitely, managing its insoluble problems without succumbing to them. Both debates miss the point. It does not matter how justified or unjustified Serbia's grievances and claims were, or how sacred its pan-Serbian cause. One simply cannot allow a small power to get away with repeated challenges and provocations to a great power neighbor without inviting a violent reaction sooner or later.

It matters still less whether Austria-Hungary deserved to die or not. So central and indispensable a member of the international community, especially in the extremely tense rivalry of the early twentieth century, could not conceivably disappear without bringing a great war in its wake, and it was almost bound to decide to fight rather than to die peacefully. The remarkable insouciance of the European powers on the Austrian problem persisted throughout the war and after; the Allies fought the war against Germany, the foe and threat they mainly feared, to defeat it and reduce its power but keep it intact, while in practical terms they fought it to destroy Austria-Hungary, which was not considered a serious menace. It was this latter outcome, far more than the treatment of Germany in the Versailles Treaty, that contributed most to the chaos of the interwar era and to the origins of World War II.

Happily, this kind of wilful absent-mindedness does not prevail in the United States now. The media reflect a lively debate both in official circles and among the educated public over the potential side effects of the war on terrorism—fears about the possible destabilization of fragile regimes in Pakistan, Saudi Arabia and elsewhere, for example. The discussion over how to carry on the war and how far to pursue the roots of terrorism includes a heated debate on whether the United States should change its policy in the Middle East and elsewhere (vis-à-vis Iraq and Israel/Palestine, for example) in order to decrease the widespread resentment that allegedly feeds terrorism.

These are important issues, but they concentrate on how this campaign can best be waged with a minimum of undesired secondary effects: they still miss deeper aspects that need to be recognized and considered. Two of these aspects concern what happens if we win. Put differently, they raise the question of whether and how we can sustain the victory and manage its wider effects. The first concerns the provenance of government, and the second the vicissitudes of hegemony.

As to the former, suppose a military campaign against the Taliban leading to its overthrow. Can we or anyone provide stable government for Afghanistan, or do we leave it and its neighbors, some of them almost equally fragile states, to deal with the mess? The scenario becomes far worse if we include other states targeted for their alleged support of terrorism, such as Iraq, Iran, Syria and Libya. What does this region and the wider world do without governments in those states that, although brutal, are stable?

Some people seem to think that states and their governments are somehow fungible, replaceable—that if one is destroyed or overthrown, another can take its place—and that if the state or government overthrown was evil and dangerous, anything that replaces it will be better. Historical experience by and large teaches otherwise. Only in a few instances (Hitler's regime in Germany, Stalin's in Russia, for example) can we confidently say that anything that could have replaced them would have been better. The normal experience is the reverse. Things get worse, at least for a good while, before they get better. Many in World War I thought Imperial Germany was as evil and dangerous as a German government could get. Twenty years later they learned otherwise. Frenchmen in 1789 thought their monarchy was an oppressive regime. In four years they had the Terror. The monarchies of Europe thought the French Jacobin Republic and Directory as aggressive and dangerous as France could become, and welcomed Napoleon's seizure of power. They soon knew better. Nationalists in Eastern Europe and many in the West believed that the downfall of Austria-Hungary would enable the nationalities questions of the region to be solved. These are now mostly solved (except in the Balkans), but only after twenty years of instability and internecine conflict leading to the greatest war in history and to two of the worst instances of imperialism in history, German and Soviet, lasting two generations and attended by massive episodes of genocide, forced shifts of populations, and catastrophic general destruction.

One thing, then, to remember throughout this crisis is that states are not fungible, easily replaceable or dispensable. There have to be powerful grounds for overthrowing any regime effectively governing a state, and a clear idea of how to replace it. This crisis is itself a striking refutation of the current talk among historians and political scientists about the alleged decline and obsolescence of the state and the takeover of its sovereignty and administrative functions by international and supranational organizations, non-governmental entities, multinational corporations, and other transnational groups and movements. When this attack came, the American people rallied overwhelmingly behind their government and expected it to act, not any of these other entities. And when the American government sought support abroad for its campaign it also looked to other governments.

It has become clear, moreover, that if this campaign against terrorism in general is to succeed in the long run, it will require strong, effective governments in control of many states where such governments do not now exist. One factor contributing to World War I was the fact that the Serbian government was not in effective control over its military officers. A major concern now is that a wider conflict could arise for the same reason in Pakistan. Part of the intractability of the Israeli-Palestinian question is the lack of effective government in the areas ruled by the Palestinian Authority and the extreme difficulty of creating it. Something of the same holds for the whole region and itself contributes to breeding terrorism.

This, like much else said here (and as suggested at the outset), is a highly conservative stance. But, under current circumstances, it is likely to arouse the most ire among certain conservatives because it does not satisfy the American demand for justice and fails to get at the root of the problem of terrorism. The short answer to both objections is that in international affairs order takes priority over justice, and that a determination to get at the root of an evil and destroy it is the precise definition of radicalism, not conservatism.

The Vicissitudes of Hegemony

One more question needs thinking about, inappropriate and distracting though it must seem amid a military campaign. Suppose that we win, by which is meant the end of Osama bin Laden, the disruption or destruction of his terrorist network, the closing of the training camps, the replacement of the Taliban regime with something at least less driven by Islamist ideology, and the cowing or replacement of other regimes who have encouraged or aided in the promotion of terrorism. Suppose, too, that victory thus defined means at least a temporary cessation of terrorist activity, so that American and other armed forces beyond those normally in the region can be brought home. Suppose, finally, that all this is accomplished with few American and allied losses, no great damage to the American economy beyond the frailty already in train before September 11, and only minimal overt destabilization of other regimes in the region. What would this achieve in the longer run?

In domestic politics, it would doubtless be a great boost for President Bush and possibly for the Republican Party. In world politics, it would produce a great near-term gain in prestige for the United States, cementing its leadership, further heightening its prestige, and making its pre-eminence in the region and in the world even greater and more unchallenged than before. But would that be a good, stable outcome? Would an even greater degree of US hegemony in the Middle East and the world represent a long-term gain for any of the parties?

One prominent theory of international politics, neo-realism, holds that hegemony is inherently unstable because weaker states almost automatically coalesce against an actual or potential hegemon as a threat to their security and thus restore the balance of power. This theory is wrong; sometimes a hegemonic power touches off efforts at counterbalancing, but it can be demonstrated that the main response of smaller powers to actual or potential hegemons has been not to balance against them, but to join them or to try to hide from them. Two other generalizations about hegemony and hegemons are true, however, and have much to say about the stability and desirability even of a hegemony so apparently unobjectionable as that which would be produced by an American victory over terrorism.

First, hegemony does not only or even mainly bring security, power and glory, but difficulty, responsibility and burden. The hegemon may or may not have to defend his leading position against challenges, but he surely will have to deal with all the quarrels into which he is drawn by virtue of being hegemon, to fend off all the demands and pleas for help from those who join his camp hoping to take advantage of it, to provide a disproportionate share of the security for threatened allies, and above all to husband the military force necessary to keep the peace in the last resort and to use that force when, but only when, really necessary.

Second, in order to be stable, any hegemony has at least to be perceived as natural, invulnerable and tolerable, if not wholly benign. It has to be natural in the sense that the hegemon is seen as belonging where it is as a leader and therefore somehow legitimate; invulnerable not in the sense that no blow can be struck against it, but that no blow will really hurt or overthrow it, and that the consequences will be worse for those who strike it; tolerable or benign in the sense that at least some who live under its hegemony feel that they benefit from it and that others, even if uncomfortable, still feel that they have room to move and air to breathe. These requirements are inescapably vague in the abstract, but they can be applied historically; when they are applied they explain why some hegemonies have proved remarkably stable and durable (that of the United States in the Western Hemisphere, that of Britain on the seas and in the colonial world from about 1750 to the early twenieth century; that of the United States in Western and now Eastern Europe since 1945), while others that for a time represented overwhelming power (the Spanish Habsburgs in the sixteenth and early seventeenth centuries, that of Louis XIV's France, Napoleon's, Hitler's, that of the Soviet Union) crumbled fairly quickly and disastrously.

The question Americans need to ask themselves now, while this campaign is still in its early stages, is whether, if and when it is victorious, the American hegemony that it will inevitably further promote in the world, and especially in the Middle East, will be natural, invulnerable, and tolerable or benign—and therefore desirable and sustainable—or not. That question must arise; indeed, it is asked already, and bound up with our understanding of the terrorist attacks. There has been endless talk about why these terrorists attacked the United States, and why so many Arabs and Muslims in the Middle East and elsewhere evidently hate us. Do they hate and target us for what we have done, our alleged sins; or for what we are, our alleged values and virtues?

The President and evidently the majority of Americans come down solidly on the latter side, yet this conclusion misses the most obvious and central point: The terrorists attacked us *here* because we are *there*. Yes, they undoubtedly hate us for what we are and for all the values we consider best, but they would not attack us and would not enjoy the sympathy of others in the region for doing so if there were not a powerful American influence and presence in that region that is felt by many as alien, oppressive, and corrupting. No one can suppose that the attack was intended somehow to convert Americans from their way of life to that of Islam. It is because these terrorists and their sympathizers see their way of life being corroded and eaten away by secular Western values and customs that we are under attack. They see America at the head of this corrosion, with most Arab and Muslim governments fecklessly collaborating with it. They see this corrosive power and influence exemplified spectacularly in such exercises as Desert Storm and less spectacularly in innumerable links between American and Western business interests and corporations and Arab and Muslim countries. They see it daily confirmed in an ongoing Israeli-Palestinian conflict in which, no matter how even-handed the United States tries to be, it is always seen as supporting Israel. The attack comes in the form of terrorism because they have no other more effective means of reprisal.

This is not in any way a defense of the terrorists or an excuse for their attack, and it does not alter what we need to do in response to it, except perhaps at the diplomatic margins. It is solely an attempt to understand the meaning of the widespread Arab-Muslim reaction to US power, and to see it as one more indication of what ought to be obvious on the face of things: an American hegemony in this region—at least a direct, intrusive, overt and coercive one—is not and cannot be natural. This is a region where local states are too weak to effectively counterbalance against US hegemony, but where cultural and historical cleavages reduce their propensity to join with it, as well. The obvious truth is that we do not belong there in the same way as we belong in the Western Hemisphere, the Atlantic, central and eastern Europe, and the Pacific. *Yet a victory in this war against terrorism will unfailingly commit us to an even more direct and intrusive hegemony than before.* All the support we are getting from the various governments in the region comes, we may be sure, with price tags and strings attached and explicit or implicit IOUs extracted that will soon be called in. We can already see what these are in respect to Russia (Chechnya), Pakistan (Kashmir, foreign debts, its nuclear arms), and other states. The full total will only become clear with time, but that they will commit us willy-nilly to more active intervention in the region's politics is unmistakable. Even more obvious and important, if victory against terrorism means preventing its recurrence, we will have to stay openly in the region in a major way both politically and with armed forces, interfering in its politics and putting constant pressures on its governments, for an indefinite future.

Such an intensified hegemony would not only be more unnatural than our present one, but also more vulnerable. In that sense it would play again into the hands of our worst enemies. One of the objects of the terrorist attack was to prove that the United States was not invulnerable—that it could be hurt even by small, relatively weak groups of dedicated fighters. The reaction of most Americans to the attack has played into their hands. By endlessly rehearsing the magnitude of the loss, labeling it a national tragedy, disaster, and even catastrophe, by hyperventilating in denouncing the action and demanding vengeance, and by panicking at the fear of still more attacks, we have encouraged the terrorists to believe that the United States really can be badly hurt by actions like these.

In fact, the opposite is true, and should constantly be emphasized. This was a monstrous crime and an individual tragedy of the deepest kind for many thousands of victims and their survivors, a genuine though less direct tragedy for all their friends and for all the businesses and employees more or less directly affected, a blow especially to all New Yorkers and a shock to all Americans—it was all these things and more. But it was not a *national* tragedy, much less a national disaster or catastrophe. On the scale of real national disasters and catastrophes in the world over the last fifty years it would not rank in the top hundred. It was a sneak punch for which we were surprisingly unprepared, but which had the effect of waking us up and making us stronger and more alert than before.

The attack does not prove that the United States is vulnerable and insecure as a nation and a world power until terrorism is destroyed. It simply adds to the existing proofs of two obvious propositions: that the whole Middle East, a region vital to our interests and even more to those of our best and strongest allies and friends, is vulnerable to crises spawned by such attacks, and that our leading position is thereby indirectly threatened; and that American hegemony in this region is not seen by many who live in it as tolerable or benign. It does not matter if this is unfair, the result of malicious anti-American propaganda and a grave distortion of the facts. Nor does it matter in the long run (though it certainly does in the immediate crisis) that we have most governments on our side and that any enemy governments are temporarily lying low. In the longer run hegemonies that are not at least accepted as tolerable by the majority of the public in the countries living under the hegemony do not last. If this is true in general, it is even truer for the era of mass politics since the mid-nineteenth century.

This suggests that the wisest course for the United States might be to declare victory at the earliest possible moment and go part way home—that is, to use a victory and the heightened prestige it will bring to reduce rather than expand our hegemonic role in this particular region. We might be well advised to try to devolve the leading roles in managing and controlling its problems upon others nearer to it, more naturally and historically tied to it, and having even more critical interests in its stability—a more mature European Union, perhaps. Doing this would not be easy, and it may not even be practically possible. But a recognition that a heightened hegemonic role in the Middle East for the United States as the result of victory over terrorism could be a danger rather than an asset would at least steel us to do the difficult.

There is nothing particularly objectionable, to my mind, about American hegemony, and plenty objectionable about a return to anything like isolationism. But in drawing on historical experience to distinguish between workable, durable, and tolerable or benign hegemonies (which American hegemony in much of the world since 1945 has mostly been) and unworkable, unstable, and intolerable ones, we may alert ourselves to ways to save, improve and prolong American leadership in the world. Still less has this argument anything to do with excusing the terrorists or blaming America for creating the conditions that led to terrorism, or even criticizing the policies that have made us the target of terrorist malcontents. It is an attempt merely to face facts and to calculate their probable consequences, to correlate means and ends, to know the enemy and oneself—in short, to apply long-term thinking and rational calculation to a field, international politics, that desperately needs it precisely because it is in many respects so resistant to it.

There are good reasons, to be sure, why this kind of analysis is unlikely to have an effect on policy. Beyond the simple fact that policymakers are too busy to consider these kinds of arguments, this particular one runs counter to the public mood, which still seems concentrated on self-pity over our loss, self-congratulation over our virtues, and calls for dissenters to shut up. There is another reason, too, why policymakers cannot afford to give much consideration to arguments based on long-range historical reflection, even if they had the time to do so. They must act quickly and decisively on the basis of imperfect information in situations full of uncertainty, and having chosen a certain course must stick to it lest a reversal generate even greater costs than those already in store. Too much reflection on all the possible consequences could lead to paralysis. Thus by historical reflection the native hue of resolution would be sicklied o'er with the pale cast of thought, and history would make cowards of us all.

Nonetheless, this kind of thinking is neither idle nor worthless, even or especially in wartime. In wartime above all times it is important constantly to reflect on what we are really doing and to calculate what the likely long-range results will be. Two Latin axioms neatly express the tension in wartime between the need for immediate decision and the need for long-term reflection: *carpe diem* ("seize the day"), and *respice finem* ("remain mindful of the goal"). One frequently must seize the moment; one always must remain mindful of the goal. A sense of history can be invaluable in balancing the two, not for prescription but for perspective and insight; or, as the Swiss historian Jacob Burckhardt once said, not to make us more clever for this or that occasion, but wiser for all time.

A final word: One subject on which we could use some wisdom concerns the nature of fanaticism. Our war, insofar as it is a war, is against fanaticism. But one definition of a fanatic is someone (to paraphrase Winston Churchill) who, facing evidence that he has lost sight of his objective or is headed in the wrong direction, redoubles his efforts. We can see that clearly in our enemies. They believe fanatically that they are serving their religion by their actions, where they are only discrediting and dishonoring it. They believe they have struck a powerful blow against us, when in fact it will mean far more powerful blows against them. Even in the face of evidence of this, they can be expected to try harder.

But we have less to fear from their patent fanaticism than from our own latent variety of it. We can do even more damage to ourselves than they can, not because we are worse—for all our faults, we are genuinely far better—but because we are so immensely more powerful. The chief danger for the United States lies in its impulse to use its power to wipe out this evil regardless of the consequences; it inheres in what George F. Kennan has called "the blind egotism of the embattled democracy." In the fight against this tendency, we could do much worse than to appreciate perspectives gained from history.

4

The Case against Preemptive War

2002

Most Americans seem little concerned at the prospect of an American war on Iraq.* This is surprising considering that, of America's friends and allies, only Israel openly supports it, while other states in the Middle East, including longtime rivals and enemies of Iraq, warn against it, and the Europeans view it with alarm and growing frustration. Those challenges to the planned war now being raised, moreover, tend to center on prudential questions—whether the proposed attack will work and what short-term risks and collateral damage might be involved—rather than on whether the war itself is a good idea.

The practical risks are indeed serious. The attack would entail a new military campaign while the so-called war against al-Qaeda and terrorism is far from over, involving many thousands of American troops in ground fighting with corresponding casualties, fought with few allies or none and paid for entirely by the United States in troubled economic times. Across the Muslim world hostility toward America is already inflamed, and radical Islamic movements are active. The global economy—particularly the oil and stock markets—is vulnerable to shock. Such a war would also come at a time when America's alliances in Europe and the Middle East are strained, certain fragile Middle Eastern and South Asian regimes are at risk, and other international dangers (tensions between India and Pakistan, North and South Korea, and China and Taiwan, and economic crisis in Latin America, to name a few) are looming. If the war succeeds in toppling Hussein, the United States will be saddled

---

* I wish to thank Dr. Levin von Trott zu Solz and Professors Edward Kolodziej, John Mueller, Margaret L. Anderson, Juan Cole, and David Kaiser for helpful comments and suggestions.

with the new responsibilities of occupying, administering, rebuilding, democratizing, and stabilizing Iraq (beyond its existing responsibilities in Afghanistan), tasks of unreckoned costs and manifold difficulties for which neither the American public nor the administration have demonstrated much understanding, skill, or stomach. In the light of all this, the enterprise merely on practical grounds looks remarkably rash.

Yet even these grave considerations should not take priority over questions of principle: Do we have a right to wage preemptive war against Iraq to overthrow its regime? Would this be a necessary and just war? What long-range effects would it have on the international system? If the answers to these questions make this truly a necessary and just war, Americans ought to be willing to make sacrifices and undergo risks for it.

On these critical issues the administration has so far won by default. The assumption that a war to overthrow Hussein would be a just war and one that, if it succeeded without excessive negative side effects, would serve everyone's interests has gone largely unchallenged, at least in the mainstream. The administration's justification for preemptive war is the traditional one: that the dangers and costs of inaction far outweigh those of acting now. Saddam Hussein, an evil despot, a serial aggressor, an implacable enemy of the United States, and a direct menace to his neighbors must be deposed before he acquires weapons of mass destruction that he might use or let others use against Americans or its allies and friends. A few thousand Americans died in the last terrorist attack; many millions could die in the next one. Time is against us; once Hussein acquires such weapons, he cannot be overthrown without enormous losses and dangers. Persuasion, negotiation, and conciliation are worse than useless with him. Sanctions and coercive diplomacy have failed. Conventional deterrence is equally unreliable. Preemptive action to remove him from power is the only effective remedy and will promote durable peace in the region.

This essay proposes to confront this case for preemptive war on Iraq head on. My argument stresses principles and long-term structural effects rather than prudence and short-term results. It rests not on judgments and predictions about future military and political developments, which I am not qualified to make, but on a perspective missing from the current discussion, derived from history, especially the history of European and world politics over the last four centuries. Rather than criticizing the proposed preemptive war on prudential grounds, it opposes the idea itself, contending that an American campaign to overthrow Hussein by armed force would be an unjust, aggressive, imperialist war which even if it succeeded (indeed, perhaps especially if it succeeded), would have negative, potentially disastrous effects on our alliances and friendships, American leadership in the world, the existing international system, and the prospects for general peace, order, and stability. In other words, a preemptive war on Iraq would be not merely foolish and dangerous, but wrong.

This essay attempts to build a case against the war on systemic grounds; it cannot for reasons of space hope to treat all-important aspects of that systemic case or answer all possible questions and challenges. It talks about the damage a preemptive war would do to the existing international system, but not about the equally important impacts it could have in terms of side effects on nascent changes in the international system needed to meet new problems already looming on the horizon. It draws on international history in regard to preemptive wars, but will not take up a legitimate though tricky question of counterfactual history, i.e., whether certain preemptive wars, had they been waged in the past, might have averted disasters as the advocates of such a war against Iraq claim a war will do now.[1] While

---

[1] I will mention only one such argument in passing here: the superficially plausible idea that a preventive war launched against Hitler's Germany in 1936 at the time of Germany's reoccupation of the Rhineland or in 1938 at the annexation of Austria would have prevented all the horrors of World War II and the Holocaust. (A war at the time of the Munich Crisis would not have been preemptive, but rather a legitimate defensive war fought by France and the Soviet Union in fulfillment of their clear alliance obligations to Czechoslovakia, with Britain joining in for the same balance of power reasons that had brought it into World War I.) My reply, in sketchy thumbnail fashion, would be that asking French and British statesmen in 1936 or early 1938 to launch a preemptive war against Germany on the basis of what Germany had done to that point would amount not only to asking them to commit political suicide, but to demanding that they play God or be God. No one could know in 1936 or 1938 the true, horrible extent of future Nazi crimes and therefore know or predict that preemptive war would prevent a world war of catastrophic

examining the official case for a war on Iraq, it will not take up, except in passing fashion in the last footnote, what is possibly the unacknowledged real reason and motive behind the policy—security for Israel.

Even with these limits, this is a tall order for a short essay; the argument must be highly compressed and asserted rather than demonstrated here. But it can be condensed into four fairly simple propositions that a preemptive war on Iraq would be illegitimate, because it cannot be justified on any of the grounds by which preemptive wars are and should be judged and would represent and promote dangerous, lawless international behavior; incompatible with the purpose, spirit, and aims of the worldwide military and political alliances which the United States leads, and therefore harmful both to these alliances and to American leadership; incompatible also with the two central principles by which the international system has evolved over centuries, namely, the right of all states to be recognized and treated as independent, and the simultaneous and corresponding need and requirement for states to become part of associations for common purposes and to follow the rules; unnecessary, unhelpful, and utopian (better, dystopian) because some of the goals the administration proposes to achieve by preemptive war are impossible to achieve by any means, and because the essential, legitimate American aims and the requirements of the international community vis-à-vis Iraq can be better realized by other means.

---

dimensions or a Holocaust. The predictable and calculable evils of launching a preemptive war at that time, in other words, outweighed the predictable, calculable evils of waiting and trying to prevent war entirely. The real criticism of British and French policy is not their failure to launch preemptive war, but their failure or refusal to take either the Rhineland occupation or the Anschluss seriously and to undertake a resolute course of deterrence and collective security. In fact, both events caused them to abandon the half-hearted efforts at deterrence of Germany they had initiated and go over to appeasement. Thus the argument for preemptive war in the 1930s really supports the case made here for deterrence.

Why Preemptive Wars Are Rarely Justified, and This One Cannot Be

Whether starting a preemptive war is justified in a particular instance is not primarily a question of international law. The critical question is whether the action is one of aggression or of legitimate self-defense, and no law can answer that. There are, however, criteria for judging the action, deriving from something more basic in international politics than specific international laws: the unwritten understandings international actors reach on an ongoing basis as to what is within the bounds, is permissible or not under the rules of the game. These understandings change with time and circumstance, of course, but a fairly wide and stable consensus on this particular issue has developed, especially in recent centuries.

To justify a resort to preemptive war, a state needs to give reasonable evidence that the step was necessary, forced upon the initiator by its opponents, and also that it represented a lesser evil, i.e., that the dangers and evils averted by war outweighed those caused the international community by initiating it. This requires showing that the threat to be preempted is (a) clear and imminent, such that prompt action is required to meet it; (b) direct, that is, threatening the party initiating the conflict in specific concrete ways, thus entitling that party to act preemptively; (c) critical, in the sense that the vital interests of the initiating party face unacceptable harm and danger; and (d) unmanageable, that is, not capable of being deterred or dealt with by other peaceful means. These criteria are naturally open to interpretation and contest. They represent, however, a consensus of enlightened international opinion, make sense of historical experience, and are easily illustrated with historical examples. They have helped actors in the past judge claims and weigh arguments for preemptive wars and have had some effect in deterring illegitimate resorts to it.[2] They are stringent; most

---

[2] For example, it was these general criteria that guided Prince Bismarck in rejecting the urgings of General Count Waldersee, the Prussian army's Chief of Staff, for preventive war on Russia in 1888–89, and that led Emperor Franz

claims made to justify preemptive wars do not pass the test, which is as it should be. But the criteria are not unrealistic or utopian, and do allow for preemptive war in certain particular cases.[3]

In fact, the rhetoric of administration leaders and their supporters urging a preemptive war against Iraq indicates that they are generally aware of these criteria and attempt to justify it on these terms. But they cannot; their arguments everywhere break down.

To show that the threat is clear and imminent, the president and his supporters repeatedly insist that Saddam Hussein has long wanted weapons of mass destruction and tried to develop them. Since 1998, he has prevented the United Nations' international

---

Joseph and several of his chief ministers to resist up to 1914 the various schemes for preventive war promoted by the Austro-Hungarian Chief of Staff General Conrad von Hoetzendorf.

[3] Let me flesh this out with a little history, not to prove my points (impossible in a short essay) but to illustrate them and keep them from being naked assertions. Four examples of preemptive wars that I consider justified are Prussia's attack on Saxony in 1756, which set off the Seven Years' War, Japan's attack on Russia in 1904, and Israel's resort to preemptive attacks on Egypt in 1956 and 1967. In every case all the stated criteria are met. Note, however, that even in these cases those who chose preemptive war were not necessarily blameless, or fighting purely in self-defense. Prussia had largely created the Austro-Russian-French threat against it by its lawless seizure of Austrian Silesia in 1740. Japan, though genuinely threatened by Russian imperialism, also had its own program of imperialism in East Asia. And, as revisionist Israeli historians have proved, territorial expansion was a part of Israeli aims in starting both these wars. Still less do these examples or others make preemptive war, even when justified, necessarily a wise choice or indicate that if victorious it will have good results. The attacking state in all these instances of justified preemptive war won the resulting war or at least did not lose. But each of these preemptive wars, even though successful, led to more conflict and complications later, and the more normal results of preemptive war are much worse. Austria, for example, tried preemptive war twice in the nineteenth century—against Napoleon in 1809 and against Sardinia-Piedmont in 1859—and once in the twentieth—against Serbia in 1914. In the first and last instances, I would argue (though many historians would disagree) that the Austrians had a pretty good case justifying preemptive war as their only way to remain an independent great power. Yet all three ended disastrously. In other words, preemptive war can occasionally be justified as a last resort, but it is never inherently a good policy—only in certain cases the least bad one available.

inspectors from returning to Iraq. He may therefore already be close to acquiring such weapons. The United States must stop him before he succeeds.

Seriously examined, this proves the opposite of what is required—that the threat is not clear and imminent. It indicates what, under pressure, administration spokesmen must admit: we simply do not know whether Iraq has developed weapons of mass destruction, or whether it will, or when. Still less do we know what Hussein would do with them if and when he obtained any. What is more, we do not seem greatly interested in finding out. Pleas from our closest allies, including even Tony Blair in Britain, that there must be a real effort to get UN inspectors back into Iraq before taking any other action against it, meet with impatient skepticism; any suggestion from Iraq that it might agree to this demand is dismissed as a bad joke; Vice President Richard Cheney insists that even actual UN inspections would not be enough. In short, the administration really does not know whether there is a clear and imminent threat from Iraq, cannot prove that one exists, and resists proposals for finding out because the answer might undermine its plans for war.

To show that the threat is direct, i.e., specific, concrete, and pointed at the United States, administration spokesmen and other advocates of preemptive war deduce from Saddam Hussein's criminal record and evil character, especially the fact that he used poison gas in his war against Iran and against his own people in the 1980s and has resorted to brutal repression since, that if and when he obtains weapons of mass destruction he could and would use them against the United States or its allies in the region.

In so doing, they ignore certain inconvenient facts—that the United States generally supported Iraq in its war against Iran, may have known and winked at his use of chemical weapons, and never at that time considered Hussein's attack on Iran or the atrocities perpetrated in it grounds for overthrowing him, and that the people whom Hussein brutally repressed in 1991 were mainly Kurds whom the United States encouraged to rise against him and then failed to support. The main point, however, is that again these arguments fail to prove what they are supposed to—i.e., that the threat from Iraq is concrete, specific, and directed against the United States or any American ally. They prove only what hardly needs proof, that Saddam Hussein is a ruthless despot who will do anything to stay in power, including using poison gas against external and internal enemies in a losing war or slaughtering his rebellious subjects. He might indeed use weapons of mass destruction against anyone for reasons of political survival—a point which counts if anything against attacking him and putting him into that kind of corner. But this says nothing about what he might do with them under other circumstances for other purposes and certainly fails to show that he would use them against the United States or its allies or allow terrorists to do so. Stalin had nuclear weapons, was a worse sociopath than Hussein and even more paranoid about threats to his reign, and his record of atrocities against his own people was far worse than Hussein's; yet none of this gave any indication whether or how he would use nuclear weapons in his foreign policy. On that score, he was demonstrably cautious.

In fact, it is extremely unlikely that Hussein would do something so suicidal as to attack the United States or one of its allies directly, or allow a proxy to do so, and the administration knows it. One expert witness at the Senate hearings on the proposed campaign against Iraq, frankly admitting this, remarked that the real danger was that possessing such weapons would give Hussein and Iraq more influence in the region (a significant admission).

The administration's case thus fails both the imminence and the directness tests. Its attempts to prove that the threat is critical are no stronger. They consist mainly of repeatedly invoking the memory of 9/11 and the war on terrorism, the right of American citizens to security against terrifying new threats revealed by that attack, the duty of their government to provide that security at all costs, and (once again) the possibility that Hussein, if he does get control of nuclear or other weapons, will supply them to terrorists for use against the United States. All this lays the basis for the general doctrine, repeatedly proclaimed, that the United States has a right to prevent weapons of mass destruction from coming into the hands of evil, hostile regimes by any means necessary.

I reserve for later some discussion of how novel, dangerous, and subversive of international order and peace this new, unprecedented American doctrine is. Here the point is that these arguments the administration and its supporters use again undercut the case for preemptive war.

How? Because they prove that the threat of international terrorism, even if it were the critical danger the administration claims it to be, does not stem from Hussein or Iraq and will not be met by ousting him. Despite many efforts, no one in the administration has ever proved a connection between Hussein or others in the Iraqi regime and September 11 or al-Qaeda and its terrorist activities. The evidence and probabilities, all well-known, point the other way. Hussein's regime and his ruling party are secular rather than Islamist. He rules a country deeply divided along ethnic and religious lines, and belongs to a branch of Islam (the Sunnis) that is a minority in Iraq. He has good selfish reasons to fear radical Islamism and terrorist activity just as other governments do. Why should a ruler obsessed with maintaining his power collaborate with some of his most dangerous enemies?

The only way to argue that overthrowing Hussein would help protect Americans from international terrorism would be to claim a beneficial ripple effect from it. By demonstrating American resolve and leadership, it would discourage terrorists from targeting us and frighten off hostile regimes from helping or harboring them while encouraging other governments to join us in the fight. This is pure guesswork and very unconvincing. Our allies and friends consider a preemptive war on Iraq a proof not of resolve and leadership, but of recklessness and unilateralism and want no part of it. Terrorists and their sympathizers would find in it more weapons with which to vilify the United States, recruit followers, and bring down the traitorous Arab and Muslim regimes cooperating with America.

And so the administration's case fails again. The more one thinks about it, the more implausible it becomes to claim that the United States, a superpower with an historically unprecedented position of unchallenged military superiority, is threatened by an impoverished, ruined, insecure state halfway round the world. Yet surely, one might object, the administration's case is right in one important respect: that whatever threat, great or small, an Iraq ruled by Saddam Hussein and possessing weapons of mass destruction would present would be impossible to manage or deter by normal peaceful means. No moral scruples, religious or philosophical principles, or appeals to the long-range interests of his country would stop him from using them against us or any other enemy, and ordinary means of negotiation, coercion, and deterrence have manifestly failed in dealing with him. Therefore, overthrowing him by war (the administration's euphemism for this is "regime change") is the only remaining choice.

Well, yes, this argument is correct—in one limited sense. If our basic problem is that Saddam Hussein is an evil ruler with hostile and dangerous attitudes and purposes, and if the only solution to that problem we will accept is to get rid of him right now, then the problem is indeed insoluble by peaceful means. All our past methods of dealing with him—first conciliation and appeasement, then war and crushing defeat, then extreme economic, political and military sanctions, and now massive overt threats—have failed. He remains a villain and remains in power. But to claim that any ruler we consider evil and hostile represents a danger to peace and American interests and security such that he should be overthrown by American military power is a really extraordinary claim—one that the rest of the world must sooner or later find intolerable and one out of keeping with central American traditions and values. We have not reached our position in the world by dealing with evil, hostile rulers and regimes through this policy of "regime change." (To be sure, we have sometimes used it, but mainly in dealing with small, weak governments in our own hemisphere, and these exercises in "regime change" have had, to put it charitably, very mixed results.) In dealing with real, major evils and threats both to the United States and the world such as those once represented by the Soviet Union, China, and their allies, we have won not by waging preemptive war for "regime change" but by deterring opponents from aggression and relying on outliving them, proving the superiority of our own system, and ultimately inducing peaceful change. That is the real American way.

Equally important, one simply cannot argue on the mere ground of Hussein's survival that coercion and deterrence have failed with Iraq and must be replaced by preemptive war. The purpose of coercion and deterrence in international relations is to stop dangerous regimes and rulers from actually doing things that harm or threaten others—not to make such regimes disappear or such rulers commit suicide. For purposes of deterring Iraq, the coercive measures imposed since 1991 have worked well. Before 1991, Hussein did many things in foreign policy that were clearly aggressive, above all his war on Iran and his seizure of Kuwait. Since then, Iraq, greatly weakened and restrained, has done nothing that could be called aggression against its neighbors. This is successful deterrence—effected, to be sure, at some cost to the United States in terms of effort and reputation, and enormous cost to the Iraqi people in terms of lives and standard of living, but, from a purely power-political point of view nonetheless the desired overall outcome. That Iraq and Hussein himself are not the regional menace they once were is shown by Iran's rapprochement with its old enemy and by the warning Iraq's historic rival for leadership of the Arab world, Egypt, now gives its American patron against war. They fear another war on Iraq more than they fear Iraq.

Thus the administration's case for preemptive war on Iraq fails the test on every criterion. But who cares? Why should we care if what America does in its own interest for its self-defense and that of its friends fails to satisfy some arbitrary legalistic criteria concocted by some liberal theorists and professors? What relevance do these arguments and examples drawn from history have in a world completely changed by weapons of mass destruction, instantaneous global communication and interpenetration, globalization of the economy, and the prospect of modern weapons and tools being used against us by fanatics driven by extremist ideologies?

We had better care. Norms, rules, standards of conduct, understandings about what is and is not permissible still count in international relations, now more than ever. They govern the expectations and calculations of statesmen; they influence public opinion and play a major role in the struggle for hearts and minds, increasingly important in this age of rising democracy, mass participation in politics, and instantaneous global communication. They form a central component of essential values in international politics—those universal values we constantly claim to be defending against the enemies of humankind. These norms, rules, and standards are vital not because they are immutable, unchallengeable, and enduring, but precisely because they are not. They are changeable, fragile, gained only by great effort and through bitter lessons of history, and easily destroyed, set aside, or changed for the worse for the sake of momentary gain or individual interest. And the fate of these norms and standards depends above all on what great powers, especially superpowers and hegemons, do with them and to them. The actions of great powers above all shape norms, mold expectations, provoke reactions, invite imitation and emulation, uphold or destroy or change the prevailing rules.

Consider what norm the administration's planned attack will set for the world. The United States will be declaring not simply verbally but by using its overwhelming armed force that a state may justly launch a war against another much smaller and weaker state even though it cannot prove that the enemy represents an imminent, direct, and critical threat, or show that the threat could not be deterred or managed by means other than war. It need only claim that the regime and its leader are evil, harbor hostile intentions, were attempting to arm themselves with dangerous weapons, and might therefore attempt at some future time to carry out their hostile aims, and that this claim as to an opponent's potential capabilities and intentions, a claim made solely by the attacking state and not subject to any international examination, justifies that state in eliminating the allegedly dangerous regime and leader preemptively.

A more dangerous, illegitimate norm and example can hardly be imagined. As could easily be shown by history, it completely subverts previous standards for judging the legitimacy of resorts to war, justifying any number of wars hitherto considered unjust and aggressive. It would, for example, justify not only the Austro-German decision for preventive war on Serbia in 1914, condemned by most historians, but also a German attack on Russia and/or France as urged by some German generals on numerous occasions between 1888 and 1914. It would in fact justify almost any attack by any state on any other for almost any reason. This is not a theoretical or academic point. The American example and standard for preemptive war, if carried out, would invite imitation and emulation, and get it. One can easily imagine plausible scenarios in which India could justly attack Pakistan or vice versa, or Israel any one of its neighbors, or China Taiwan, or South Korea North Korea, under this rule that suspicion of what a hostile regime might do justifies launching preventive wars to overthrow it.

We cannot want a world that operates on this principle, and therefore we cannot really want to use it ourselves. In a real, practical sense, Immanuel Kant's famous ethical principle that one must so act that the principle of one's action could become a universal law must also influence the conduct of states in international politics, above all the policy of the world's only superpower. Without some application of it especially in critical cases like this, a sane, durable international system becomes impossible.

Why a Preemptive War Would Undermine Our Alliances and World Leadership

The previous discussion makes it possible to answer this question more quickly. Many practical, prudential reasons explain why our allies almost unanimously oppose the idea of preemptive war on Iraq (some of them grounds already mentioned that ought to worry Americans as well). Europe has special reasons for concern: the large Muslim communities within many European states and the effects an American attack would have on their domestic politics; the fact that Europe's relations with the Arab and Muslim world geographically, historically and culturally, and even economically are much closer to the Middle East than ours, so that the repercussions of war (an oil shock, for example) could easily be far worse for them than for us.

In other words, Europeans see the United States riding roughshod over many European interests in a critical area where they have more at stake than do the Americans. And if that holds for Europeans, it holds trebly for the countries of the Middle East itself, Israel excepted. Turkey and Iran, for example, are directly, vitally interested in avoiding a war in which Iraq might break up and the Kurds fight for their independence. No Arab leader, however opposed to Saddam Hussein, wants to see Iraq destroyed or another Arab state crushed and humiliated by a Western power. And of course no moderate or pro-Western Arab or Muslim regime, vulnerable precisely because it is pro-Western, wants to stoke the fires of radical dissent and revolution with more television pictures of more Arabs being killed and their country subjugated by the Great Satan, infidel America.

Yet prudential considerations, powerful though they are, do not exhaust the reasons for the European opposition. (I cannot speak about Arabs and Muslims with any confidence.) The basic reason is precisely the one identified and discussed above: the sense that this will be an unjustified, unnecessary war, and that regardless of how it turns out militarily it will have bad long-range political consequences.

Many Americans explain away this opposition in Europe as the product of instinctive anti-Americanism, envy of American power, cynicism and world-despair (*Weltschmerz*), a war-weariness that makes them not merely eager to avoid more war, but ready to appease third-world dictators, the sense of their own decline and relative unimportance in the world, an inability to unite behind a common European foreign policy and defense capability accompanied by a tendency to carp at America for acting without them, and sometimes even anti-Semitism or a bias against Israel.

This is unfair, even where there is a modicum of substance to the charges. Americans ought to heed the advice of logician Morris Cohen: "First, if you can, refute my arguments. Then, if you must, impugn my motives." How little real, deep anti-Americanism there is in Europe and how ineffective it has been in influencing government policy have been repeatedly demonstrated in the past fifty years, right down to the reaction to September 11. Europeans, like Canadians, are not really envious or afraid of American power per se—at least their governments are not, which is what counts. These governments have been, if anything, too cautious in confronting the United States and asserting their views, rights, and interests as allies. What they fear is what they see as an ignorant, arrogant American hubris and recklessness in the use of that power increasingly evidenced by this administration, especially on this issue.

If this is true, it bodes ill for the future of the Atlantic alliance, a crucial element of world peace and stability over the last fifty years. No doubt this uniquely durable and flexible alliance has survived innumerable challenges and stresses and already outlived the predictions of its obsolescence and demise since the end of the Cold War. It is also true that differences between the US and its partners have always existed, and that there were European and Canadian complaints of American unilateralism and excessive reliance on force, answered by American charges of appeasement and indecision leveled against them, long before this issue became acute. But this is different. Other issues on which the two sides have disagreed during this administration (capital punishment, the Kyoto Protocol, the International Criminal Court, issues of trade and tariffs, etc.) do not really concern the central security and foreign policy aspects of the alliance. This issue goes to its heart. When the United States makes publicly clear that it intends to launch military action to overthrow the regime in a key state with which Europe has important relations regardless of what its alliance partners and other friends (e.g., Russia) think of the idea, this touches the core of the alliance as a joint instrument for security, peace, and freedom as nothing else has done in the past.

How? Both because the unilateral American planning of preemptive war against Iraq concerns the central collective security purposes of NATO and its machinery for joint action and alliance solidarity in critical situations, and also because here the general European approach to international peace clashes headlong with the American version (at least that of this administration). It will not do for the administration to say, as it often has, that it will be glad to consult with its European allies, but will do whatever it considers necessary for the defense of American interests regardless of what anyone else thinks. An essential element of any alliance relationship is that allies must exert influence on the foreign policy of their partner(s) and that the joint alliance policy must take account of the concerns of all the partners. The administration's stand on Iraq flatly contravenes that basic requirement for a durable alliance.

If this persists, it will not necessarily mean the formal end of NATO, but it will mean its hollowing out, as America's partners search for other combinations to defend their interests and find refuge from the likely consequences of America's actions and as America's opponents are encouraged to seek partners and form coalitions against it. America's power and position are strong enough and its margin of error wide enough that it can get away with a good deal of what one administration spokesman described as "internationalism à la carte," calling for support where it wants it, going its own way when it wishes, and insisting on having its way as the leader. But there are limits, and on this crucial issue the United States could well overstep them.

Why This Preemptive War Would Attack the Foundations of the International System—and Why We Should Care

This is a bit more abstract and needs a little more thumbnail history of the current international system to explain, but the basic point is not hard to understand. The planned war would violate and weaken the two basic principles which, developed over the past five centuries and combined in a fruitful tension, have enabled the international system to work and peace to grow in our own time.

Since the sixteenth century, the international system, first confined to Western Europe, then expanding to all of Europe, then becoming global under European domination, and now simply global, has developed inexorably though unevenly, with many advances and retreats, in two fundamental directions, different and divergent from each other, but nevertheless inextricably united. The first direction is the recognition and acceptance of the idea that the system must consist of independent units (in the main, states) coexisting in a coordinate system of equal juridical status and rights, as opposed to the medieval hierarchical system in which power and authority descended in ranks from God to Emperor to kings and princes down to the lowliest peasant. The triumph of this principle is usually ascribed, not wrongly but too simply and prematurely, to the Peace of Westphalia in 1648 ending the Thirty Years War and the era of religious wars in Europe.

The second major direction of development appears directly contrary to the first. It is the movement toward the association of independent units in international relations into unions (leagues, alliances, confederations, associations, etc.) for common vital purposes that could be realized only through such associations, the most important of these being stable peace and security. The fundamental story of that movement toward association, allowing for all the ups and downs, advances and retreats, is that this movement, though hopeless and marginal in its effects in the sixteenth, seventeenth, and much of the eighteenth centuries, nonetheless experienced a major early flowering in the nineteenth, and, after apparently disastrous setbacks in the early twentieth has ripened and borne unprecedented fruit in the late twentieth century.

I am aware that the notion that the history of international politics over the last four to five centuries has been one fundamentally of the growth and development of international peace will strike many as absurd, if not perverse. Yet I think it can be demonstrated (though not here). The central point is that while it may be difficult and controversial to document a decline in the incidence of war and other violent international conflict, including organized terrorism, there is no question or difficulty at all in demonstrating the reality over the centuries of a huge, immensely valuable growth in international peace. Critical areas of modern international relations—trade and business, communications, travel by land, sea and sky, the commercial use and exploitation of the sea and sky, international tourism and travel, international science and scholarship, immigration and emigration, the control of state borders, international property rights and business practices—even human and civil rights and religion—which were once in the realm of war, that is, governed solely by power, force, fraud, and individual state self-interest, have now throughout the developed world been generally brought into the realm of peace. That is, they have been brought under the governance of international treaties, conventions, common practices, and institutions to enforce jointly accepted rules. Where this is not true in certain parts of the world, we notice, it makes a critical difference, and we try to do something about it. The modern world in which we participate, from which we profit, and of which we boast could not operate without this enormous expansion of the realm of peace in international affairs. And this expansion is the product of a long-sought, dearly bought, highly fragile combination of these two fundamental principles of modern international relations: the recognition of state independence, and the willing acceptance by most international actors of the necessity and benefits of international associations and their requirements and rules.

This structure is what the intended American preemptive war on Iraq threatens and would violate. It would do so in two ways: by denying the right of Iraq to be treated as an independent state, and by rejecting the obligation of the United States to comply with the requirement bearing on all states to join in international associations and to abide by certain rules. The fundamental offense committed by Iraq against the United States is not any particular aggression or criminal act. The only one of these in the litany of Saddam Hussein's crimes and to which we decided to respond was his occupation of Kuwait, and that was duly reversed and punished. The offense has been and still is that Iraq, under the leadership of someone we consider an international criminal, has purportedly been trying persistently to acquire the same weapons that both we and some of our best friends and a number of neutral states already possess, namely, weapons of mass destruction. Note that our argument is not that these weapons (nuclear, biological, chemical) are inherently illegal and dangerous and should be banned universally by the international community. We could not argue that without condemning ourselves along with our friends, as we are notoriously the world's largest possessors of such weapons and have no intention of giving them up. The charge is rather that states like Iraq, because they have undemocratic governments, unjust social structures, dangerous ideologies, and criminal leaders (all according to American criteria) have no inherent right to seek or possess the same weapons of mass destruction as law-abiding democratic states possess, and deserve to be restrained, punished, and finally militarily overthrown by the United States if they persist in developing them, regardless of what other states think about this procedure.

Only deliberate effort enables one fully to grasp the implications of such a position. It is as clear a negation of the fundamental principle of the juridical equality and coordinate status of all recognized states within the international system as one could imagine. To put it bluntly, it declares that there is one law for the United States and other states of which it approves, and another law for all the rest. It is Orwellian: all states are equal, but some, especially the United States, are vastly more equal than others. There is no state, allied, friendly, neutral, or hostile, that will not note this implication, and fear it.

This position and policy is more than Orwellian; it is imperialist. I know full well how slippery, ill-defined, and emotionally loaded this term usually is, and how often and easily it is abused. Let me, at the risk of personalizing the discussion, state quickly the standpoint from which I make this claim. I consider myself by every standard save that of the current one-sided American political spectrum a conservative, especially in political outlook and general world view. I have no sympathy with the view that America has been historically an imperialist power. There are major imperialist chapters and aspects in its history, of course, and it was a full participant with others in the great wave of late nineteenth- and early twentieth-century European imperialism, but its founding ideology was and remains anti-imperialist, it has passed up more tempting opportunities for imperialist gain than it seized, and its overall record is more anti-imperialist than imperialist down to this day. Nor do I share the left-wing denunciation of American hegemony as per se a great menace today. It has its dangers and negative aspects, but on balance American leadership has done much more good than harm in the decades since World War II, and I want it in general to continue. It is precisely from this conservative, pro-American stance that I claim that this would be an imperialist war.

I do so because there is no defensible definition of imperialism that would not fix that label upon it. Imperialism means simply and centrally the exercise of final authority and decision-making power by one government over another government or community foreign to itself. Empire does not require the direct annexation and administration of a foreign territory or its people; in fact, it usually does not mean that at all. Imperial rule is normally indirect, exercised through local authorities co-opted by the imperial regime. This was the case with the Roman Empire, the so-called Holy Roman Empire, the British, the Ottoman, the Napoleonic, and many others one could name—even Hitler's short-lived one. All that is required for an imperial relationship is that the final authority and power over crucial decisions of foreign policy, war and peace, and the place of the territory and people within the international system lie with the imperial power.

This is the relationship between America and Iraq that this war intends and is designed to establish. We intend to use armed force against Iraq in order to acquire the power to decide who shall rule Iraq, what kind of government it will have, what kind of weapons it will develop for its own security, what kind of foreign policy it will have, and whose side and what stance it will take in the crucial questions affecting it and its region (Israel, terrorism, Islamism versus secular rule, even for some Americans what kind of economy it will develop and what kind of educational and social systems it will erect under American tutelage). This is clearly imperialism, even if we claim and really believe that we are doing it for noble ends—liberation, democracy, capitalism, human rights, whatever. Nineteenth-century imperialism was also conducted under the banner of noble ends—Christianity, civilization, an end to the slave trade, economic development, etc.

Let no one reply that this is what we did to Nazi Germany and Imperial Japan after World War II, with great benefit to them and the rest of the world. We went to war with these powers because they attacked us and many other nations. That was a justified defensive war, and the dimensions of the war, the enormous damage it did, the crimes and atrocities Germany and Japan committed in it (though we and our allies were not blameless), and the dimensions of their defeat justified and virtually compelled an occupation and period of tutelage. A preemptive war on Iraq is a totally different proposition.

Besides being imperialist in violating one fundamental basis of world order, the recognition of the independence and equal status of states, this war also would violate its counterpart, the principle of association and the need to observe community rules and bounds. In planning and preparing for this war, the United States is declaring to the world that it really does not consider this principle of association binding upon it; that the American government intends to decide what is best for the United States itself, on its own, listening perhaps to what allies and friends have to say, but acting strictly for its own self-defined interests; and that we do not need the sanction of the UN, NATO, or any other association or institution to which we belong and lead to justify it—this despite our knowledge that in this issue and decision the vital interests of many other countries, some of them our closest allies, are at stake even more than our own.

Once again, we cannot want a world that operates by these rules—but that is the world we would be promoting.

Why a Preemptive War on Iraq Is Unnecessary and Unhelpful for Security

One possible response to this argument might go as follows: "If you are right that we should not do this, what do you suggest as the alternative—that we simply sit on our hands and let Hussein and other dangerous leaders develop weapons of mass destruction with no control on their possible use by themselves or by terrorists? Must we really wait until we (i.e., the United States and allied countries it protects) are actually attacked or at least overtly, directly, demonstrably threatened before we may justifiably respond?"

That this does not guarantee perfect security for us or anyone else is true—but nothing can, least of all preemptive war. We have, however, powerful means of defense and deterrence both within our own hands and available through the international system—another good reason for not wrecking it by preemptive war. If new, more effective means to check new dangers are needed, this system is the way to develop them. If we use these means and this system sensibly, we can enjoy a measure of security far greater than most of the rest of the world has enjoyed in the past or enjoys now.

If this seems not good enough, it is because of our own unrealistic perceptions and expectations. There can be no perfect security against either terrorism or weapons of mass destruction—especially not through the use of military force. Trying to eliminate all the possible nests and sources of terrorism through military action is like trying to kill fleas with a hammer: it does more damage to oneself and the environment than to the fleas. (This does not at all rule out armed police actions like those against the Taliban or identifiable rebel groups.) The idea of eliminating all evil regimes that might use weapons of mass destruction or let terrorists use them is impossible and counterproductive, a bad dream.

What too many seem to forget, however, is that we and others have lived through this sort of danger before, and that defensive measures short of war can work. The menace of having nuclear weapons in the hands of mortal enemies who might use them against us was far greater during the Cold War than it is now. A few then called for preventive war to eliminate it; they were, thank God, not heeded. Terrorism has been around for centuries, and several countries in the nineteenth and twentieth centuries, notably Spain, Russia, Italy, and the United Kingdom, survived worse terrorist campaigns and threats than we have experienced or are likely to experience. Right now the threat of terrorism is greater for the Philippines, Israel, Colombia, Peru, Nepal, and Sri Lanka than for us. Terrorism, like nuclear war, is an evil we must of course combat, but cannot hope to extirpate and must learn to endure and outlive.

In other words, a preemptive war against Iraq would be unnecessary as well as wrong, and would serve no useful purpose while doing us, the Iraqi people, the world, and the international system great harm.[4] When the great American historian Charles

---

4   There is one possible (in my view, likely) motive for the planned war that I will mention only in this footnote, not because it is unimportant but because it involves too many delicate issues to be discussed adequately here. Some have ascribed President Bush's determination to oust Saddam Hussein to certain personal or domestic political aims, among them his desire both to emulate his father and to surpass him while avoiding his mistakes, especially the alleged mistake of failing to finish the job of destroying Hussein's regime in 1991. Without claiming any privileged sources of information, I doubt that these are more than contributing factors. Much more plausible is the suggestion that this plan is being promoted in the interests of Israel. Certainly it is being pushed very hard by a number of influential supporters of Israel of the hawkish neoconservative stripe in and outside the administration (Richard Perle, Paul Wolfowitz, William Kristol and others), and one could easily make the case that a successful preventive war on Iraq would promote particular Israeli security interests more than general American ones.

If this is an important factor, then I would make just two comments. First, it would represent something to my knowledge unique in history. It is common for great powers to try to fight wars by proxy, getting smaller powers to fight for their interests. This would be the first instance I know where a great power

A. Beard was asked at the end of his career what was the most important thing he had learned from history, he replied, "That the mills of God grind slowly, but they grind exceeding small, and that chickens always come home to roost." He was an agnostic, and so presumably meant only that this was the way history ultimately worked out, and that long-range systemic consequences were the most important. He was right. If we carry out what we are now planning, then regardless of any short-term success we may have, our chickens will ultimately come home to roost.

(in fact, a superpower) would do the fighting as the proxy of a small client state. Second, while Israel's survival and security certainly represent a vital interest for the United States, the Middle East, and the world, I am convinced that a preemptive war on Iraq would be as counterproductive in the long run as the Israeli occupation of Lebanon engineered by Ariel Sharon or the current Sharon/Likud efforts to destroy Palestinian resistance and terrorism and abort any independent Palestinian state by sheer military force. There are better ways for America to insure Israel's survival, including, for example, a full, formal military alliance and territorial guarantee. But that is a separate though closely related topic too vast and complex to open here.

5

A Papier-Maché Fortress

2002

Philip Bobbitt's *The Shield of Achilles* is a bad book.* It is error strewn, it suffers from grand delusions of theoretical adequacy, and it is unscholarly. This judgment, however, being evidently a minority one, imposes an obligation not only to render the work's aim, thesis, and argument fairly before criticizing it, but also to account for the book's evident appeal to the public, as well as to several distinguished historians who have endorsed it.

The former task is not easy, given the book's great length and convoluted development, but is aided by repeated statements of the author's aims and theses. The book, Bobbitt writes in his prologue, concerns the evolution of the modern state, in particular "the *relationship* between strategy and the legal order as this relationship has shaped and transformed the modern state and the society composed of these states." Wars and the attendant revolutions in military affairs, he argues, have been the engine of change in the constitutional order of states since the Renaissance: "*each* of the important revolutions in military affairs enabled a political revolution in the fundamental constitutional order of the State."

Bobbit holds that four great epochal wars transformed the dominant constitution of states in previous eras (Habsburg-Valois, the Thirty Years' War, the wars of Louis XIV, and the French Revolutionary wars). Now the most recent epochal war, the Long War of 1914–90, has "brought into being a new form of the state—the market-state"—and put "the constitutional order of the nation-state . . . everywhere under siege." Major new developments—human rights as a universal norm, weapons

---

* Philip Bobbitt, *The Shield of Achilles: War, Peace, and the Course of History* (New York, 2002).

of mass destruction, global and transnational threats, globalization of the economy, and global communications networks penetrating all states and societies—threaten both the sovereignty of individual states and the legitimacy of the international order by making it impossible for nation-states to fulfill their legitimating purpose—namely, to maximize the welfare of their citizens. What Bobbitt calls market-states, however, promise instead to maximize opportunity.

In an instance of the elliptical exposition that characterizes the book throughout, Bobbitt begins the substantive historical defense of this thesis at the end, presenting 1914–90 as a single Long War between fascism, communism, and parliamentarianism to decide the dominant constitutional form of the modern nation-state. A brief excursus summarizing the historiographical debate over the revolutions in military affairs in the fifteenth to eighteenth centuries is followed by three longer chapters covering the history of the state from the Renaissance to 1914. These chapters, together with the one on the Long War, comprise the historical core of the book, called Book I: The State of War, and the basis for its projections about the present and future. With them come five "plates" that depict in simplified form the patterns and correlations the author detects in history and that encapsulate his essential arguments.

Plate 1 lists six distinct constitutional orders of the state since the Renaissance—princely, kingly, territorial, state-nation, nation-state, and (emerging) market-state. Plate 2 links these to Bobbit's five epochal wars that "brought a particular constitutional order to primacy." Plate 3 lists the peace treaties that "end epochal wars [and] ratify a particular constitutional order for the society of states"—Augsburg, Westphalia, Utrecht, Vienna, Versailles, and Paris (1990).

The last two plates concern Bobbitt's most crucial theses, those that tie strategic, military, and constitutional factors tightly together. Plate 4 illustrates how "each constitutional order asserts a unique basis for legitimacy." In the princely state "the State confers legitimacy on the dynasty," whereas in the kingly state "the dynasty confers legitimacy on the State." The territorial state is legitimated by its claim to manage the country efficiently; the state-nation by its claim to forge the identity of the nation; the nation-state by its promise to better the welfare of its citizens; and the emerging market-state by its promise to maximize the opportunities of its citizens. Plate 5, "Historic, Strategic, and Constitutional Innovations," illustrates how "a constitutional order achieves dominance by best exploiting the strategic and constitutional innovations of its era"; it does this by linking the claimed innovations and dominant political characteristics of each era with their respective military innovations and leading features. For example, the absolutism and secularism characteristic of kingly states is linked to the gunpowder revolution, lengthy sieges, and standing armies, while the trade control and aristocratic leadership that feature in the territorial state are tied to professional armies and limited cabinet wars, and so on with the other main types.

This historical basis laid, Bobbitt turns to the current crisis. The challenge to the nation-state from the current revolution in military affairs, and the nation-state's rapid loss of legitimacy, demands deep thought about the concrete transformations this will require of the new market-state in terms of security, politics, and welfare. He surveys what he typologizes as the five policy choices now being offered for the United States after the Cold War—new nationalism, new internationalism, new realism, new evangelism (i.e., democratic peace), and new leadership (i.e., permanent American world hegemony)—but argues that none offers the new paradigm needed. Of three possible forms of the market-state (mercantile, entrepreneurial and managerial)—yet another typology—he concludes that the United States will be an entrepreneurial market-state, as it should. He ends Book I with speculation on the likely character of wars in the coming era of the market-state.

Book II, "States of Peace," is about what Bobbit calls the society of states. It rests on a key assertion: "that international law derives from constitutional law—and thus follows the same periods of stability and revolutionary change charted in Book I." Thus, "contemporary developments in limiting sovereignty are a consequence of the change in the constitutional order to a market-state." This returns us to the grand historical pattern, once again unfolded from the end rather than the beginning. Two long and strange chapters then develop Bobbitt's argument that the nation-state era in world society, founded on the Wilsonian premise of self-determination, has now run aground on its inability to solve central problems presented both by nationhood itself and the new world emerging since the Cold War. The first of these describes Versailles and the entire post–World War I settlement primarily through the personality and activities of Wilson's adviser Colonel Edward M. House. The second links the famous Kitty Genovese incident (a gruesome murder in New York City in 1964, which bystanders did nothing to stop) to the war in Bosnia (culminating in the failure of the UN or NATO to stop Bosnian Serb atrocities at Srebrenica in July 1995), in order to demonstrate the death of the society of nation-states.

Book II then returns to earlier history to show how "the great peace settlements of the epochal wars have shaped the constitutional order of the society of states." Brief chapters on the peace settlements of Augsburg, Westphalia, Utrecht, and Vienna, and longer ones on Versailles and Paris (1990), summarize the provisions of the treaties and their supposed constitutional impact on the society of states. Accompanying each are short discussions of the interpretations given each settlement by leading jurists and theorists, and in the last section an analysis of various American schools and approaches on the relations between international law and international politics. These discussions are by far the most interesting and instructive parts of the book, demonstrating Bobbitt's expertise and authority in his own field and his ability to construct a tight, coherent narrative and argument. But the relation of these segments to his main argument is unclear.

The final section of Book II, entitled "The Society of Market States," speculates further on the challenges to the new international order of market states, and the nature of war and peace in the coming age. The bewildering variety of the propositions offered and the absence or impossibility of proof or substantiation would seem to put this section beyond summary or critical evaluation, at least for historians. The author insists, however, that his arguments and prescriptions for the present and future derive from the historical scheme earlier developed and schematized, so even Bobbitt's futurology invites evaluation according to the standards of historical scholarship.

A Reach Too Shallow

As history, Bobbit's work unquestionably presents a broad panorama and offers a bold, arresting, and apparently coherent set of theses and arguments relevant to the world today. The historical scheme seems compelling, the analysis of the current crisis cogent, the predictions and scenarios for the future important to consider. The overall recommendation—that America strive for market principles globally and in domestic politics, and continued American military domination and the ability to fight a series of low-level contests as the only way to avoid the next epochal war—offers a program congenial to many Americans today. These qualities, one supposes, have recommended the work to many lay readers and some distinguished scholars. What is wrong with it?

As historical scholarship, a great deal. The book suffers from so many grave defects of an evidential, logical, and methodological character as to render it unreliable both for fact and interpretation. Stating such a verdict flatly, while being unable for reasons of space to bring full evidence for it, is uncomfortable. Since it is not possible to comment inclusively on over 900 pages of text in a review of a few thousand words, only a few of the book's technical historical flaws, though they are crucially important, can be discussed.

The first of these is inadequate research. Sixty pages of notes and eleven of bibliography may seem impressive, but the reading required to undergird so sweeping a reinterpretation of history as Bobbitt offers would have to be at least ten times as great and yet also more discriminating—a nearly superhuman demand, to be sure, but one that is inseparable from the undertaking. Apart from discussions of Bobbitt's specialty, constitutional law, the only topic among the many huge, controversial ones he discusses on which his reading is adequate is that on the fifteenth- to eighteenth-century revolutions in military affairs.

Inadequate research contributes to other defects but cannot wholly account for them. Ungrounded generalizations, naked assertions, logical leaps, vague language, conceptual confusion, contradictions, arbitrary definitions, exaggerations and distortions, and major omissions of vital material abound. Then there is the problem of outright factual errors.

Factual errors are bound to occur in any book as broad and ambitious as this one. What counts is the level of their incidence and significance, and it is unacceptably high. Some errors do not directly affect the overall theses, but others demonstrate a general misconception of a problem important to the story. As to the former, for example, when Bobbitt writes that in 1798–99 France attacked and conquered Switzerland, the Papal States, Piedmont-Sardinia, and Naples (which is like saying that the Soviet Union in 1947–48 attacked and conquered Poland, Czechoslovakia, and Hungary), the factual error shows only that he misunderstands the nature of French expansion and the allied response in a crucial period of one of his epochal wars. But the statement that after 1815 the majority of Poles lived under Prussian and Austrian (rather than Russian) rule is not an incidental error. It shows that the author cannot have understood the Polish question either in its domestic or international aspects. It would be like trying to understand the American race problem if one believed that after 1865 the majority of freed blacks lived in the North.

Still other errors reveal the vagueness and vacuity of certain core concepts. When Bobbitt writes that the Congress of Vienna "recognized the state of Switzerland as a single state-nation," he demonstrates not only a misconception of what the Congress did, but the meaninglessness of his category of the state-nation.[1] Similarly, when Bobbitt contends that Russia was able to withstand Napoleon's onslaught in 1812 through strategic retreat because "she [Russia] was not a territorial state, and her dynasty did not constitutionally depend on the support of the nobility and the army," he not only gives an absurd explanation for the strategic and tactical decisions made in 1812 and betrays an ignorance of major facts about Russian history, but again

---

1 If one can call the Swiss Confederation of twenty-two independent cantons legitimated and neutralized by international treaties under guarantee of the great powers a state-nation—meaning a state acquiring its legitimacy by forming its people into a nation and putting the people at the service of the state—then one can do anything.

demonstrates how malleable and hence meaningless his concept of the "territorial state" is.[2]

Finally, certain factual errors reveal misconceptions so basic that they raise questions as to the author's ability to deal with a whole complex of central problems and issues. Bobbitt describes European feelings about war and peace at the end of the nineteenth century as follows: "There seems to have been widespread agreement on two expectations: that science and technology would make war impossible and that international law would govern the relationships between states." This is like saying that the general late nineteenth-century view on the solar system was that the sun revolved around the earth. A misconception so fundamental and so contradictory to central, well-known facts established by a massive literature disqualifies Bobbitt from being taken seriously on the international order in prewar Europe or the origins of World War I, the start of the most important of his epochal wars.

Even more disturbing in certain ways than factual errors are instances of Bobbitt's twisting the clear meaning of evidence to fit his theory. Two examples: he praises Hedley Bull's "pathbreaking" book, *The Anarchical Society*, for describing the international world in Hobbesian terms as without law, "a world of all against all and each one against every other one." Bull's book was indeed important—for precisely the opposite reason. His whole emphasis was on the international system as a *society*, anarchical solely in the sense of having no recognized lawgiver but otherwise involving real community, norms, rules, and elements of law. Bobbitt similarly takes a statement by Bismarck defending his policy of pure *Realpolitik* in the interests of Prussia against his opponents' charge of lack of principle and makes it into something Bismarck then opposed: a manifesto for nationalism as "the authentic voice of the nation-state."

---

2 The Russian government aspired to improve its efficiency every bit as much as eighteenth-century Prussia or Austria; Peter the Great and Catherine II were enlightened despots in the same mold as Frederick II or Joseph II. The statement that its dynasty did not depend on the support of the nobility and army—in light of the history of Russia's eighteenth- and nineteenth-century crises—is nonsense.

A Reach Too Far

Instances of Bobbitt's bad scholarship could be multiplied, but simply to indict the book in that fashion ignores the big picture: the book's theses and argument. Could they not be mainly right and very much worth thinking about, even if Bobbitt is not a good historian? A good question; but the answer is no. The broad scheme of war, peace and the course of history given here is equally flawed. It is, in fine, an imposing fortress of papier-maché.

The first problem is that nothing in Bobbitt's very grand scheme is ever proved. Nothing major in it—neither categories, concepts, fundamental assumptions, alleged links, and causal connections nor definitions of critical terms—is rigorously analyzed, hypothesized, and operationalized. Nor is any of it tested against contrary evidence and alternative views and shown to be more solidly based than competing schemes and interpretations. If one believes it, one does so essentially because it looks good, or because one wishes to believe it.

The second point is that under close examination the grand scheme falls apart. Central categories develop fissures and cracks and their contents leak out and mingle with others. Crucial concepts, when tested, prove tautological or simply empty. Vital causal connections and links between phenomena in different spheres prove nonexistent or unconvincing. Major generalizations central to it prove untenable. An example: One of Bobbitt's main contentions is that epochal wars and their peace settlements establish the dominant constitutional form of the state and the constitution of an era's society of states. The first of these, the Habsburg-Valois wars and the Peace of Augsburg, meet none of the requirements of the theory. These wars were not epochal but local and sporadic, and did not end in 1555 but continued underground until once more breaking out openly in the 1630s and ending in 1659. The Peace of Augsburg had nothing to do with them; it established only a temporary and unstable truce in Germany's religious conflicts, and led to no new constitutional order either in Germany or elsewhere.

Or take Bobbitt's concepts of different state constitutions—princely, kingly, territorial, and so forth. Not only is each of these fuzzy in definition and the distinctions drawn between them arbitrary and artificial, but at least one and perhaps two (the state-nation and the territorial state) are figments of Bobbitt's imagination, corresponding to no historical reality whatsoever. Of the five great powers at the Vienna Congress that supposedly established and legitimated the dominant state-nation form, not one remotely fits his definition of it—and not one wanted or dared to do after 1815 what he says state-nations do, which is to put their people at the service of the state. As for the territorial state, its supposed legitimating principle—the more efficient use of the state's resources—would fit some states and not others in any era; and some of the central defining characteristics Bobbit ascribes to its era as opposed to others (e.g., the unimportance of dynastic succession, a coolly rational secularism in regard to religion, and the waging of only limited cabinet wars) are all flatly untrue.

Indeed, the whole notion that each different constitutional form of the state rests on a particular distinctive legitimating principle—so that nation-states try to maximize the welfare of all their citizens while market-states try to maximize opportunity—is unhistorical to the point of absurdity. Had Bobbitt done any serious study of his eighteenth-century territorial states, he would have seen that many of them, at least, saw their *raison d'être* in promoting the welfare of all their subjects as they saw it, and they tried to do so in part by maximizing their opportunities within the established order.[3]

Alas, most instances of incoherence and conceptual confusion in *The Shield of Achilles* come down, ultimately, to the central one involving Bobbitt's notion of what drives the course of history. He vastly exaggerates and distorts the roles of war and peace settlements in constituting states and the international system. Yes, states to a considerable degree are *made* by and for war; but states *exist and endure* by and for governance. The

---

3 See, for example, Marc Raeff, *The Well-Ordered Police State* (New Haven, CT, 1983); and C. B. A. Behrens, *Society, Government, and the Enlightenment* (New York, 1985).

constitutional changes that states have undergone over time (in a way far more uneven, contingent, and complex than Bobbitt indicates) have had more to do overall with trying to meet challenges of governance than those of war, and those demands, while changing enormously in detail over time, remain essentially the same in kind: order, welfare, and legitimacy. How rulers, governments, and peoples conceive and try to meet these needs varies; their need to do so in order to endure remains constant.

As for epochal wars and major peace settlements settling major questions about the international order, yes, they sometimes have—but mostly in a negative rather than positive way, doing more to clear the ground and establish what cannot be done than to establish what the new order will be. This is true of all the genuine epochal wars and peace settlements that Bobbitt discusses. The Thirty Years War, for example, ended any possibility of Spanish Habsburg dominance in Europe as a whole and of Austrian Habsburg-Imperial-Catholic rule in Germany; it thereby cleared the way for France's rise and for a different kind of confessional though not secular order for Germany. *Mutatis mutandis*, the same holds for the War of the Spanish Succession and the Peace of Utrecht: they ended Louis XIV's bid for hegemony and opened the way for a balance of power system, but they did not really establish it. That took fifteen years of further war, crises, major adjustments, and new or revised settlements. The same holds even for the far greater French Revolutionary and Napoleonic Wars and the most ambitious and comprehensive peace settlement ever attempted, at the Congress of Vienna. Together they ended the Napoleonic bid for empire and laid the basis for a new order based on legality and solidarity, but even this genuine effort to solve all Europe's problems at once did not really establish a durable constitutional order per se. Within five years the solidarity eroded; within fifteen the settlement underwent major challenges and revisions.

This points up a further weakness in Bobbitt's world-historical scheme: its neglect of what follows the epochal wars and peace settlements he tries to link too neatly together. What counts most in every case is not simply the war itself and its results, or the provisions of the peace settlement, but what actually happens thereafter, what states and peoples do with the opportunities and challenges presented. In other words, the determinist strategic-constitutional paradigm makes less difference than the contingent responses and adaptations made by many different actors.

The same observation applies to Bobbitt's epochal war and settlement, the supposed single Long War of 1914–90 between parliamentarianism, fascism, and communism over which would be the dominant constitutional form of the nation-state. In the end, words are defenseless things, and so is history, at least in some hands. Anyone may choose to see this period as one long war over this central issue if one wishes. But this pattern may not be used to explain the origins of World War I and II, as Bobbitt seeks to do, or explain away the great issue that was settled by those wars and the settlement of 1945. World War I was not caused by a clash between supposedly proto-fascist Germany and parliamentary France and Britain. The war arose out of power-political strategic rivalry between Germany, Austria-Hungary, and Russia, resulting from the fatal breakdown of their long triangular restraining alliance and leading to an acute security crisis for all three—especially for Austria-Hungary, which actually precipitated the war. The confrontation between parliamentarianism, fascism, and communism was one result of the war, not its cause; and it was not the chief issue or cause of World War II either. In both wars, the central issue was a German bid to dominate the continent by power-political means, and that issue was finally solved once and for all in 1945. In the most important sense, therefore, 1914–90 was not one Long War.

A Saving Grace?

One question remains: If the main historical paradigm is not sound or helpful, what about the argument for an emerging new order based on a new kind of state, the market-state, and Bobbitt's discussion of new policies, strategies, and paradigms necessary for that new era? How much is that worth?

Many of Bobbitt's individual thoughts and arguments seem to me sensible and insightful, many others foolish, some wrong, and one or two dangerous and even a bit sinister. The problem, however, once again, is that the whole discussion of the emerging market-state and the market-state international system is one long question-begging exercise; it assumes the point at issue that needs to be proved and argues from it as though it had been proved. Bobbitt greatly exaggerates the death of the nation-state, but more important, he does not render even comprehensible, much less probable or proved, the emergence and existence—indeed, the very definition and possibility—of his market-state. It is never defined by anything more concrete than an advertising slogan—"maximizing opportunity for all its citizens"—as if that were not a means by which many states of various kinds have often tried to promote welfare, improve their powers to govern, and gain legitimacy. No serious attempt is made to show that the market, efficient for individual and corporate economic activity, can be made the basis for the governance of the state. The main evidence given for its emergence consists of selected extracts from speeches and press releases by Bill Clinton and Tony Blair, and the evidence offered to show that the historic transition to it has occurred is almost too ludicrous to discuss: the difference between the UN-NATO failure to stop the Bosnian Serb massacres at Srebrenica, supposed to prove the failure of nation-state principles to meet problems arising from nationhood, and NATO's intervention to stop Serbian "ethnic cleansing" in Kosovo three years later, supposed to arise from new market-state principles. This is like arguing that the shift from Anglo-French appeasement of Hitler beginning in 1936 and the decision for war in 1939 shows a fundamental shift in the constitution of the society of states.

Readers may choose to believe that a new market-state society of states is emerging, and they may read this book for counsel on how to meet its challenges. They should not believe, however, that the course of history supports this prophecy.

6

International Order and Its Current Enemies

2004

In this essay I propose several sweeping propositions about international order: that it is structurally prior to international peace and justice and required for it; that in the anarchical society of international politics any order must be based on the principle of voluntary association and exclusion, with their attached rewards and sanctions; that such a working order has been emerging over centuries and has resulted in an undeniable growth of world peace, though without ending war; and that this emergent international order is now under attack from various directions. One such attack—not the worst or most dangerous in the long run but very grave at present—is the current foreign policy of the United States, which directly denies or indirectly subverts the principles and trends that have led to the emergence of a promising international order.

I fear that I may be reprising here the role I remember playing in the conferences that led to Glen Stassen's book *Just Peacemaking*—that of a skunk at a garden party.[1] Although most of the conference attendees were speaking of peace, justice, and other related noble goals and virtues, a few, including me, kept talking about international order and, in my case, arguing for the necessary, inevitable priority of a quest for order over a search for justice and peace in international affairs.

Such language was bound to seem suspect in a discussion of just peacemaking—and still is today. The Scriptures undoubtedly

---

1 Glen Stassen, ed., *Just Peacemaking: Ten Practices for Abolishing War* (Cleveland, OH, 1998).

speak far more about peace and justice than about order. Calls for law and order are constantly used by authoritarian leaders and institutions and by privileged elites in general to defend and perpetuate an unjust status quo. All systems of order involve injustice; many are based on it, and innumerable crimes have been committed in the name of law and order. Nonetheless, I want to defend once more a certain priority of order over peace and justice in international affairs—not a normative priority, as if order were a higher or better good than peace and justice, or even a chronological priority, as if one first had to have order and then wait some indefinite period for some peace and justice to grow out of it, but a structural and logical priority. International peace and justice are impossible and unthinkable without international order in the way liberty is unthinkable without law or good health without a sound physiological system.

I urge this order, moreover, not as an abstract academic or theoretical exercise but as an intensely practical matter. Although I have no practical, positive steps toward healing the world's ills to suggest, as a historian I do want to share my conviction that the worst danger to international peace and justice today lies in current threats and assaults directed against the existing international order—an order with centuries of costly development invested in it, that has begun to ripen and bear fruit especially in recent decades, and for which we have no viable replacement. The most important task in promoting peace and justice, therefore, must be to defend that international order against its current enemies. We must reform and change that order, to be sure, but we must also defend it against threats and attacks from various quarters—one of the most serious of which, and one we and others in the United States can readily do something about, stems from current US ideas, attitudes, and policies.

This argument requires saying something very quickly about this emergent world order from a historical perspective. Some of this description will be familiar—in fact, it rehearses briefly certain points made in my chapter of *Just Peacemaking*— but some is not and reflects what has happened and is happening to that order in recent years.[2] One begins by recognizing that the

---

2 Paul W. Schroeder, "Work with Emerging Cooperative Forces in the

current international system—though enormously expanded, transformed, and rendered incomparably more complex and interdependent since its origins centuries ago—still constitutes, as ever, an anarchical society. It has never been either simply a Hobbesian world of war of everyone against everyone else or a world of clear relationships structured and governed by law. It is anarchical in the sense that there is no one recognized lawgiver; it is a society in the sense that its members are inextricably connected and constantly interacting in unavoidable, necessary, and important ways and that means must be devised—rules, norms, conventions, common practices, and even laws—for making those relations and transactions at worst tolerable and calculable and at best mutually beneficial. In this anarchical society, some competition and conflict are inevitable, and violent conflict—including war—is always possible. This is so not simply or mainly because some players do evil things for evil purposes, though that is clearly true, but because the goods all the players are seeking in international politics are scarce, diverse, and badly distributed. Moreover, the general goods all seek—order, welfare, and legitimacy—are defined differently, sought in different competing ways, justified by different irreconcilable claims and rights, and pursued from different starting points in terms of power and advantage.

This description is old and conventional, but it leads to an unconventional conclusion. As a general phenomenon, war is not a puzzle, difficult to understand and explain; peace is. It is understandable that scholars, especially historians, constantly investigate and debate the causes of wars, but in a way this analysis inverts reality. Wars are natural, can just happen, and are easy to understand in the context of international politics. As a historian, I never have met a war that after a little reading I could not easily understand and explain in the broad sense of why it happened at all. Peace is artificial: It always is devised and contrived; it never just happens.

Thus, peace is the puzzle. Why have there not been more wars? Why have so many been avoided or long postponed? More important still, why has peace grown? The mystery is not the

International System," in Stassen, *Just Peacemaking*, 133–45.

persistence of war or the occurrence of great, terrible wars but the very existence of peace; the occurrence of longer and longer periods of relative general peace; the undeniable reality of the growth of peace; the expansion of a zone of international peace over more and more of the globe; the shift in history of vast, vital areas of human activity in the world arena from the zone of war to the zone of peace—that is, from being under sway of force, fraud, and violence to becoming calculable, normal activities regularly conducted under international rules, laws, normative principles, and regulated procedures. The number of these activities carried on internationally that used to be in the sphere of war and now are mostly in the sphere of peace is staggering: trade of all kinds; communications; travel by land, sea, and air; movements of peoples; health and sanitation; ownership of property; protection of one's person and rights; even civil rights and religion—the list goes on and on.

Therefore, for scholars and for everyone who is interested in pursuing just peacemaking, the central question is not so much what causes war and how it can be avoided as what makes peace grow and how this growth can be fostered. The basic answer I suggest to this question is that peace grows through the gradual, tortuous, uneven, yet nonetheless undeniable growth of international order.

Although in this essay I cannot describe the evolution of that international order or evaluate its present state, there is a fundamental principle on which the evolution of peace has rested since the beginnings of the modern international system in fifteenth- to sixteenth-century Europe: the principle of voluntary association. If one looks at all the great schemes and plans for peace in Europe and the world since 1500 or so (here speaking of peace in the usual more restricted sense—an absence of organized violence between settled communities under stable governing authorities), they all rest on a single principle: forming durable voluntary associations of like-minded rulers and governments for the collective purposes of preserving peace among themselves and defending themselves against external threats and dangers. I refer here not to the essentially military alliances so common in history that rely principally or exclusively on the use or threat of force to maintain peace. Historically, these alliances have sometimes worked temporarily but almost always proved fragile and temporary and have done as much to provoke counter-alliances and conflict as to promote durable peace. I mean here leagues, associations, confederations, or unions that rely for their long-term efficacy and durability mainly on the inherent benefits of belonging to the association and the penalties of exclusion from it.

The immediate answer, of course, is that these associations haven't worked. This notion represents the typical woolly headed idealism of the academic peacenik. From the leagues for perpetual peace dreamed up by the Duke of Sully or the Abbé de St. Pierre through Immanuel Kant or the Concert of Europe to the League of Nations and the United Nations, such groups and institutions have not stopped war and aggression, and relying on them to do so can only make war and aggression worse. That assessment is a very wrong, one-sided view of history. True, these leagues and association—and their underlying principle of association/exclusion—have not eliminated large-scale war or the possibility of war, but that is like saying that the science and/or art of medicine that has developed over ages has failed because it has not eliminated disease or the possibility of recurrent epidemic disease today, ignoring all that it has done to prolong and improve human life. Such a perspective comes from concentrating one's attention solely on the occurrence and possibility of war rather than the evolution and reality of peace. More important, where we can see that this method of voluntary association and its underlying principle have failed in the past, as they doubtless often have—sometimes in dramatic and tragic fashion—we also can see why these failures have happened; we can analyze the structural as well as individual causes for failure, just as we can see why the art of medicine simply could not work until certain structural deficiencies in knowledge, techniques, and organization were overcome.

These structural deficiencies that in the past made this principle of international order inadequate for durable peace (not useless, simply not good enough) can be recognized and named—insufficient carrots to induce states to join; insufficient sticks to sanction defectors and rulebreakers; inadequate means of distributing the benefits and burdens of membership fairly; fears of costs and risks exceeding the benefits of membership; insufficient unity of beliefs and purposes; and insufficient adaptability to allow the association to gain new members, change goals, and meet new needs. These problems are structural in the sense that they are inherent and not just incidental, but not structural in the sense that they are insoluble or unmanageable, as some observers insist—that they derive from the very structure of international relations and therefore cannot be overcome.

History, I am convinced, shows the opposite. These structural deficiencies have been largely overcome and are still being overcome by powerful, fundamental changes in modern international relations—trends and developments long under way that have ripened and accelerated in recent decades. The four major trends I would emphasize—though again I cannot discuss them here—are the decline in the utility of major war as a tool of statecraft; the rise of the trading state—that is, the fact that where once it was true that war made the state and the state made war, it is now more true that trade makes successful states and successful states make trade; globalization and the attendant dramatic increases in the volume, density, and speed of international communications and exchanges of all kinds, along with an equally startling increase in the number and activity of international and transnational organizations, institutions, and actors; and the gradual emergence of a broad consensus on some form of guaranteed civil and human rights, constitutional democracy, and market economy as the norm for membership in the international community.

I do not contend that these developments have eliminated the danger of war, force, and violence in international relations or the need to guard against them. I do claim that they have made a worldwide international order that is based primarily on this principle of voluntary association possible, feasible, and to an increasing degree a practical functioning reality. The benefits of this order and its associations and the need for governments and societies to belong to it have become so compelling and the disadvantages and dangers of exclusion from it so great that even ideological enemies of this order and rogue states have to find ways to integrate themselves into it. The evidence in recent history—the North Atlantic Treaty Organization (NATO), the pacification and integration of Europe, the European Union, the end of the Cold War, new relations with states such as China or Vietnam—is obvious and overwhelming. Moreover, the process continues. Given time, I would argue, what has happened and is happening with Libya, Syria, Iran, even North Korea and Iraq demonstrates the vitality and power of this principle of association/exclusion.

Yet in the past decade, especially recently, the very idea of such an emergent international order has come to seem ridiculous—at best a delusion of utopian idealists and cranks, at worst a treasonous plot against the United States and the free world. This reaction is the result partly of an organized propaganda campaign against it, but it also draws strength from real threats to that emerging order and assaults on it—threats and assaults that again can be identified and named.

First, most frequently discussed, is terrorism—or, more precisely, the fear that terrorist organizations or rogue states or both could acquire weapons of mass destruction and use them against the United States and other countries. In my view the actual and potential danger of terrorism in this sense to world order and the basic stability of the world's leading countries, especially the United States, is overrated. Historically, terrorism is neither new and unprecedented nor more dangerous than ever before—to the contrary. The threat undoubtedly exists, however, and represents an attack on this international order or any decent one.

Second—more important, though less recognized—is the threat arising from a structural deficit in stable, decent governance in much of the world as a result of failed states, states broken or riddled by civil war and ethnic or other conflict, or states and regions that simply are too poor and undeveloped to function within an international order, yet whose deadly problems are impossible and wrong to ignore.

Third—even bigger but far less recognized, especially by the United States and many of its closest associates—is the danger arising from massive inequities and deformities in this current world order: the North-South divide; the gross imbalances in wealth, power and security, and know-how among different members of the world community; and the consequent ability of some to manipulate the system and its institutions to their advantage at others' expense, building tensions, creating rivalries, deepening already great inequalities, and failing to meet looming worldwide problems (e.g., environmental degradation, global warming) or making them worse.

The fourth threat is not structural at all but nonetheless presents an immediate danger to the emergent international order: the current international stance, policies, and actions of the US government, reflecting the attitudes and outlook of a large segment of the American people. This sweeping claim has to be made more specific. The reasons current administration policy constitutes a threat to international order and an assault go beyond the obvious—that the US government waged a war of choice on Iraq against widespread world disapproval without United Nations sanction on the basis of justifying claims that were always highly dubious and have now been shown to be untrue. US policy represents a general threat to world order in that it openly rejects or more subtly undermines the very changes in the structure of world politics and society that have worked and are working to make a viable international order that is based on the principle of voluntary association possible and increasingly real.

The administration of George W. Bush explicitly rejects the notion of the declining utility of war and military force. Instead, it expressly bases its pursuit of US and world peace and security on maintaining a permanent, overwhelming American military superiority over everyone else combined and demonstrating the United States' determination to exercise that military superiority whenever and wherever it decides to do so. This policy, the heart of the Bush Doctrine, is being reinforced by a massive, organized publicity campaign that is designed to rehabilitate and glorify war, the use of military force, as the necessary, right way to peace and security.

This policy constitutes a frontal American assault on one of the pillars of world order. The other actions are more subtle, sawing away at the foundations of the other pillars. Although the administration of George W. Bush constantly proclaims the expansion of world trade and commerce as a prime benefit and goals of its Pax Americana, it also has made clear by words and actions that such a Pax Americana rests on military and political domination, not peaceful trade, and that it will use that domination to assure a world economic system that favors and protects US economic interests anywhere and everywhere it chooses. The administration acts this way with such regularity and nonchalance that it ceases to astonish. For example, we have learned that the US government has declared the oil resources of the Sudan a vital American strategic interest.

The administration similarly praises the technological, scientific, cultural, and commercial globalization of the world while exploiting it to enhance its power and influence and rejecting it whenever the mechanisms of globalization tend to check what it wishes to do. It insists on the United States' right to lead every international organization and institution to which it belongs, but it also declares that it will not accept decisions of these institutions that infringe on what it considers its sovereign rights and will defy them whenever it thinks doing so is in its own interests. Finally, although the Bush administration constantly declares that worldwide peace through democracy and free-market capitalism is its goal, it flatly repudiates the notion that democratic decision making might apply to the United States within the international community or that any serious international control could be exerted over US decisions wherever it claims sovereignty.

This record of doctrine and action unmistakably constitutes a repudiation of the emergent international order and an assault on it. How serious a threat and assault it is depends both on one's point of view and on how long and how far the current policy is allowed to go. My own view is that it is a greater long-term danger to world order, peace, and justice than terrorism or any actions by so-called rogue states or axes of evil, though probably less dangerous than other basic problems—namely, the deficiency in stable governance and development in much of the world and the grave imbalances between various members of the world community in terms of their wealth, power, security, and ability to achieve their minimum goals within the system. The reality of the current US challenge to the emergent world order is unmistakable, however. A world order resting primarily on the principle of voluntary association sustained basically through rewards from association and penalties and sanctions from exclusion cannot last if the leading, dominant member of the association—under the banner of consultative unilateralism or instrumental multilateralism or internationalism à la carte or whatever—repudiates and violates that central principle at every turn.

Moreover, the current American threat to world order, though perhaps not the worst one, clearly is the one we as Americans can do the most, the most directly, to correct. I have no prescriptions for action to propose. Nor do I want to turn this essay into a political forum—at least not any more than I already have. Therefore I close with a couple of exhortations, a bit of cheerleading, instead. The first bit of cheerleading is an old phrase from the liturgy: *Sursum corda*—"Lift up your hearts." I have painted a fairly gloomy picture, and I do not think I exaggerate—but it is a one-sided picture. Despite the current threats and assaults against the international order, that order is still a long way from being destroyed or ruined. The chances for general relative peace and some greater measure of justice in the world, though not rosy, are still far brighter than they were during any of the first eight or nine decades of the twentieth century—or, for that matter, any of the centuries I know anything about going back to the fifteenth. Moreover, the kind of system and order I have tried to depict has not disappeared or stopped working; it is still working underground and above ground in ways we may not recognize now but may have powerful effects later. What that means for Americans is that the very international order our government is now threatening may help contain us and save us from ourselves. In this sense there may still be, in Prince Bismarck's phrase, a special providence reserved for fools, drunkards, and the United States of America. Space considerations preclude me from providing supporting details for these sweeping statements.

The other exhortation is, "Gird up your loins." This will be a long struggle and probably for a good while a lonely, losing one. It will not be decided by one national election or a change in leadership, for two central reasons. The first is that this is not simply a question of choosing leaders who understand better that the United States must seek its goals through the international system, not in defiance of it or over its head. It also is a question of finding leaders and parties with the will, courage, and skill to sell the necessary sacrifices, choices, and changes in outlook to the US public, at very considerable political risk. It means not merely getting the US government to adopt a different, better style of leadership in the world but changing America and Americans so that they can exercise a different, better kind of world leadership—overcoming the ignorance, provincialism, self-absorption, and self-satisfaction that now handicaps the United States for such leadership. This kind of change, this reeducation, cannot come without costs, and a major part of the cost must be an experience and recognition of failure that is sufficient to prompt a general willingness to turn around—in a word, repentance. In short, one who believes that his or her country is on a wrong, dangerous course has to hope that the country will fail—moderately now so that it does not fail disastrously later; it must fail so that it can turn round and succeed—but nonetheless it must fail. It is hard enough to come to terms with that idea oneself—to realize that in a sense one has to expect and welcome losses that really hurt one's own countrymen; it is much harder to do so openly from a position of responsibility and accountability. It is easy for me; I am an old man with nothing to lose or gain by speaking openly. It is much different for leaders in all walks of life—politicians, educators, clergypeople, businesspersons—anyone with constituencies to answer to, responsibilities to meet, and consequences to face. For them, I recognize, what I call for takes real courage, conviction, commitment, and patience for the long haul.

7

For Shame

2004

We already know the administration's strategy for damage control on the latest erupting scandal in occupied Iraq, the abuse of Iraqi prisoners of war. The tactics have served more or less successfully, at least in America, to cover up and survive every earlier scandal and fiasco of this administration at home and abroad. President Bush has already raised his hands in holy disgust, pronouncing the actions contrary to his and the country's principles and the Army's policy, the work of a handful of miscreants whom Donald Rumsfeld solemnly promises to pursue and punish. We are already hearing the predictable excuses employed by defenders of corporate corruption, high-paid criminal athletes, and this administration—"This does not represent us or America and its values," "mistakes have been made," "no one claimed we or democracy are perfect." A few obvious culprits will be punished, a few mid-level superiors reprimanded or demoted, dangerous questions held at bay at hearings, a commission possibly named to study the problem, administrative changes promised, and then the administration, denying involvement and responsibility, will move on to other things to distract the public.

They must not get away with this. Not only is this episode more sickening and shameful than others that have already stained the occupation of Iraq. Not only will it have an even more shattering effect on America's image and ability to lead abroad. Not only does it end any surviving hopes that Americans can be seen by Iraqis and other Arabs and Muslims as liberators, models, leaders, and friends. It reveals as nothing has before the true character of this venture and of the whole policy by which this administration has chosen (allegedly) to fight terrorism and evil in the world. It ought finally to force every American, even the most loyal and patriotic, to face what this country under this leadership has done and is doing in this war. Where is it leading us?

This was not an isolated incident caused by a few bad apples, a shocking but minor and exceptional digression in an otherwise heroic and humane enterprise. This fish that now stinks to heaven began to rot long ago from the head down.

Consider when this happened—in October to December 2003, five to seven months ago. Think about how long many in the Army and outside have known about it; how long the official report investigating it has been in preparation and circulation; how long and often rumors and reports about this and other incidents of abuse of prisoners or civilians have appeared in the foreign press, especially the Arab press our authorities seek to control or repress. Yet in all this time, and to this day, all the higher officials in the Army, the Pentagon, and the White House responsible for policy insist they knew nothing about it. It is not a question of whether there will be a cover-up. There already has been—we are now beginning to learn the extent.

Consider why it happened—not in the superficial sense of why it was allowed to happen rather than prevented, but in the deeper and more important sense of what concrete purpose this abuse served, where it fit into what overall policy. These incidents were not simply a case of a few reservists getting their sadistic kicks or a result of indiscipline, bad chain of command, or other incidental administrative snafus. That would be bad enough and would constitute one more indictment of the incredible levity and mismanagement demonstrated by this administration in the war and occupation. Anyone who knows anything about the history of war and military occupations knows that this is precisely the sort of thing likely to happen, and that if one's goal really is liberation and winning the hearts and minds of those occupied, this kind of conduct has to be prevented at all costs.

A historical aside: in the summer of 2003, when the Iraqi insurgency was just beginning and the administration still hotly denying its existence, Donald Rumsfeld and Condoleezza Rice insisted that the problem was merely last-ditch resistance by fanatical dead-enders like Nazi resisters in Germany in 1945. The assertion was false, of course—no civilian resistance worth mentioning developed in postwar Germany—but easily buried and forgotten under other more important administration untruths and deceptions. A different resemblance between the two occupations, however, is now dismayingly germane. By far the worst problem the Army faced in 1945 in the relations between troops and German civilians was American soldiers raping German women. The fact has gone relatively unnoticed except by historians, both because Americans at home closed their eyes to it and because it was overshadowed by far worse and vaster Soviet crimes in the Eastern Zone. Yet the Army and the Pentagon should have learned from that experience and from military history everywhere how grave the danger of this kind of conduct was.

The larger point is not, however, that they failed to prevent the abuse at Abu Ghraib prison and elsewhere. It is that they allowed and indirectly encouraged it, in pursuit of a wider and supposedly more important mission. This operation was an integral part of intelligence gathering by both military intelligence and private firms hired by the government for this purpose. The abuse was thus deliberate and purposive, intended to make prisoners psychologically ready for interrogation.

Consider further the context of that interrogation and intelligence gathering. The aim then was not simply or mainly to root out pockets of resistance and ongoing subversion or new terrorism and thereby pacify Iraq and protect American lives. This was the time when the administration was frantically bent on finding proof of the stocks of weapons of mass destruction and the alleged pre-war links to al-Qaeda that were advanced (as we now know, falsely) to justify the war. It was also part of a more massive program of detention of supposed evildoers in Iraq, numbering 10–12,000 by different accounts, an unknown number of them still held without charge or notification to their families—a little-known story with its own cargo of abuses. It fits into the broader pattern of the so-called War on Terror in which the United States covertly and overtly supports a Gulag Archipelago of detention camps and interrogation centers over the Middle East and Central Asia, either on its own bases or on the territory of other regimes, mostly repressive ones, with whom America works.

Consider the ethos behind this massive effort, and how it characterizes and shapes the administration's entire view of the world and foreign policy. It flows seamlessly from the prevailing Ollie North or (to borrow a phrase from Professor George Lopez of Notre Dame University) Dirty Harry Callahan theory of international politics. It's a dangerous world out there; hordes of fanatical evildoers are bent on committing unspeakable crimes against us. If we play by the rules they despise, we will lose. We must play dirty to win, and ultimately only winning counts. The end and the unquestioned fact that we represent the forces of light and they the forces of darkness justify the means.

Consider the incentive structure this collective mentality held at the highest level of government creates for people down the line called on to wage this kind of campaign on the ground. Consider what it means to reservists, thrown into a situation for which they are wholly untrained, to be instructed to induce in prisoners a suitable physical and psychological readiness to yield information they were doubtless would save their country or their fellow soldiers' lives. Consider what it means for military intelligence officers to know that their promotion and careers depend on coming up with the right stuff; for so-called civilian intelligence agents to know their paychecks and their company's contracts depend on the results, and that nobody higher up worries too much about the methods used to obtain them. Consider what it means for a general commanding a large system of prisons to be told not to obstruct this critically important job of intelligence gathering, knowing that her career is on the line.

Consider also what it says about the administration as a whole when, on top of the many previous outright lies, false promises, failed predictions, abrupt changes of course, and multiple evidences of bad or no planning, corruption, confusion, and failure that have already plagued the occupation of Iraq, this supremely ugly scandal breaks, and no one at the highest level—not Richard Meyers or Wolfowitz or Rumsfeld or Rice or Cheney or Bush—takes responsibility, resigns, is fired, demoted, or even publicly reprimanded. In a government like that of Japan or some other countries, a sense of shame alone would suffice to bring about resignations; in an earlier era it might have meant suicide. But to this crew apply the words that brought Senator Joe McCarthy down in 1954: "Has it come to this, at long last? Have you no shame—no shame at all?"

Consider finally what it must say about the American public, or at least a major portion of it, if this does not at last produce an overdue and overriding sense of revulsion against leaders and a policy that have led their country to this shameful pass. The Republican slogan in 1996 was "Where's the outrage?" That outrage, understandable given the disgusting though essentially private misdeeds of President Clinton and important in the 2000 election, today seems strangely absent on the Right. Liberals can now ask conservatives, "Where's the revulsion?" What must it mean if good, loyal, religious, family-values conservatives—the segment that George W. Bush overwhelmingly commands and that this journal appeals to—find even this degrading spectacle something they can swallow? What if at least a sizeable contingent does not deliver to Bush in November the message that Oliver Cromwell addressed to the English Long Parliament in 1649: "You have been here too long for any good that you have done. In the name of God, go!"

The nineteenth-century Danish philosopher Søren Kierkegaard wrote in an essay that a sign of malfunctioning of the digestive system was the inability to become nauseated or to vomit upon eating spoiled food, and that the remedy was to take an emetic. The disorder that offended him then was spiritual, the failure of Danish Lutherans to share his revulsion at a complacent established church that he believed was betraying real Christianity. His analysis and advice apply in a different way to Americans today. Anyone who does not feel revulsion against this administration for what it is doing and has done in Iraq and elsewhere has something seriously wrong with his political digestive system.

8

Misreading the 9/11 Report

2004

The 9/11 Commission Report draws praise for valid reasons. But the remarkable plaudits, publicity, and sales it has garnered do not prove that it has been correctly understood. The public discussion of the report in fact suggests that Americans are missing its central point and purpose.

This results in part from the report's virtues. The thorough, well-documented, and often gripping description of the events surrounding 9/11 tends to focus attention on what are essentially historical questions of causes and responsibilities, while the report's main purpose is to make recommendations for the future. Even more important, its penetrating analyses of the failures and inadequacies in America's counterterrorist system before 9/11 and its proposals for reforming that system tend to reinforce perceptions already dominant. America is now the frontline in the anti-terrorist struggle, and the central battle involves keeping Americans safe from further attack, primarily by improving security at home and carrying the fight to the terrorists by military action and intelligence work elsewhere. The administration naturally promotes this perception, believing it yields an electoral advantage, and Democrats, not daring really to challenge it, only contend that they could wage the battle better.

No one could complain about this perception and its likely electoral consequences if it were correct. If the report actually confirmed that the American homeland constituted the main battleground in the so-called War on Terror, then the verdict of "safer but not yet safe" endorsed by the administration would be reasonable. (I say "so-called" because this "war" consists of two distinct though connected things: a real if unconventional war against particular terrorists and their organizations and a wider non-military struggle against terrorism in general in favor of a decent civil society. Why this distinction is crucial will become clear later.)

In fact, the report says something different. It demonstrates clearly if indirectly in its narrative and analysis and directly in its conclusions that the struggle against terrorism is not centered in America. It is essentially global, therefore any strategy that concentrates on homeland security, military action, and counterterrorist intelligence and policing while neglecting the foreign-policy aspects of the struggle will fail. Repeatedly it stresses how much international organization, communication, financial activity, travel, training, and recruitment went into the planning and execution of the 9/11 attacks. Time and again it emphasizes how those terrorist strikes and others were connected to wider issues of international politics, economics, religion, and society. Constantly it points out the transnational nature and reach of terrorist organizations.

The most important recommendations of the book, ignored in the public discussion, come near the end in Chapter 12, significantly entitled, "What to Do? A Global Strategy." These recommendations start from the clear recognition that even though the United States is al-Qaeda's avowed prime enemy, and America's homeland has become an important target for terrorist attacks, the central front lies elsewhere—Pakistan, Afghanistan, the Arabian Peninsula and nearby East Africa, Southeast Asia, Indonesia and the Philippines, West Africa, and European cities with large Muslim populations. (Iraq is mentioned only in passing, with the remark that it would go to the head of the list were it to become a failed state.) The report goes on to argue that the main task of finding and destroying the terrorist networks must be done by local governments and forces that the US cannot command but can only aid and persuade. Success depends on active co-operation from friends and at least noninterference or partial help from neutrals and opponents.

Even more crucial advice, real dynamite expressed in calm factual prose, comes in Section 12:3, entitled "Prevent the Continued Growth of Islamist Terrorism." Note the ominous verdict implied in that title and backed by a quotation from Donald Rumsfeld: since 9/11, despite three years of American effort and two wars, Islamist terrorism has continued to grow. Even more startling admissions follow: the US needs a long-range strategy giving foreign policy as much attention as the military and intelligence aspects of the struggle and does not have one; American engagement in the Muslim world is both deep and resented; throughout the Muslim world "support for the United States has plummeted"; our task is to "help defeat an ideology, not just a group of people, and we must do so under difficult circumstances"; and most arresting, "among the large majority of Arabs and Muslims . . . we must encourage reform, freedom, democracy, and opportunity, even though our own promotion of these messages is limited in its effectiveness simply because we are its carriers."

These statements do not represent new revelations. They are commonplaces, supported almost daily by ongoing developments. Their importance lies in their devastating indictment—within an expert, moderate, bipartisan report—of the existing policy on combating terrorism and in their call for radical change.

This report says that the United States needs but does not have a long-range strategy that recognizes the centrality of foreign policy. In the vital global struggle with the terrorists over ideas, influence, allegiance, recruitment of followers, and commitment, we are losing. Our world influence and image have deteriorated so badly that measures we need others to take for our mutual benefit become less likely simply because we urge them. A more decisive verdict of policy failure is hard to imagine.

The report does not discuss what caused this deterioration in our world position. That was not its mandate. It does offer advice on what might be done to reverse it, but the suggestions are, understandably, rather general, sometimes amounting to little more than restatement of the problem. One point about the actions proposed to help prevent the continued growth of Islamist terrorism is, however, significant: they are all international, that is, they represent things that the United States cannot do without help and in many instances cannot do as a prime actor or mover at all—actions it can only encourage others to do, restricting itself to paying for them, giving them international legitimacy, and sometimes just getting out of the way and concealing its role.

What does this reading of the report tell us about the current American discussion of it, concentrated on homeland security and intelligence reform? Indulge me in a parable.

There once was a very rich man who lived on a lavish country estate, well away from a teeming nearby city plagued by gangs, crime, poverty, and violence. He was the richest and most powerful businessman in that area, owning extensive properties in the region and exercising a leading influence in its politics, economic activity, and society.

One day the worst gang in the city, led by a particularly dangerous thug who had earlier attacked some of the landowner's businesses, made a daring assault on his country estate, causing major damage. The landowner responded by declaring war on the gangs and promising to take the fight to their lairs in the housing complexes of the city. The first raid, enjoying the consent and support of local authorities, many fellow businessmen, and even some residents in the complex, succeeded brilliantly. The housing complex was quickly seized, some gang members, though not the most important leaders, were killed and captured, the managers of the complex were replaced, and some order was restored. But a succeeding raid on another larger housing complex went much differently. It was not approved by the local authorities, was supported by only a few businessmen, and was condemned by almost all others in the city. Though this housing complex was also easily overrun, no evidence of gang activity could be found, the problems of occupying and running it proved unmanageable, living conditions became worse, the residents resisted, and gang members who had not been there before now filtered in.

Under pressure from his family and associates, the landowner reluctantly agreed to let an independent expert analyze the situation and advise him how best to wage his war on gangs. After careful study, the expert gave him this report: "Lax security on your estate under both the previous and the current management was one factor enabling the gang to attack it. That situation already has been improved, but not enough. I have a list of more things to do. Your main challenge, however, lies not in defending your estate but in doing something about the gangs themselves and the environment in which they live. The gang leaders are not mainly trying at this time to kill you or destroy your estate. They are trying to distract and discredit you, ruin your reputation, wreck your businesses, drive you out of the region, and isolate you on your estate—and then kill you.

"You therefore cannot win this war on gangs by yourself. The more you try this, the more you give them the war they desire. The local authorities have to do the main job of finding these gangs and rooting them out. You can help, urge, pay, bribe, and coerce them into doing it, but beyond a certain point if you make it too dangerous to their interests and lives, they won't go along. You also need to enlist more of the other businessmen in the task, not just to help pay the costs but even more to make clear that this is not just your war. Above all, you have to get the people in the city on your side. Persuade them that the way you and your friends do business will make their lives better, that what the gang leaders promise is false.

"As of now, the local authorities do not really trust you. Your fellow businessmen have concluded that your method of fighting threatens their interests. Worst of all, people in the community, including many who work for you and used to support you, have come to see the gang leaders as Robin Hood and you as King John—so much so that if you urge them to do something, they will be less likely to do it simply because you are urging it. Unless you change your strategy, you will lose."

The wealthy landowner listened to the expert, thanked him, assured him that he would consider his recommendations carefully—and went back to concentrating on strengthening the security of his estate and finding out what new attacks the gangs might be planning.

Some weeks ago, an editor of this journal asked readers to respond to this question: What should voters who generally oppose Kerry and the Democrats and favor Bush and the Republicans on social and domestic issues, but oppose Bush on Iraq and foreign policy, do on November 2?

The differences between Bush and Kerry in personal qualities, beliefs, and abilities, though important, need not be decisive here, and the differences in their announced programs, goals, and policies for Iraq and elsewhere are notoriously not that far apart. But this commission's analysis and recommendations call for major change on the foreign-policy side of the struggle against terrorism, and to do any good a change must be perceived as credible—not just in America but especially in other parts of the world. Re-electing Bush rules it out.

This president cannot change himself or his administration's foreign policy. That would contradict his style, character, and self-image, and overthrow his whole campaign and appeal to his base. He must go on as he has, insisting in the face of every evidence of failure that things are going well, that he and America are right and good and that only evildoers fail to see it.

Moreover, even if he could change, if by some miracle he and his whole administration underwent a road-to-Damascus conversion, it is too late. No one would believe him—and this is decisive. Hard though it is for Americans to accept, when it comes to the main front in the struggle against terrorism, it matters far less whom Americans trust to ensure their safety than whom Arabs, Muslims, Europeans, and even Asians trust enough to join in the common endeavor. On that score, the verdict is in. Like Belshazzar, Bush and his policies have been weighed in the balance and found wanting. Polls, demonstrations, defections, diplomatic defeats, restlessness among allies, glee among enemies, and continued terrorist activity demonstrate a massive, almost worldwide distrust.

Where Kennedy, Reagan, and the elder Bush could be acclaimed in Germany as heroes and use that acclaim to accomplish important ends, Bush cannot now find an audience there safe to speak to. Clinton visited Dublin and was surrounded by 100,000 cheering Irishmen. Bush could briefly visit Ireland, the most pro-American country in the world, only when surrounded by 10,000 security guards.

It does not finally matter what caused this, and how much Bush is to blame. Saying so is not attacking him personally but recognizing facts and drawing inescapable conclusions. The slogan "Anybody but Bush" need not arise from blind Bush-hatred but from a sober appreciation of the international situation. Most of the world has reached that conclusion, and as Bush says, results matter.

The same facts that make serious change in the direction of American foreign policy impossible under Bush make it possible under Kerry. The crucial factor is not whether he is better qualified by education, experience, intellect, and temperament. It is rather that he is not burdened by the crushing baggage Bush carries—the Bush Doctrine, the open disdain for international institutions and law, the choice of preventive war, the misleading arguments for it, the botched occupation of Iraq, the stains of Abu Ghraib and Guantanamo. Kerry already enjoys in much of the world, especially Europe, such credibility as a harbinger of change that some call for toning down the praise so as not to create a backlash in the United States.

One more thought, intended to sweeten slightly for conservatives the bitter pill: many think that voting out an incumbent president in wartime shows national irresoluteness, even cowardice. Rationally and historically this makes no sense. It is no more a sign of weakness to change leadership in wartime if success depends on it than it is to remove a baseball pitcher who is getting shelled in order to prevent the game from becoming hopelessly lost. Switching to the elder Pitt helped Britain win the Seven Years' War; switching to Churchill helped win World War II. Clinging to failed leaders and policies often contributes to disaster. Germany might have benefited in World War I by getting rid of Bethmann earlier. Exchanging Daladier for Reynaud earlier might conceivably have helped France in 1939–40. Examples could be multiplied. And this switch can be made without personal vindictiveness or betrayal of one's deep convictions and party loyalties, if a greater good and overriding need justify it. The case of Chamberlain and Churchill illustrates this. Even in 1940, Chamberlain was still more trusted by many Conservatives and Labourites than Churchill, widely seen by Conservatives as a maverick and by Labour as a warmonger. What brought Churchill to power was simply the conviction that Chamberlain, though he meant well, was unsuited to lead the war effort, while Churchill was—and once the war in Europe was over, the voters promptly kicked him out. There would be nothing dishonorable in conservatives voting for Kerry now as a necessary evil while vowing to oust him in four years.

But enough of argument—a final plea: do not let America continue to play the rich landowner in the parable. There is still ample chance to turn things around now. After four more years there may not be.

9

The War Bin Laden Wanted

2004

George W. Bush's re-election campaign rests on three claims, distinct but always run together: that the United States is at war against terror, that it is winning the war, and that it can ultimately achieve victory but only under his leadership.

The second and third propositions are hotly debated. Critics of Bush contend that the US is losing the struggle against terror on the most important fronts and that only new leadership can bring victory, but except for a few radicals, no one denies that the struggle against international terrorism in general and groups like al-Qaeda in particular constitutes a real war. The question comes up in the campaign only when Republicans such as Vice President Cheney charge that Democrats view terrorists as mere criminals and do not recognize that the country is at war. The charge, though false—no Democratic leader would commit political suicide by even hinting this—is effective politically.

Some experts on international law and foreign policy object to calling the struggle against terrorism a war, pointing for example to the legal problem of whether under international law a state can declare war on a non-state movement and claim the rights of war, or arguing that terrorism constitutes a tactic and that no one declares war against a tactic. Both arguments indicate the sloppy thinking that pervades the rhetoric of the War on Terror. The first point, moreover, has important practical consequences for such questions as the treatment of detainees at Abu Ghraib, Guantanamo Bay, and elsewhere, and for our relations with allies, other states, and the UN. Yet these kinds of arguments seem too academic to matter. The general public can hardly understand them, much less let them influence their votes.

Other reasons, however—different, more powerful, highly practical, and astonishingly overlooked—argue against conceiving of the struggle as a war and, more important still, waging it as such. The reasons and the logic behind them are somewhat complicated, but the overall conclusion is simple: by conceiving of the struggle against international terrorism as a war, loudly proclaiming it as such, and waging it as one, we have given our enemies the war they wanted and aimed to provoke but could not get unless the United States gave it to them.

This conclusion is not about semantics or language but has enormous implications. It points to fundamentally faulty thinking as one of the central reasons that America is currently losing the struggle, and it means that a change in leadership in Washington, though essential, will not by itself turn the course of events. What is required is a new, different way of thinking about the struggle against terrorism and from that a different way of waging it.

Osama bin Laden and al-Qaeda repeatedly and publicly declared war on the United States and waged frequent attacks against its property, territory (including embassies abroad), and citizens for years before the spectacular attack on 9/11. This admission would seem to destroy my case at the outset and end the discussion. If bin Laden and al-Qaeda declared war on the United States and committed unmistakable acts of war against it, then obviously the US had no choice but to declare war in reply, just as it had to do so against Japan after Pearl Harbor.

No, not really. Some other obvious facts also need consideration. First, states frequently wage real, serious wars of the conventional sort against other states without declaring war or putting their countries on a war footing. In the latter twentieth century, this practice became the rule rather than the exception. Korea and Vietnam are only two of many examples. Second, revolutionary and terrorist organizations and movements have for centuries declared war on the governments or societies they wished to subvert and overthrow. Yet even while fighting them ruthlessly, states rarely made formal declarations of war against such movements. Instead, they treated these groups as criminals, revolutionaries, rebels, or tools of a hostile foreign power, not as organizations against which a recognized legitimate government declares and wages war.

The reasons are obvious. A revolutionary or terrorist movement has much to gain from getting a real government to declare war upon it. This gives the movement considerable status, putting it in some sense in the same league with the government with which it is now recognized as at war. No sensible government wishes to give such quasi-legitimacy to a movement it is trying to stamp out. Consider Napoleon's treatment of the insurrection in Spain from 1808 to 1813. The insurgents had powerful claims to belligerent status and even legitimacy. They maintained a government in a small corner of Spain, represented the former legitimate Bourbon government Napoleon had overthrown, included the regular Spanish army, and were supported and recognized by a major power, Great Britain. But Napoleon always insisted they were nothing but brigands, used this designation as justification for the brutal campaign he waged against them, and acknowledged a state of war with them only when, defeated in Spain and on other fronts, he decided to cut his losses, evacuate Spain, and make peace with them and the Bourbon regime.

Other reasons further explain why legitimate governments have not declared war on terrorist or revolutionary organizations that waged war against them—for example, the fact that when one declares war one has to operate under the prevailing laws of war, and these can be constricting for a legitimate government, as the United States is currently finding out in Iraq, Afghanistan, and elsewhere. Thus declaring a war on terrorism and waging it as a genuine war has to be justified as an exception to a powerful rule, not accepted as the obvious response to a terrorist attack.

Readers may find this an impractical, academic argument and respond, "So what? This is a unique situation. Our country never faced a threat just like this before. Besides, what difference does it make what you call a campaign against terrorism if in fact you intend to wage an all-out fight to exterminate terrorist organizations with every weapon at your command? In practical terms, that is war, whatever name you use for it, and it is good for the American public, the world, and the enemy to face it."

Again, not so fast. The issue is not whether the American public after 9/11 needed squarely to face the fact that the United States had been attacked by a dangerous enemy and had to fight back. It still needs to understand this—and does. Neither is the issue whether in fighting back the US had a right to use military force against that enemy anywhere (though only where) it was sensible and practical to do so. Those points are not in dispute. The relevant, practical questions instead are, first, whether it was necessary to declare war on that enemy in order to confront the attack and fight back with every useful means, including military force. As just indicated, the historical and practical answer to that question is no. Second, was a public declaration of war against terrorism in general needed to prepare psychologically for a serious campaign against the enemy? The reaction of the American public and virtually every other government and people to the 9/11 attack and the subsequent American counter-attack makes clear that for this purpose a formal declaration was unnecessary. The support in America and abroad for a powerful campaign against al-Qaeda was overwhelming.

The only question left is the one central to the argument: Did the American government, by constantly and solemnly declaring the nation at war against terrorism and repeatedly summoning the rest of the world to join up or else be ranked among America's enemies actually help or hurt the campaign against the terrorist enemy?

The natural response might be, "How could the declarations of war possibly have hurt? Even if they were not strictly necessary, they served to unite the American people and gird them for possible sacrifices and losses and to rally the rest of the world behind the American effort. What harm did they supposedly do?"

It was never in dispute that Osama bin Laden deliberately, repeatedly, and in the most spectacular way possible provoked a war with the United States. What should that tell us? Why did he do this? What was he after?

Once again this looks like an intellectual befogging the issue and ignoring the obvious. Osama bin Laden did this because America is his enemy. He hates America and its ideals, America stands in the way of his creating the kind of world he is fanatically determined to bring about, and so he declared war on America and tried to destroy it and kill as many Americans as possible. This interpretation is perfectly understandable and defensible from a moral and emotional standpoint. Unfortunately, it is counterproductive from the standpoint of rational analysis and policymaking.

Two vital principles in foreign-policy thinking are, first, know the enemy—this means doing one's best to enter into his thought world and decision-making processes, to think from his presuppositions and standpoint—and second, expect a hidden agenda and look for it. Assume that the enemy's decisions and actions have a purposive rationality behind them, that he hopes to achieve by them some concrete result that is rational in terms of his goals and worldview, however fanatical, irrational, or simply evil his actions may seem.

Apply these two principles to the question here. Take for granted that Osama bin Laden is an evil fanatic, totally determined to pursue his goals and wholly unscrupulous in the means he is willing to use to reach them. But assume also that he is highly intelligent, shrewd, patient, and focused in his strategy. Supposing this and knowing that he is the leader of a relatively small, highly secret terrorist organization, strong in devotion to its cause but weak in both numbers and weapons in comparison to the resources available to any major state, much less the world's one superpower, ask yourself: Why would he go out of his way to challenge that superpower with its awesome array of resources and weapons, deliberately provoking it into declaring war to the death upon him and his organization? The enormous risks are obvious. What were the potential gains?

Any serious and unemotional consideration of this question makes it apparent that the answer "He hates America and wants to destroy it" will not do. If that were his concrete strategy and end, that would make him a fool, which he is not. Any fairly intelligent person would know that an attack like that of 9/11, or even ten such attacks, would not suffice to defeat the United States or make it give up the struggle against terrorism and accept the unhindered spread of radical revolutionary Islam in the world. Any intelligent person would instead expect the attack on the American homeland to have precisely the political, psychological, and military effects it actually had—to mobilize the government, the American public, and many of its allies around the globe for an all-out struggle against al-Qaeda and international terrorism. Anyone with intelligence would also have anticipated the huge risks to himself and his organization from the inevitable counterattack—a military campaign by an overwhelmingly superior foe against his political base and secret camps in Afghanistan, blows to his cells wherever they could be found, international police, intelligence, and financial measures against his organization on a vastly increased scale, heavy pressure on regimes that had secretly supported or tolerated his activities to crack down on them, the imprisonment or death of anyone in al-Qaeda's ranks from bottom-top—in short, all the measures that the Bush administration carried out and has trumpeted as successes in the War on Terror. Why would bin Laden knowingly risk all this for the sake of an attack, however spectacular, that he knew would not seriously damage the United States as a nation?

Two replies frequently offered need to be considered before getting to the real answer. Each, though superficially more plausible than "He did it because he's evil," is fundamentally no more satisfactory. The first is that bin Laden did it to demonstrate the power, bravery, skill, and fanatical resolve of his organization and thereby gain new recruits and allies. This is undoubtedly true in a sense but far too vague. As just noted, the overwhelming surface probability was that the attack would result in gravely weakening and threatening al-Qaeda. That is certainly what the Bush administration confidently promised. Why precisely did bin Laden expect, against all probabilities, that the attack would eventually expand and strengthen his organization and cause?

The second reply is that the 9/11 operation was intended as only one step in a long campaign against the United States, a kind of dress rehearsal for worse blows, perhaps with weapons of mass destruction—nuclear, biological, or chemical. Once again, this argument makes no sense. If one intends to start a long campaign to destroy the enemy, one does not begin with an action that can be expected to galvanize rather than cripple the enemy and make him more prepared to anticipate, prevent, and counter new attacks. It would be as if Japan in 1941, having decided to fight the United States and needing first of all to cripple American naval power in the Pacific, chose to attack by bombing buildings in San Francisco and Los Angeles.

The only sensible answer, once the foolish and inadequate ones are discarded, is that Osama bin Laden anticipated the American reaction and wanted it. His purpose in attacking the United States directly in its homeland was to get the American government to do what it had not done in response to his previous attacks: to declare an all-out war against him and al-Qaeda and a worldwide War on Terror led and organized by the United States, with every other country in the world summoned to follow and support or be considered an enemy. That seems to deepen the puzzle. Why thus deliberately multiply the ranks of his enemies and organize their efforts under the leadership of a single, powerful, aroused country?

The answer, if one thinks about it free from emotion and preoccupation with oneself, is clear. Deliberately provoking the United States into open, declared war against him, his forces, radical Islamism, and worldwide terrorism was bin Laden's way of expanding a struggle he was already waging but losing, one he could not win on account of its insoluble contradictions, into a larger war free from internal contradictions that he could hope ultimately to win. To put it in a nutshell, Osama bin Laden needed the United States as a declared enemy to enable him to win his war against his primary enemies and thus achieve his goals.

To understand this, we need once again to take bin Laden's fanatical ideology and his hatred for the United States and the West for granted and concentrate on his situation and the purposive rationality behind his tactics. Consider his central goal—a Muslim world ruled by true Islamic law and teaching, purged of all evil, materialist, secular, infidel, and heretical influences. Of course he regards the West, especially the United States, as the source of many of the evils corrupting and oppressing Islam and would like ideally to destroy it, but the immediate obstacles to achieving his vision and the main foes to be overcome have always lain within the Muslim world itself. (There is a good parallel here with sixteenth-century Europe. The Ottoman Turks were the great military and religious threat to Christendom, but the most bitter quarrels and wars were between Christians of different creeds, churches, rulers, and countries.) The obstacles he faced consisted of the divisions in sects, beliefs, and world visions within Islam; hostile governments ruling in Islamic countries, virtually all of whom regarded his kind of Islamic radicalism as a threat to their rule and were determined to repress it; and the attitude of most Muslims, loyal to their creed but unwilling to sacrifice what security and well-being they had in his kind of jihad. Osama bin Laden tried to overcome these obstacles and foes directly but the struggle, besides being difficult, dangerous, and largely unsuccessful, was inherently divisive and counterproductive. It meant pitting Muslim against Muslim, alienating more followers and potential recruits to the movement than it attracted, and giving free rein to the spread within Islam of infidel influences from outside while Muslims fought each other.

There was, however, one good way to overcome these obstacles—that is, to unite Muslims of divergent beliefs, sects, and visions against a single foe; to discredit, paralyze, and possibly overthrow secular Muslim governments; and to galvanize more believers into that suicidal zeal that al-Qaeda and its kindred organizations need as a baby needs its mother's milk. That way was to make the United States, already the Great Satan in much of the Muslim world for a variety of reasons—its support of Israel against the Palestinians, its support of corrupt dictatorships and secular regimes, its encouragement of Iraq's war against Iran and toleration of Saddam Hussein's atrocities, its later conquest, humiliation, and ongoing punishment of the Iraqi people through sanctions, its long record of imperialism, its greed for Arab oil, its military occupation of sacred Muslim soil, its penetration of Muslim societies with its decadent culture and values—declare open war on him and his followers united in a true, heroic Islamic resistance movement.

The solution, further, was if possible to provoke the US into actually attacking Muslim countries, using its awesome weapons against pitifully outmatched Muslim forces, destroying and humiliating them, killing and wounding civilians and destroying much property, occupying more Muslim land, and miring itself in an attempt to control what it had conquered and to impose its secular values and institutions on Arab and Muslim societies. From this would arise the chance to demonstrate that faithful Muslims under leaders and movements like bin Laden and al-Qaeda could be David to America's Goliath. If they could not immediately slay the oppressor, they could survive its onslaught, grow and spread despite it, and gradually reduce it to a helpless giant, isolated from its former friends, trapped in an interminable occupation of hostile territory and peoples, with its armed forces stretched thin and its awesome weapons unusable, while al-Qaeda and similar groups could continue to launch even bolder attacks against it or anyone still associated with it.

That, I believe, is a reasonable rendition of Osama bin Laden's hopes and strategy. It was a tremendous gamble, of course, and he could not possibly have predicted exactly how it would turn out. But it is beyond doubt that his gamble succeeded, that for more than three years after 9/11 things have generally been going his way, and that he could not have achieved this huge, improbable victory without indispensable American help. In declaring and waging a War on Terror with al-Qaeda as its initial announced focus and the United States as its self-acclaimed World Leader, America gave bin Laden precisely the war he needed and wanted.

One can anticipate at least three reactions to this conclusion (three that are printable, that is). Starting with the least important, they are: first, this is all hindsight, Monday-morning quarterbacking; second, given the circumstances, there was nothing else the United States could have done; third, even if this is all true, it is water under the bridge, useless in deciding what to do now.

The first is easy to answer. Hindsight is a good exercise in politics, especially for the public at election time—but this is not that. Quite a few observers warned about these dangers at the time, and I was among them. In an article written just after 9/11 and published in November 2001 ("The Risks of Victory," *National Interest*, Winter 2001/2002) I argued, among other things, against allowing a necessary and justified military campaign in Afghanistan to draw us into leading a general War on Terror in the wider Middle East and the world. More warnings were included in my "Iraq: The Case against Preventive War," appearing in this journal in October 2002. Mine was only one voice in a steady, growing chorus, though one always drowned out by crowds of raucous hawks.

The second objection has a little more substance. Certainly 9/11 required strong action including military measures against al-Qaeda in Afghanistan, and the natural, inevitable war psychology pervading the country had to be reckoned with. Yet as was pointed out earlier, these needs required actions like those taken initially more than words. As far as the public rhetoric and justification was concerned, nothing hindered the administration from conceiving and explaining the undertaking differently both to the American public and the world, especially the Arab-Muslim world that was Osama bin Laden's real target.

There is little point now in drafting the kind of address Bush should have delivered to Congress and the public. But one can readily imagine an American president (though not Bush) persuasively making the two cardinal points. First, the United States intended to pursue al-Qaeda with all the weapons at its command on grounds of legitimate self-defense and, while respecting the rights of other countries, would allow no one to interfere with these actions. It would not, however, dignify al-Qaeda's atrocious crimes by calling them acts of war or give Osama bin Laden and his fellow criminals what they obviously wanted, a pretext to portray themselves as soldiers in a holy war against the United States. Instead, it would pursue them ruthlessly the way civilized nations had always pursued criminal organizations, as international outlaws and pirates, enemies of all governments and of civilization itself, and it expected other countries to co-operate in this struggle.

Second, the United States recognized that though it was the direct target of this attack and that in one sense it represented al-Qaeda's final enemy and target, it was not the country most menaced by the current threat from al-Qaeda and international terrorism generally. As bin Laden well knew, neither this attack nor possible future ones, tragic though the individual deaths and losses were, could really hurt the United States, much less deter it from its purpose of hunting down the criminals behind the atrocities. The attack instead had already had just the opposite effect. It had strengthened the country and united Americans and their friends throughout the world for a long struggle against him and his fellow terrorist criminals. America's government, institutions, and civil society were rock solid. It had no homegrown terrorist organizations to fear or ethnic and religious differences for terrorists to exploit. Its relatively small Muslim population was well integrated and overwhelmingly loyal to the United States, thankful for its blessings and freedoms.

Many other countries in the world could not say this, especially the Arab and Muslim countries that Osama bin Laden wanted to subvert and revolutionize as he had already done in Afghanistan. These countries and governments had the most to fear from al-Qaeda and international terrorism; they and not the United States were the real targets of the 9/11 attack. Even America's European allies and friends, sound though their countries and institutions were for the most part, had more to fear directly from terrorism than the United States, given their large unassimilated Muslim populations and their proximity to the Middle East. The United States was, of course, vitally concerned with the general problem of international terrorism. It had interests around the world to protect, including those in the Middle East and other threatened regions. Nonetheless, this was not first and foremost America's problem, nor was it America's place primarily to provide the solution. The terrorists wanted to make the United States appear an imperialist Great Satan imposing its will and its solutions on others and forcing them to follow its lead. America would not fall into that trap. The US had a particular right and duty to its citizens and the world to pursue al-Qaeda and exterminate it as a criminal organization. It would help, advise, support, and even where specifically desired lead others in the global struggle against terrorism. But it would not try to force others who had an even greater and more immediate stake in that struggle to do what their own self-interest ought to compel them to do, nor would it try to dictate the kinds of internal measures and reforms they needed to take to combat the common enemy.

That kind of language would have done everything language can do both to free the United States to attack al-Qaeda and to put pressure on other governments, especially in the Middle East, to confront their own problems and responsibilities and seek help if necessary from the United States, rather than hiding behind it. It also would have undercut the al-Qaeda strategy of making the United States into the main enemy, helped place responsibilities where they belonged, and galvanized genuine world support in the struggle against terrorism. What is more, it would have been entirely consistent with the campaign against terrorism the United States actually waged at the outset. That was very much an international effort, a largely proxy war directed but not mainly fought by the US and focused strictly on destroying al-Qaeda's organization and governmental base—until this focus was foolishly abandoned to attack Iraq.

To heighten the irony, this kind of language would have conformed to the actual wartime policies the administration has followed. Let us be honest: the "War on Terror" in America is basically a sham, a charade. While great, even ultimate sacrifices have been demanded of relatively few, chiefly those in the armed forces, for the overwhelming majority of Americans having the country at war has meant massive tax cuts, exhortations to spend and consume, enormous deficits, politics and government spending as usual—in short, no wartime sacrifice at all. The rest of the world knows this and sees the hypocrisy, if we do not.

As for the last reply, that this argument now represents water under the bridge, useless for current or future policy, if that were true, it would constitute the most devastating indictment of the Bush strategy possible. It would mean that the administration had so ruined America's position that nothing could now remedy it. But it is not true. This administration's policy deserves harsh condemnation for the reckless incompetence that has made the way out now much more painful and costly, but a way out still lies in recognizing that the United States needs to abandon not the struggle against international terrorism but the conception of that struggle as a war fought and led mainly by the United States, making itself the chief target of the enemy.

This is a change only a new administration could make, though obviously not during the electoral campaign, when it would be suicidal. Once in office, however, it could claim that it had found things to be even worse than it knew and could make the kind of 180-degree turn Bush executed after his election. A gradual disengagement from Iraq and re-concentration on Afghanistan and Pakistan in the pursuit of al-Qaeda, a devolution of tasks onto the UN and NATO on the grounds that even the best meant efforts of the United States are frustrated by the fact that it is seen as the enemy by too many in the region, a willingness to admit past mistakes and agree to focus co-operatively on other problems as well—all this would become possible, though not easy, if only the current American war mentality and psyche gave way to a saner one. This still could happen—but of course not under Bush.

10

Liberating Ourselves

2006

The Bush Administration originally sold the Iraq War to the public, Congress, and the world with two propaganda packages appealing respectively to fear and hope. One drew a horrifying picture of The Disastrous Consequences of Inaction in Iraq; the other depicted The Bright Promise of Victory in Iraq. Everyone remembers the absurd predictions, false promises, and outright lies these packages contained.

Today both have been totally discredited by events. The president, administration officials, and loyal supporters in the Congress and media spin the ongoing disaster in Iraq and looming one in Iran as signs of coming victory, but only true believers are convinced. With rebellion rising even among Republicans and control of Congress in jeopardy, the president is touring the country with a series of speeches designed to refurbish the old propaganda of fear. This newest package, The Disastrous Consequences of Failure in Iraq, seeks to terrify the public, mobilize the base, and vilify the opposition by portraying worse disasters sure to arise should cowardly, cut-and-run Democrats cause America to fail.

It should be easy for opponents of the war to refute this fear-mongering campaign with The Disastrous Consequences of Staying the Course. Though any such exertion comes hard to a divided party with its so-called moderates pulling in the opposite direction, the evidence showing the current campaign to be as illegitimate and self-deluding as the original pro-war campaign is overwhelming. But such a counterattack, though necessary, will not defeat the White House's strategy by itself and could even play into its hands.

The reasons are simple. Like other Bush-Cheney ploys, this one is not designed to educate or persuade rationally but to arouse and exploit patriotic emotion. Any counterargument, however solidly grounded in logic and evidence, will be politically and emotionally distasteful to many voters. Moreover, Americans want not merely to be warned of impending disaster but also to be told how it can be averted. To Republican true believers, "Stay the course" still represents the answer, simplistic and delusional though it is, while the majority skeptical about this answer demand something positive in its place.

The Republican electoral strategy thus rests on two pillars: on Bush's reported private quip during the 2004 campaign, "You can fool some of the people all the time, and those are the ones you have to concentrate on," while keeping the rest distracted, divided, and on the defensive; and on the opposition party's tearing itself apart trying to devise a positive alternative policy, with some leaders, including Hillary Clinton, still endorsing John Kerry's message in 2004, The Bright Promise of Letting Us Handle Iraq Better. This approach, now even more than in 2004, will divide the Democrats, confuse the public, and fail to rally supporters. Worse still, it would continue to obscure the central point and the first critical requirement for any solution in Iraq or progress toward one: that the current American venture has decisively failed, cannot be rescued or reformed, and must be abandoned.

This essay proposes an answer to this problem—not to the tactical electoral dilemma faced by the Democratic Party but to the policy dilemma faced by the country, an answer not offered by either party and almost certain to be denounced and repudiated by both. By frankly acknowledging failure in Iraq and acting quickly, decisively, and prudently on that recognition, the US not only could avoid further disasters there but might also achieve a kind of success. Call it The Bright Promise of Accepting Failure in Iraq.

Be warned: the success to be described bears no resemblance to the glowing predictions made by neoconservative hawks before the war. Participating in their game of false promises and self-delusion would mean violating the most critical requirement for any ultimate success for American policy in Iraq and elsewhere—that Americans get over their habit of spreading and believing comforting lies. The main weapon for opponents of this war and this policy must be ruthless honesty, and the great strength of that weapon now is that the war's proponents cannot use it. Therefore I begin by admitting, indeed insisting, that the light that could be kindled by accepting failure in Iraq resembles a flashlight with limited battery life rather than a locomotive headlight. But like a flashlight in a dark cave, it may be bright enough to show the way out.

It is idle to discuss the administration's refusal to recognize failure in Iraq and its insistence on the goal of victory as if this represented a serious military strategy or foreign-policy plan. "Victory" is not really defined and cannot be. Virtually all the concrete goals of the original Bright Promise of Victory in Iraq propaganda have already been tacitly abandoned and are no longer mentioned. The "success" talked about is not merely indefinable and unattainable but incoherent as a concept. The ends sought are self-contradictory and incompatible with the means used to attain them. All this could be demonstrated at length, accomplishing nothing but to further the administration's purposes of distraction and obfuscation. For the denial of failure and insistence on pursuing victory, insofar as it is a product of something more than pure fantasy, is not designed for military and foreign-policy purposes but for domestic politics, especially the 2006 elections. There the strategy could succeed by limiting the Republican losses just enough to keep control of both houses, avoid the congressional investigations the administration dreads, and delay the final collapse in Iraq until after 2008, when the presumably victorious Democrats could be blamed for it.

The possibility of such a success rests on more than Rovian electoral wizardry. It exploits roots deep in the American heritage and character—the special difficulty many Americans have in coming to terms with limits in international politics, the feeling that admitting failure and wrong choices especially in wartime is un-American. Add to this the portrait the administration and a largely compliant press paint of what failure in Iraq would bring—civil war, chaos, and radical Islam dominating the region, terrorism triumphant, Iran emboldened, Israel threatened, the oil supply imperiled or cut off, America humiliated, isolated, and impotent, and (the most dishonest but politically effective claim of all) the brave Americans killed or wounded in the fight for Iraqi freedom and American security betrayed. Against this lurid background Bush & Co. challenge the Democrats: if you are serious, show us your plan for meeting these dangers, solving these problems, and avoiding these disasters while getting us out of Iraq.

It is easy to show how absurd in logic and fact this demand is. It is like insisting that a man who shows you that your $100 bill is counterfeit owes you a real one, or—to use Molly Ivins's illustration—to argue that those who warned against hitting a hornet's nest with a stick must now, after the administration has done so and caused the hornets to swarm and attack everywhere, either propose a concrete plan for getting the hornets back into the nest or else join in efforts to kill them with the stick. Worst of all, the demand calls on others to solve the problem the Bush administration created while rejecting the fundamental condition for any solution, a recognition that wrong policy and failed leadership created the problem and that both must first be changed.

Yet outrageous as this tactic is, it may still work with many voters because making failure in war acceptable to Americans is like putting lipstick on a pig. That is the ungrateful task of this essay, and it requires a series of steps. First, I must show that the option of trying for success through acknowledging failure is the only rational chance to avoid further failure and worse disaster. Then that option must be made plausible and meaningful—plausible by seeing that this often happens in history as in ordinary life and meaningful through redefining and better understanding the nature of the contest and the meaning of victory or success.

The argument starts with two generalizations from history, obvious and familiar but often ignored. The first, that the worst disasters in history arise from a refusal to recognize and admit failure and deal with it, needs no proof. History is full of striking instances. Here is just one: the causes and factors that drove Germany deliberately to launch World War II and inflict unspeakable crimes on the world and on Germany itself were diverse and complicated, but one was basic—a refusal to admit that Germany had really lost World War I and must accept the consequences of defeat. Essentially, the German decision for war in 1939 was a decision to stay the course—to resume in a radical new form the effort of 1914–18 to make Germany dominant in Europe through military power. Similar instances from history could be cited almost ad infinitum.

The second generalization is also easy to document from history. Often—not always—a timely recognition of failure and the willingness to abandon or alter a wrong course leads in unexpected ways to success. Sometimes the change in course enables one to achieve the original aims by a different route; more often it leads to the discovery that the original goals were not that great or cost too much and that the country was actually better off with a different outcome—that sometimes one could win by losing.

American parochialism and the privileged, triumphant course of American history make this point hard for Americans to grasp. Yet in at least four major instances during the Cold War, the US had to come to terms with failure, accept the consequences, and change course, sometimes by 180 degrees: Korea and the Korean War, China and the recognition of the Communist regime, Vietnam, and strategic parity with the USSR. In every case, accepting failure served to avoid further losses and potential disasters and led to an outcome different from what the US was originally trying to achieve, but better. America would be worse off now had it won any of those contests in the way it originally tried to.

There is no mystery about why this happened to the United States as it has many times to other countries. A timely recognition of failure helps cut losses, stop rot, and cease wasting vital resources. It magnifies contradictions between goals and misfits between means and ends, helps us better understand the reasons for failure, and changes views of what outcomes may be acceptable. By admitting that one cannot solve the problem with the resources and methods one has, one may discover or create new, useful ones. Stop swimming upstream, and the current may carry you somewhere safe, if not to your original destination. Acknowledging that the problem is beyond your capacities may get you help—old or new allies and partners with common interests who cannot afford to let you entirely fail. A recognition that the way you are fighting the battle is making things worse may teach you that the struggle is not the kind you supposed it was and that there are better ways to fight it if necessary or to avoid it entirely—all simple lessons, but true, and these cases illustrate them.

The harder part is to show that this Bright Promise of Failure scenario can work in regard to Iraq and the Middle East and the struggle against terrorism. I offer no guarantees of success. Yogi Berra is right: it is always dangerous to prophesy, especially about the future. I also make no claim to expert knowledge of Middle East politics or access to intelligence. My expertise is as a historian, a bird that flies backward and knows where it has been better than where it is going. Oddly, however, my analysis and predictions on the Iraq War and the so-called Global War on Terror in articles published since 9/11, a good number in this journal, hold up better now than those of most of the supposed experts.

There is a reason for this. The main intellectual defect in current American foreign policy is the lack of any sense of history, particularly as the British historian Lewis B. Namier defined it: a trained intuitive sense of the way things do not happen. (How they actually happen depends on the evidence.) America's leaders and their advisers, including some so-called historians and political scientists, not only are ignorant of history and insensitive to it, they despise and repudiate it. Their favorite epithet for opponents is to accuse them of having a pre-9/11 mentality, of believing that history before September 2001 still tells us something.

Neither having a sense of history nor wanting one, their calculations and policies are thoroughly infected with that disease fatal for good policy, for which a sense of history is the best prophylactic and cure—utopianism. It is the blind optimism, the utopianism of this administration, along with its dishonesty, that accounts for its record of repeated promises and calculations that anyone with a sound historical sense could tell were not going to work. Their particular brand of utopianism, moreover, combines its two worst forms—a radical utopianism that believes that the evils to be fought are simple, readily identified, and easily capable of being rooted out and replaced with good, and the utopianism of Machtpolitik, the belief that with enough power resolutely applied one can do anything.

One requirement for reaping any profit from accepting failure in Iraq, then, is a clear anti-Utopian sense of history, a willingness to recognize and respect limits and reject self-delusion—something any reasonably educated, sensible person can develop. It also helps if we avoid some natural but erroneous assumptions about what accepting failure in foreign policy involves. It is not simply a first preliminary step, a matter of seeing that you are in a hole and should stop digging. It involves a rigorous, active search for the deeper causes of failure and thus becomes a strategic maneuver, a way of seeking and creating conditions needed for climbing out of the hole.

Another natural assumption would be that harvesting success from failure requires a clear policy delineating the principles and steps that will lead from failure to success. Most Americans and a majority of observers worldwide recognize that staying the course to victory in Iraq is not a real policy and that recent proposals by neoconservatives to up the ante by attacking Syria and/or Iran and having the president declare that America is in World War III are certifiably insane. But thoughtful persons looking for a way out are confronted with at least four alternative lines of policy, each strongly advocated and all at least sane and intellectually defensible. These approaches can be broadly characterized as semi-isolationist/libertarian, realist balance-of-power, leftist-reformist, and internationalist or (misleadingly) Wilsonian. The differences between them are not trivial, and the debate over which is best is not inappropriate—except at this time when the critical issue is whether the country will face the fact of decisive failure in Iraq at all. On that score their differences make no real difference; advocates of all four of these approaches today agree on rejecting the current course and taking some initial steps for recovery and ultimate success. Disputes over the merits of these approaches at this point only confuse the public and help the administration and its neocon prophets to propose their nostrums as no-nonsense remedies.

Even more necessary than this "first things first" basis for consensus among opponents of the war is a better understanding of the nature of the broad global contest the US is now engaged in and the definition of success in it. Nothing in this discussion so far suggests a good slogan for a bumper sticker or a banner in an antiwar demonstration. That is as it should be; international politics is too complicated for slogans, and the slogans of the simplifiers in the administration have contributed to the terrible mess they have made. But for understanding the nature of the contest, one slogan would fit: "It's Not a War, Stupid!"

Words are defenseless things. Any kind of struggle can be called a war—on drugs, poverty, crime, illiteracy—so long as one does not take the metaphor literally and wage the contest as if it really were a war. An NFL coach who urges his players to go to war with the opposing team does not expect them to start shooting. Yet Bush & Co. insist that all their campaigns—against al-Qaeda, the Taliban, Saddam Hussein's regime, the insurgency and sectarian violence in Iraq, Hamas and Hezbollah, terrorism in general, and potentially against Syria and Iran—are literally wars and all are against the same generic foe, terrorism; that America is under military attack; and that these enemies, all lumped together, must be fought primarily by military means.

This incessant beating of the war drum is enormously important. It has served as the main propaganda weapon for Republicans at the polls; the rationale for every expansion of executive authority now leading the country toward a constitutional crisis; the justification for every violation of international law; the cover for all the abuses, atrocities, and instances of collateral damage in civilian casualties and destruction attendant on military action; the excuse for massive expenditure, waste, and corruption; and the main weapon used to silence critics, vilify opponents, and cover up illegality, fraud, and incompetence in government. The insistence that America is at war, combined with a persistent refusal to pay for it or require sacrifices of most Americans, has contributed to a massive distortion of public spending, huge and growing deficits of every kind, a dangerous militarization of American thought and society, and the destruction of any sense of responsibility in both the government and the public.

Worst of all, the propaganda campaign has worked and is still working politically. Though a majority of Americans polled believe the wars on terror and in Iraq are not going well and now consider the war in Iraq a mistake or at least not worth its costs, few Americans, including opponents of the war in Iraq and

Bush's general policy, doubt that 9/11 put America in a state of war, and most still believe that this war must be prosecuted and ended successfully, even if they cannot exactly define victory.

This belief that the United States is now genuinely in a state of war against terrorism, still the president's greatest electoral asset, represents at best massive misconception and confusion. The United States, along with many other major governments and advanced, orderly societies, is engaged in a struggle to defend the rule of law, order, and security at home and to sustain a decent international system abroad against irregular attacks and crimes by individuals, groups, and factions within various countries. This is therefore essentially a struggle of governments against a diverse assortment of criminal anti-government groups. Those who oppose terrorism and terrorist groups have a prime interest in promoting this view and in keeping as many governments as possible united and engaged in the struggle against terrorists as a legal international campaign against criminal enemies of all regular states and governments.

Proclaiming this a war and waging the struggle primarily by military means works concretely against this purpose and helps terrorists. The fact that terrorist leaders and groups may have declared war on the United States and other countries and carried out attacks against them makes no difference. They have a major interest in making this a war. It legitimizes them, ennobles their cause and their actions in the eyes of followers and sympathizers, gives them international stature, and lures opponents into the kinds of overreactions that delegitimize them, alienate their natural allies and the neutrals, and split the antiterrorist governmental front.

A little history to illustrate: throughout the nineteenth century, conservative regimes in Europe, especially Austria and Russia, waged a mortal struggle against revolutionary groups and organizations. They hated and feared these enemies as much as Americans do terrorists today, and given the weakness of these regimes and the genuine threat revolution posed to them they had far better reason to do so. Their efforts to suppress revolution, often counterproductive and finally ending in failure, included the use of their armies at various times against revolutions at home or in allied regimes abroad. But they never made the blunder of justifying their repressive actions at home and abroad by saying they were at war with the revolutionaries. They knew that this would elevate the status of their foes, alienate friends and neutrals, and negate the strongest card in their hands—their claim to be enforcing law and defending civilization against international criminals.

This is not a matter of diplomatic-legal terminology or an academic distinction. The American insistence on calling its campaign against particular terrorists a Global War on Terror has gratuitously given its enemies an important victory in a struggle in which politics, image, and propaganda are more than half the battle. The decision to attack Iraq, a state clearly no threat to the United States, multiplied that propaganda victory many times over, and the impression of America it created—that of a country ruthless and powerful in military conquest but incompetent and impotent in civic follow-up—has multiplied it again. Americans, led by their government, seem incapable of understanding that this worldwide contest is not a shootout at the OK Corral but judo. The object is not to eliminate the opponent but to unbalance and overthrow him, using his own offensive lunges to do so. Osama bin Laden, the Taliban, the Iraqi insurgents, even Saddam himself understood that, with the result that America, though incomparably stronger, has been thrown off balance far more than they.

This understanding of the contest as a long-term political, legal struggle to uphold the rule of law rather than a war, and judo rather than a gunfight, must also change the American definition of success. The administration, with most of the media and many voters in tow, has consistently defined victory in terms of missions supposedly accomplished, positive gains allegedly achieved. Time and again it has hailed particular triumphs as breakthroughs and turning points, proof that the US is on the road to victory—military victories in Afghanistan and Iraq, installation of "friendly" regimes, introduction of "democratic" institutions and reforms, capture or killing of particular enemies, defeat of certain insurgent forces or risings, conduct of elections, adoption of constitutions, formation of a "permanent," "sovereign" government in Iraq, a roadmap for peace in Palestine, the death of Yasser Arafat and democratic elections in

Palestine—only to have every glorious victory quickly turn to ashes in the mouths of the administration and its followers.

Why? Lack of planning, incompetence, poor intelligence, insufficient manpower, bad decisions, inexperience, unfamiliarity with an alien environment? Yes, all these and more, but the deeper reason for failure is a wrong concept of victory. In this contest, as in the nineteenth-century contest of legitimate regimes against revolution, victory cannot mean crushing the evil and establishing the reign of Freedom and Democracy throughout the world by glorious victories on the battlefield or elsewhere, but (in the words of Austria's Prince Metternich) outliving the evil. That is not compromise or surrender. It means ensuring that one's own values, institutions, and way of life survive and ultimately thrive while those who would overthrow them are gradually marginalized and ultimately die out. That is the only kind of victory in this contest America can achieve or should aspire to.

History does not repeat itself, but it does show repetitive patterns. In looking for clues from previous instances where Americans harvested success from acknowledged failure—the Korean War, Vietnam, recognition of Communist China, and accepting strategic parity with the Soviet Union—it makes sense to start with the assumptions behind the original policies that ultimately failed and had to be abandoned. In all four instances American policy rested initially on certain common assumptions: the threat being confronted was uniquely grave; failure to meet and defeat it now would have a domino effect, leading to its becoming steadily worse and potentially unstoppable; the danger could not be met by normal international politics but required either the direct application of military force or the possession of clear military superiority and willingness to use it as a deterrent; and finally, the US, if it acted with the necessary resolve, would bring most of the rest of the world into line with its action or at least deter others from opposing it, that the tide of history threatening to turn against America would thus be turned back in its favor, and that the defeat of this particular enemy on this particular front would decisively promote the ultimate victory of the good cause.

These assumptions were not obviously irrational, stupid, or cover for a hidden agenda. The North Korean invasion, regardless of its origins out of an emergent Korean civil war rather than a worldwide Communist offensive against the free world, was a serious military attack on an American ally and a threat to the American position in East Asia that needed to be met with force. Much of Southeast Asia did seem ripe for Communist takeover from Vietnam. The regime of Mao Zedong was one of the most revolutionary and ruthless in history. The USSR was a superpower with a tyrannical regime, oppressive empire, formidable military, and the nuclear power to destroy the world.

Yet after a half-century or less, these original assumptions can be seen and acknowledged as having been wrong—not dead wrong, wholly without foundation or excuse, but flawed, exaggerated, one-sided, and hence when used as the basis for policy destined to make things worse rather than better.

That recognition did not come automatically nor was it a precondition and cause of the reversal of policy. In all four instances what came first was a recognition that the task assigned America by its current policy—uniting Korea under American control, defeating the Viet Cong and preserving an independent anti-Communist pro-American South Vietnam, defending Taiwan as the legitimate government of mainland China, and denying the Soviet Union its status as a strategic equal with equivalent military power—was not feasible, that the goal was not attainable at any acceptable risk and cost. Only then did the majority of decision-makers and the general public begin seriously to question the assumptions on which the strategy of the impossible rested. Yet this recognition of failure and the resultant gradual changes in policy inevitably entailed and produced a change in thinking as well as in strategy and tactics—the kind of turnaround needed in America now.

In each instance, the US gave up unachievable goals and settled for temporary, provisional, managerial solutions, truces, or standoffs; accepted or deliberately sought multilateral, negotiated outcomes based on compromise; and sometimes made major concessions to its opponents to reach them.

These were more than mere tactical moves forced by hostile pressure. They simultaneously produced and were accompanied by a change in thinking and approach. The US government, in practice if not in overt proclamation or ideology, ceased viewing each particular danger primarily in global terms as part of an overarching worldwide threat and instead aimed to handle each as a local, limited challenge, isolating it where possible from the putative global contest, even where and when Americans believed that the global contest was real and serious. This enabled it consciously to induce divisions among its opponents and exploit these.

At the same time this shift enabled the US to control and reduce its commitments to its subordinate allies, persuading or forcing them to make compromises, share or assume burdens and risks, and give up their particular goals in order to retain general American support. The South Korean regime had to abandon its goal of unifying Korea through American arms. Taiwan had to accept American recognition of its worst and most threatening foe as the legitimate government of China and ultimately of Taiwan itself. The South Vietnamese regime had to accept destruction. West Germany had to give up any prospect of German unification for the foreseeable future. In a sense, America made others pay the main price for the success it achieved by accepting failure.

Why did this work? Because once Americans woke up to the impossible character of their aims and the flaws in their basic assumptions, they cleverly adjusted themselves to reality and managed their problems with skill and moderation? Not mainly. It would do little to correct the radical utopianism of the Bush administration and its followers to encourage Americans to think that even if they cannot win simply by being militarily all-powerful, they can achieve whatever they want through clever and forceful diplomacy. The US succeeded for a number of reasons that had little to do with its own power and skill and far more with favorable international conditions not under American control.

Our main opponents, though formidable and impossible to destroy or defeat by military force, were neither as powerful nor as stable internally nor as aggressive and revolutionary in their foreign-policy aims nor as incapable of compromise and coexistence as we supposed. In other words, normal international politics could work with them. Besides that, these opponents were less united than we imagined, more riven by internal rivalries and disputes they had to manage and the US could exploit. In contrast, the US had genuine partners rather than satellites, allies who were ready to help promote compromise solutions where they could not support the American quest for victory. As for our client states and those we defended, in all these cases save that of South Vietnam, they were not merely willing under pressure to accept the sacrifice of particular aims for general peace but in certain instances actually welcomed and co-operated with these aims (e.g., West Germany's promotion of détente and the Helsinki Accords in the 1970s and Japan's welcoming of the recognition of China). It was also important that on both sides governments were able and willing to control and marginalize their own extremists pushing for aggressive measures to achieve decisive victory over the enemy.

Most important, however, is the fact that this different approach changed the arena and rules of the contest from one that the US could not win at any acceptable cost, and that its allies and friends did not want to fight, into one that the US and its side of the world were far better suited to wage: a contest over what kind of government, society, economy, and politics was best at peaceful coexistence.

Critics insist that this is all old history, rendered obsolete by 9/11. What the US now faces is a wholly different situation and array of foes—rogue regimes like Iran and North Korea, terrorist organizations with global reach immune to sanctions or pressure because they have no address or permanent interests to defend, the possibility of WMD being used by fanatical ideologues with purely destructive aims and suicidal followers deterred by no moral restraints or civilized codes. To talk of diplomatic strategies for dealing with these is the worst kind of self-delusion.

Most astonishing about this ubiquitous response is not the lack of historical sense it reveals but the absence of memory. Again allowing for changed circumstances, these arguments were used time and again, at even greater volume and with better reason, to argue the futility of dealing with the North Koreans, the Chinese, the Soviets, and the Vietnamese except by force. The extremist hawks were wrong then and they are wrong now. The global terrorist threat is no more real now than the global

Communist threat was then. Terrorism is mostly concentrated on particular local and regional aims and directed against particular local enemies. The identifiable terrorist groups and organizations are fragmented and divided by serious fault lines and disagreements. Iran is hostile and verbally belligerent but tactically and strategically more concerned with its defense against the United States and Israel and its influence in the Shi'ite world than with holy war against infidels. Hamas and Hezbollah have particular goals; so does Syria. Everyone now recognizes—though Bush will never admit it—that the insurgents and resisters to the American occupation in Iraq are very much divided and often hostile toward each other. The point is not that they are harmless or should be ignored or pampered but that using the tactics of the gunfight against them only drives them together and increases their number, while combating them with judo would divide them and decrease their threat.

Above all, recognizing failure in Iraq means seeing not simply that the US has not succeeded to this point but that it cannot ever succeed in what it set out to do by this war—supplant the regime of Saddam Hussein with a stable, democratic, friendly Iraq—because the strategy was fundamentally flawed, the execution worse, and the consequences by now such that anything American occupiers do, however well-intentioned, must make things worse. The longer America stays, the more it fuels the insurgency, the latent and growing civil war, the sectarian divisions, and the pervasive degradation of Iraq's civil society.

As to concrete steps for turning this situation around, I offer no blueprint. Few blueprints in history are ever followed or work when they are. The rule in statecraft and warfare is improvisation guided by a general goal. In this case the general goal, to turn accepting current failure into eventual success, requires more than simply an exit strategy. Certainly one is necessary and overdue, but it should be more than a way of getting Americans out of harm's way. Combined with other measures of strategic retreat, it can be a measure of active defense and offense, like apparently yielding to the opponent's lunge in order to throw him off balance for a countermove.

An even better way to understand America's task is to use a historical model full of relevance and potent lessons but so politically incorrect that neither party could embrace it and that those who would, chiefly radicals on the Left, would misuse it: to see the new policy as an attempt at successful disimperialism. Regardless of whether one considers the war in Iraq as continuing a longstanding American imperialist tradition or (as I do) a departure from America's main Cold War tradition, two conclusions are inescapable.

First, the Iraq War originated in an attempt at American informal empire in the Middle East and remains mired in it. When one powerful country invades and conquers a small, weak country thousands of miles away with a very different culture, language, history, religion, and society in order to replace its regime permanently with one resembling the occupier's own, change its economic structure, control its most important resource, and use it to dominate and change other regimes in the region, that is classic, unalloyed imperialism. To refuse to admit this and cover it up with transparent dodges of liberation, democratization, self-defense, and Global War on Terror is to indulge still further in the comforting lies that are ruining America's capacity for world leadership and even for democratic self-governance.

Second, that imperialist effort has failed disastrously, America's so-called unipolar moment is past, rotten before it was ripe, and the task before it now is disimperialism. Like Britain and France after World War II and the USSR after 1989, the goal has to be not merely to give up an untenable imperialist position but to do so in such a way as to protect vital interests, maintain a necessary position of leadership, and lay a new basis for eventual useful relations with the countries of the former or would-be empire.

That is bound to be a distasteful, delicate, and sometimes humiliating task, with many apparent setbacks and only long-range payoffs. But as history shows, it can be done, and there are at least some fairly concrete ways to approach it. The trick is making the decision to abandon the imperial venture clear and convincing to one's own people and the rest of the world (including opponents), while at the same time showing that this is a strategic decision dictated by good sense and done from strength, not the product of weakness, despair, or disorientation.

A good place to start is with the public renunciation of failed, misconceived, counterproductive policies. There are three obvious candidates, favorites of Bush and the neoconservatives.

The first is the administration's much trumpeted goal of transforming the Middle East through democratization, something impossible from outside, especially through military intervention and hostile pressure by the perceived main enemy of the region, and destabilizing and dangerous even where apparently successful. Political scientists and historians have long known that immature democracies are more unstable, aggressive, and war-prone than traditional regimes. Promoting democracy in Iraq has led to civil war and the nascent collapse of the country and in Palestine and Lebanon to greater power for radicals and terrorist groups.

The second is democratization's twin—promoting regime change, particularly by military force or support for dissidents. Where this fails, as it usually does—witness Cuba—it discredits both the US and the dissidents; where it succeeds, as in Afghanistan, it generally promotes failed states and rule by warlords, militias, and rival factions. Both outcomes contradict the main US interest in working with regular, stable governments against terrorism and violence.

The third is promoting Western values in the Arab-Muslim worlds by public diplomacy, in particular attempts to sell the American way of life and convince others that Americans are truly friends and protectors of Islam and can serve as honest brokers. This whole project only serves to make the US look ridiculous and discredit the moderates in Islam who would like to adapt to modernity, thus aiding the radicals. What will it take to convince many Americans that much of the world currently hates and fears the US not because of its values but because of its policies and actions and that the only way to change that perception is to change those?

This part is fairly easy, a matter of discarding useless baggage. The next, announcing a genuine change in policy in convincing fashion without making it appear an act of desperation, is trickier. But there are ways to approach it. One is to announce a clear general goal not subject to conditions or compromises—in this case, the entire removal of American armed forces from Iraq in the near future and a comprehensive review with all the host countries of the status of American forces and bases throughout the region with an eye to reducing them—accompanied by an offer to work out the timing of these moves with the other parties concerned, including the current Iraqi government and any successor ones. The purpose of this, of course, is to change the American military presence from being publicly an albatross around the necks of these governments and privately a crutch they lean on to something that, if they want it, they need to seek, compete for, and acknowledge.

Along with this open announcement of a change in course needs to go some striking symbolic action to make the announcement credible. Here is an obvious candidate: publicly scrap the plans for the billion-dollar-plus American Embassy/fortress-city in the heart of Baghdad and commit America unconditionally to no military bases, bastions, stationing agreements, or other ways of staying on militarily in Iraq.

An even better political action would be for the US government to call now for an international conference under other auspices than our own to discuss how to deal with the now inevitable civil war in Iraq and the possible breakup of the state. The participants would have to include all Iraq's neighbors, including Iran, and all vitally interested outsiders besides the United States. The point would not be to achieve concrete results, which is unlikely; even getting such a conference convened would be a long shot. Instead, like these other moves, the effort would serve to prove that the US genuinely recognizes the problems its intervention helped cause, wants to share the burden of meeting them with others, and is not trying to control the outcome unilaterally.

There are other ways in which the US could, if it tried, turn a strategic retreat into pursuit of a different kind of victory by robbing enemies of their main pretexts for hostile propaganda and actions, dividing them among themselves, and helping those who have common interests with America to co-operate with or at least not oppose it. The common interests are obvious—opposition to terrorism, need for stability, equal access to the oil and gas of the region, worry about the ripple effects of civil war and sectarian violence—and the potential divisions and rivalries to take advantage of are equally so.

I do not believe that the strategy urged here will be adopted—certainly not by the current administration, probably not by any successor or any future electorate. The reason is not that such a policy would not work. As I have argued, on objective historical and practical grounds it would stand a reasonable chance. Nor is it that present American political conditions, habits, and institutions make it unthinkable. Though there is much more to this argument, it is just possible that crushing defeats for the Republicans in 2006 plus the accumulation of further bad news from the Middle East might deter the administration from more mad gambles to cover existing losses and might embolden the Democrats and the public to try something really different.

The insuperable, structural obstacle to a serious pursuit of success in the Middle East through accepting failure in Iraq, the elephant in the room that I have carefully avoided mentioning hitherto, is Israel. More precisely, it is not Israel itself or its actions, but the fact that the United States has deliberately forfeited control over its policy toward Israel and the Israeli-Palestinian and Arab-Israeli conflicts that form one critical aspect of the Middle East imbroglio. While the US could conceivably change its policy and aims in regard to all its other vital aspects—Iraq, Iran, oil, regional security, even terrorism—I see no possibility that any party, administration, or American public will take the steps needed to regain that essential control.

Obviously this is not a subject that can be opened up, much less discussed here. I mention it solely in the interests of candor and to explain why this guardedly optimistic essay ends as a Cassandra cry. Perhaps better, it calls to mind Bismarck's parting words to the third Turkish delegate to the Congress of Berlin in 1878, a Congress that rescued the Ottoman Empire from part of its losses in revolts, crises, and wars in 1875–78: "This is your last chance—and if I know you, you will not take it."

11

Mirror, Mirror on the War

2006

Fellow historians and others may recoil at the sins I commit here. I propose to draw lessons from history through an apparently inappropriate historical analogy: comparing the Dreyfus Affair, an old story (1894–1906) concentrated mainly on one individual and one country, with current developments in Iraq and their implications for American and world history.

This effort would be absurd were it my intention to discuss the broad skein of historical causality and consequence supposedly linking these two cases. My purpose, however, is to illustrate how events can be significant not mainly for their broader historical impact, but simply for what they are in themselves—for what they tell us about the essential human qualities of the actors involved and the society in which they live. At the time and ever since, most people have believed the Dreyfus case important for its impact on French history. It really had but modest impact; its chief historical importance lies in what it revealed about *fin-de-siècle* France. Most believe today that the unfolding Iraq story is crucial for the broad consequences it has had and will have on American, Middle Eastern, and world history. Perhaps. But the war in Iraq, too, may turn out to be important above all for what it is, for what it tells us about the United States today.

An Abbreviated Affair

The Dreyfus Affair began in 1894 when the intelligence service of the French Army, called the Statistical Section, discovered that some French officer was selling military secrets to Germany's military attaché. Suspicion centered on a Jew, Captain Alfred Dreyfus. A sloppy investigation and defective court-martial procedures led to Dreyfus's conviction and imprisonment on Devil's Island.

Dreyfus's claims of innocence and his family's and friends' efforts kept his cause alive, but this would not have availed had not the treasonous activity continued and a new head of the Statistical Section, Major Georges Picquart, ultimately become convinced that another officer, Count Marie-Charles-Ferdinand Walsin Esterházy, was the real culprit. Picquart's investigations prompted a concerted Army cover-up, however, during which his subordinate, Major Hubert-Joseph Henry, forged and falsified documents to bolster the case against Dreyfus. Meanwhile, Picquart's superiors tried to silence him by bribes, threats, reassignment and, when none of that worked, with dismissal, arrest, and imprisonment.

Nonetheless, as more evidence seeped out incriminating Esterházy and exonerating Dreyfus, the case became a *cause célèbre* that split France into Dreyfusard and anti-Dreyfusard camps. Before long, the question of Dreyfus's innocence or guilt became entangled with the hottest issues then dividing Frenchmen—Catholicism versus anticlericalism, militarism versus anti-militarism, conservative nationalism versus radical republicanism.

Public pressure finally forced the government to bring Esterházy to trial but, despite clear incriminating evidence, a court-martial acquitted him. The case then flared anew when Henry's forgeries were detected, whereupon Henry committed suicide, leaving behind a false "confession" insisting that he had only followed orders and was sacrificing himself for the Army's honor and France's security. Anti-Dreyfusards hailed him as a martyr.

In late 1898 and 1899, however, the flood of revelations of corruption, cover-up and malfeasance seemed to turn the tide. A new government brought Dreyfus back from Devil's Island for another trial. The military court once more—incredibly—convicted him of treason, but with extenuating circumstances. Determined to end the crisis without provoking civil and military disorder, Premier René Waldeck-Rousseau then pardoned Dreyfus, released Picquart and restored him to duty, and pushed through legislation giving amnesty to everyone involved. A moderate anticlerical campaign he also launched turned radical under his successor, culminating in the separation of church and state in 1905. In 1906, the Courts of Appeal eventually quashed the verdict of the second military court, enabling Dreyfus to return to the Army. In 1998—yes, *1998*—the French government officially proclaimed his innocence.

What can one say about the larger dimensions of all this? Dreyfusards who claimed that the Republic was in grave danger from monarchists, the Church, and militant nationalists were exaggerating threats well past their peak. The serious political problems the Republic did face at that time—ministerial instability, ideological divisions, party and class conflict, and a venal, irresponsible press—did not cause the Affair, nor did the Affair and its outcome directly address them. Anti-Semitism in France was nasty but not a real threat to the Republic or a central cause of the Affair, though the trial's outcome probably made it worse. The main issue involved the Army's threat to civil liberties and republican institutions, yet French generals were after freedom from political interference in their sphere, not political power for themselves. The reforms the Dreyfus case did eventually facilitate, chiefly the separation of church and state and a Republican purge of monarchist-Catholic officers in the Army, had mixed results; indeed, the purge may have hurt the French army at a fateful moment in August 1914.

The Affair brought obloquy and ridicule on France from abroad, but never threatened France's alliance with Russia or increased the threat from Germany (though it risked doing so). It hampered France in a humiliating confrontation with Britain in 1898–99, but France recovered and, in the 1902–06 period, made major diplomatic gains. Frenchmen could even claim that the foreign denunciation was exaggerated and hypocritical. After all, one reason French political life was so unstable was that France was freer and more democratic than any other major European state. French military justice left much to be desired, true; but other countries' systems were worse, and the crisis proved that Frenchmen did in the end care about justice and individual rights. As for anti-Semitism, then a pervasive Western phenomenon, it was much more virulent elsewhere in Europe, as French Jews themselves were well aware.

A Superficial Resemblance

Why, then, raise the Dreyfus case now? Because these comments also apply generally to the Iraq story. Though intrinsically more important, the Iraq War, too, seen in comparative historical perspective, looks less earthshaking than most commentators currently claim. For example, the abuse of prisoners and detainees by Americans or at America's behest, though morally repellent, appears relatively mild compared to many past and current atrocities around the globe. The war in Iraq is (in my view, for reasons indicated below) an illegal and unjustifiable war, but it is clearly not an old-fashioned war of conquest; and while it has caused much death and destruction for Iraqis, Coalition forces have not deliberately fought it as a dirty war and have tried hard, especially after the early months of occupation, to minimize collateral damage.

But the same historical perspective that relativizes some of the evils alleged by critics also relativizes much else. The successful initial Coalition military campaign was no more than a colonial-style victory by an unchallenged superpower over a crippled, disorganized foe. Saddam Hussein was a genuine villain, but by March 2003 he menaced only his own people, and even that threat seemed to be fading. The insurgency remains moderate by historic standards, embarrassing America more than seriously endangering it. The administration's original goals in Iraq must be characterized as imperial by the normal historical definition of this slippery term, but from an historical perspective what impresses most is how rapidly the administration's goals for the war (a stable, united, secular, and democratic Iraq; a transformed Middle East; a defeat for terrorism; enhanced American prestige, power, and influence in the region and the Muslim world; pressure on Iran, North Korea, and other dangerous states) have been scaled back in the face of an unexpectedly recalcitrant reality.[1]

---

1 Imperialism by this definition means gaining control over important political and economic decisions of a foreign country such that one can use its strategic and economic assets for one's own purposes or, at a minimum, deny them to any

As for the Global War on Terror, the all-purpose justification for every action the Bush administration takes in Iraq and elsewhere, here too there is less than meets the eye. The claim that most Americans seem still to believe—that terrorism and al-Qaeda menace the United States and the free world as they have never been menaced before—is in historical perspective simply and demonstrably untrue. The current terrorist danger is of course real and serious, but terrorism has menaced many countries and peoples in the distant and recent past. The actual terrorist attacks of 9/11, though sensational, were pinpricks compared to the losses suffered every day in many countries during both world wars, and by countless peoples and countries in great wars and insurrections for centuries. Americans merely have not experienced this, at least not since 1865, and so are practicing what might be called "existential exceptionalism."

Current nightmare scenarios of future terrorist attacks with weapons of mass destruction, though certainly not to be dismissed, involve low probabilities with high consequences. The threats endured by statesmen and peoples before, during, and especially following World War II involved much higher probabilities ("the bomber or the ICBM will always get through") with even more intolerable consequences. Current predictions of inevitably worsening terrorism are speculative and may prove as unsound as the widespread predictions of inevitable nuclear conflict during the Cold War.[2] The obvious message to Americans

---

opponent. If, as I assume, the United States overthrew Iraq's government with the aim of establishing a regime allied to the United States and dependent on it for its security in the hope (among other things) of thereby strengthening America's security and influence throughout the region, these aims must be called imperialist—though, as in most instances of modern imperialism, they were to be achieved through indirect rather than direct control. Typical instances are the British occupation of Egypt after 1882, British and French imperialism in the Middle East after World War I, and most German war aims in Europe during World War I. If these latter examples are fairly called imperial, so must be America's. This is not merely an attempt to anticipate an objection, but goes to the central theme of this essay: the critical need for intellectual rigor and honesty, a willingness to see things as they are and call them by their right names.

2 John Mueller argued years ago that 9/11 might prove an historical aberration rather than the harbinger of a new trend (*National Interest*, Fall 2002). At the time of this writing, the evidence supports his view.

here is: Get a grip. Don't let fear, anger, patriotism, or propaganda sweep you into exaggerating current dangers. Don't let them deflect you from soberly appraising what has happened and shrewdly assessing what needs to be done about it.

A Deeper Kinship

But there is more to the Dreyfus analogy than a warning against exaggerating the historical significance of one's own times. A second message from the Affair is subtler, requiring us to understand why, regardless of its relatively moderate and mixed impact on larger issues, it was important precisely because the central question really was the innocence or guilt of one man, and because the French response revealed critical things about France. Once we do understand that, applications to Iraq today come into focus, though be warned: The pictures revealed are not pleasant to view.

The Dreyfus Affair started with a serious but not particularly sinister miscarriage of military justice. Only with the later cover-up did official conduct become criminal. The driving engine in this was the French Army, dragging various civilian ministries along to protect itself from scandal.

The Army's leaders pursued this course so stubbornly for what came down to simple reasons: caste spirit, career ambition, an ethos of unwavering loyalty to one's superiors, fear of reprisal and the conviction that control of the Army by radical, anti-military, anti-Christian forces would ruin it. The public rationale was that the Army was the true embodiment of the nation and its only bulwark against a fearsome enemy; let its morale and the public's confidence in its leadership be undermined, and the Germans would soon overrun France again as they had in 1870.

This seems to proclaim, "You see? This is the kind of thinking that got America into the tragic mess of Iraq and Abu Ghraib." Not so fast. Alongside some resemblances between France in the 1890s and America today are as many or more contrasts. For example, the respective structures of military and civilian control are far different, and it was civilian hawks in the White House and Defense Department, not the generals, who drove America into Iraq. The German threat to France was very real; the Iraqi threat to America was at least grossly exaggerated.

One has to go deeper, asking why French Army leaders were not deterred from their cover-up or from persisting in it as doggedly as they did. The reason turns on what was missing from their world: namely, internal norms, such as strong loyalty to the Republic and its ideals and a code stressing individual rights and due process, that were adequate to check the lure of career incentives, group loyalty, religious zeal, myopic patriotism, and military honor. Parallel to these missing norms was inadequate civilian control over the Army. Put simply, French officers thought they could get away with their cover-up because they believed no ministry would dare confront the Army, and because they calculated that so long as just one man's (especially just one Jew's) disputed guilt or innocence was pitted against the entire Army's honor, the public would mainly take its side.

For years they seemed to be right. This calculation, that the public did not care much about Dreyfus and *did* care about the Army, accounts for many aspects of the case—not only the remarkable persistence of anti-Dreyfusards in the teeth of mounting evidence and their success in diverting attention from the central issue, but the complaints of some Dreyfusards that his defenders concentrated too much on Dreyfus's personal fate and not enough on purging the Army of monarchist officers or breaking the hold of the cursed Roman sect. This factor also explains the hesitations of the ministries and the timidity of the Chamber of Deputies. Of course, such behavior is commonplace in politics, especially in a democracy, and France was not worse than average in this regard—rather the contrary. But the Army's calculation shows clearly what the Dreyfus affair reveals about French public life at the time: a serious deficit in intellectual and moral integrity.

I put this historical verdict as objectively and dispassionately as possible; yet it still sounds moralistic, judgmental, and unhistorical. Without some such conclusion, however, one cannot get to the heart of the Affair. The initial blunder grew into a major scandal and crime because too many Frenchmen in high places were willing to ignore evidence, bend facts, and accept or do what they knew at bottom was wrong—and too much of the political public either endorsed this, or just did not care. Without recognizing this deficit one cannot explain the high level of dishonesty and deception sustained throughout the case in the anti-Dreyfusard camp and the protracted success of their dirty tactics.

Again, this sounds moralistic. Dishonesty of many varieties is obviously endemic in politics and social life and is inseparable from it. But it remains vital for analysts and leaders to judge when the level of dishonesty goes beyond normal nuisance and becomes toxic. Because he and others realized that the Dreyfus case was poisoning French public life, Waldeck-Rousseau, no crusader by experience or temperament, finally intervened to end it—and he was surely right to do so. One piece of evidence was that the case enflamed French anti-Semitism when, by all rights, it should have discredited it. Even better proof lay in Franco-German relations. Army leaders, who insisted that the Army's honor and morale must be maintained intact to enable it to defend France against the German threat, repeatedly jeopardized French security against Germany by their cover-up. Their false assertions were offensive and provocative to Germany, and gave German leaders an excuse, had they wanted one, to provoke a crisis or even to attack France at a time when it was unprepared. If that does not define dishonesty driven to a toxic level, it is hard to think of what does.

Here is where the analogy lies between the Dreyfus case and the Iraq-Abu Ghraib-Guantanamo story. America has got itself into a tragic mess by a roughly similar process with a roughly similar underlying cause: a national deficit in intellectual and moral integrity. But once again there are contrasts alongside similarities, and our deficit must be carefully defined, away from the distortions of partisanship and raw emotion.

The Bush administration's decision to attack Iraq resembles the first verdict against Dreyfus in being a blunder rather than a crime. President Bush and others seem to have genuinely convinced themselves of what they were disposed to believe from the outset: that Saddam Hussein posed a real, imminent menace that had to be removed by force. This was a mistake, and the process of making and selling this decision, carried out in public view (unlike the Dreyfus trial) therefore involved almost inevitably plenty of false statements and misleading distortions—but no cover-up.

What has happened since the war, however, has turned blunder into crime. There has been a cover-up, one bigger, more organized and more brazen than in the Dreyfus Affair. In this cover-up the American public has been to some extent lied to, for example about the real sources for the atrocities at Abu Ghraib. To a greater degree, Americans have been misled about the occupation, which has involved the administration in near constant denials of facts and distortions of reality; repeated claims, promises, and confident predictions that when falsified by events are dismissed and forgotten; the treatment of central, direct results of the war and occupation in Iraq (civilian deaths and destruction, the breakdown of the civil and economic order and security, massive unemployment, steep declines in health and living conditions) as if they never happened or were unimportant or were simply the enemy's fault; the refusal to ascribe any but nihilistic motives and purposes to all opponents, who are uniformly called "terrorists" even when they are fighting uniformed foreign soldiers on their native soil. These characteristics have been and remain hallmarks of the occupation, notwithstanding the somewhat more candid tone adopted by President Bush starting in December of last year.

These assertions will be hotly denied by some, as the current furious debate testifies. Backing them with detailed evidence would break the bounds of this essay and deflect it from its purpose, which is to contend that this cover-up, fairly successful until recently, constitutes evidence of a major national deficit in intellectual integrity.

The key word here is "national." The American public has not been an innocent victim of manipulation and distortion by the administration or the media, but in the majority showed itself a willing collaborator in the process. The same willingness to believe comforting untruths and ignore inconvenient evidence that led many in government to endorse the decision for war and support the policy thereafter also motivated many Americans and helped the cover-up succeed. To illustrate: When administration officials before the war claimed without credible evidence that there were close ties between Saddam Hussein and al-Qaeda, this was at least distortion. When Vice President Cheney continued to assert this even after the 9/11 Presidential Commission had explicitly refuted it and after the president had admitted the lack of any such evidence, this was either obfuscation or a lie. And when, according to polls, a solid majority of Bush voters still believed in such lies in November 2004, and in a connection between Saddam Hussein and 9/11, this was evidence of a powerful willingness to be deceived.

The revelations about American detention and interrogation practices at Abu Ghraib, Guantanamo, Bagram, and possibly elsewhere, along with subsequent investigations tailored to concentrate attention on individual wrongdoers in the lower ranks rather than the policies and culture of command behind these practices, add a special moral dimension to the deficit in integrity. Three aspects of this stand out.

First, though the uniformed services and Defense Department civilian leaders had the best and earliest information on these scandals, public revelations have all come from the outside—certain journalists, CBS, the FBI, the International Committee of the Red Cross, the American Civil Liberties Union, Human Rights Watch, and others. A good example is a whistle-blower, Army Captain Ian Fishback, who finally went to Human Rights Watch to make public what he knew when all his attempts to go through Army channels failed.

Second, no one in high office, either military or political, has genuinely taken responsibility for these ugly abuses or paid a penalty for them. When the French chief of staff general Raoul Boisdeffre, a convinced anti-Dreyfusard, discovered that Army officers had fabricated the evidence on which he had based his testimony to the Chamber, he resigned his post, ending his career. Boisdeffre genuinely took responsibility. Secretary of Defense Donald Rumsfeld, who knew about Abu Ghraib months before the abuses became public, finally, in order to help quell the public outcry, accepted full responsibility—and remained at his post. Rumsfeld, in effect, pretended to take responsibility.

Finally, public indignation over these scandals, despite a steady drumbeat of new revelations and charges, has never risen, especially on the Right, to anything approaching the level reached over scandals in the Clinton White House. Yet those scandals, however disgusting, cannot compare to these in national, international or moral significance.

No outsider can be certain of the motives impelling those most responsible for the cover-up, but their statements and conduct indicate ones not radically different from those in France—a mix of career concerns, loyalty to party, president, and armed forces, the drive for power and electoral success, ideological commitment, and the patriotic conviction that the threat to America justifies extraordinary means, weapons, and tactics both in fighting it and in keeping power away from those too weak or unpatriotic to do what is necessary. In any case, their motives are less important than their reasons for believing they could get away with their actions, and these too are similar—that the operation would quickly succeed and any furor die down, and that most Americans would accept as legitimate any actions claimed necessary for national defense regardless of international law, world opinion, or normal moral constraints.

Once again, as in France, this calculation, especially the latter part, seemed correct for a good while, and shows again that the deficit in intellectual and moral integrity is a national, not a partisan, phenomenon. The divided and half-hearted Democratic opposition to both the war itself and a host of issues related to its conduct usually concedes the principles involved and challenges only particular means and measures of execution. An example is the administration's detainee policy, which asserts the American government's right to capture thousands of persons abroad and, on the president's sole authority, to designate them as enemy combatants, keeping them imprisoned indefinitely without specific charge, representation, or right to a hearing on suspicion of acts they might have committed, aided, or might want to commit in the future. Most criticism of the administration on this score evades the central principle (thereby avoiding the real, admittedly difficult problem) and merely nibbles at the edges—how the policy is applied and what consequences it has had. In some quarters even this marginal critique is pilloried as unpatriotic.

A Question of Law

This argument may give the impression that the deficit in intellectual and moral integrity in both cases, *fin-de-siècle* France and America today, consists simply of dishonesty in public life raised to an unusual level. Crucially important though the element of dishonesty is, the deficit goes still deeper, into things both countries did that crossed a vital line—decisions and actions reaching to the negation of the rule of law itself.

One can break the law, even by grave crimes like murder, without putting oneself outside the law or negating the rule of law. A murderer knows that if caught he faces trial and punishment. But when certain crimes are declared legal for certain individuals or groups because, when done by them, they automatically serve a higher good—for example, when policemen or soldiers are allowed to commit murder in order to preserve public order or uphold a particular regime—this crosses a vital line and negates the rule of law itself.

France crossed that line in the Dreyfus case when Army leaders decided that deliberately perpetuating a grave injustice was a legitimate means of defending the Army's honor and the nation's security. The United States crossed that line when its leaders, some of whom may genuinely have believed that the war was legitimately preemptive—the only way to meet a demonstrable, intolerable, and imminent threat—faced incontrovertible proof from its own investigations following the military victory that rendered this justification for the war untenable. It thus became in hindsight at best a preventive war, forbidden under the UN Charter of which the United States was a leading author and sponsor.

Just as French military leaders, faced with the truth, had the option of admitting their mistake and reversing Dreyfus's conviction, so the Bush administration at this point had the option of admitting that it had made a mistake and trying to secure international cooperation to minimize the damage and retrieve whatever good was possible from the situation. This was never considered. Instead, after long denial of the facts and dispute over their meaning, the president himself refused to admit that these discoveries (or absence of discoveries, in this case) made any difference, or that he had made any mistake at all. (Even in December 2005, when the president finally spoke to the matter of key intelligence errors, he still refused to entertain the possibility that the decision to go to war had been a mistake.) After the fall of Baghdad the president reasserted even more vigorously the US "right" under the Bush Doctrine to use force against any government or movement it deemed a threat to American security. He insisted that any such operation by the United States *ipso facto* constituted legitimate self-defense because, by definition, it fought terrorism and promoted the universal higher ends of freedom and democracy. Along with this reassertion of its right to wage preventive war went a reassertion and continued exercise of its claimed right of indefinite preventive detention.

Here is where one must attempt to introduce clarity into a discussion marred (as in France during the Dreyfus Affair) by confusion, obfuscation, and deliberate evasion of the real issues. Policies of preventive war and indefinite preventive detention are wrong *in principle* and should be rejected because they are wrong, not because they may work badly or produce harmful side effects.

True, a state may under extraordinary circumstances legitimately use military force preemptively. Granted, also, that changes in military technology and in the nature of international actors affect the determination of when and whether a threat is certain, imminent, and impossible to deter except by preemptive force. Granted, further, that non-uniformed enemy combatants and suspected terrorists cause special problems for both civil and international law. Yet after all reasonable concessions are made, the distinctions between legitimate preemptive and illegitimate preventive war, and between policies of legitimate temporary detention of illegal enemy combatants or suspected terrorists and policies of indefinite preventive detention, remain valid and are too vital to be discarded. The fact that a line is difficult to draw, and may under changed circumstances have to be drawn somewhat differently, does not mean that the burden of judgment is thereby lifted. A basic principle cannot be abandoned simply because it must be applied differently and with difficulty.

When principle is abandoned, the rule of law is negated and is replaced by what amounts, in effect, to vigilantism.

This point becomes even more crucial when, as here, a war originally proclaimed and justified as preemptive is subsequently proved to have been at best preventive, and is then praised and defended as legal because of its alleged humanitarian and political achievements. This particular form of moving the goalposts suggests the extremely dangerous principle that states may engage in preventive (or even aggressive) war if some putative higher good comes out of it. It makes no difference in this case whether those who made the decision for war genuinely believed in the original rationale and still believe in the new humanitarian one. Once the case for preemptive war has been disproved, those who deny the facts, defend the action as right despite them, persist in it, and claim a right to do the same thing *again* under similar circumstances, place the country outside the law and negate the very rule of law.

Nor does the claim that Saddam Hussein had violated UN Security Council resolutions make the war legal. Neither the United States alone nor any group of nations aside from the Security Council itself is entitled to determine whether this was so and if it justified a war to overthrow his regime, any more than a bloc of Arab states could legally attack Israel militarily for allegedly violating UN Security Council resolutions. Again, this is vigilantism.

Least of all does it help to say, as President Bush regularly does, that the United States alone must decide when, whether, and how to exercise its right of self-defense. The right of self-defense cannot be used to justify everything a nation claims to do for its security. True, the United States for much of its existence has enjoyed an extraordinarily privileged position within the international system and has developed an extravagant understanding of its right of self-defense. In part we learned this from our elders: Just as for several centuries the British believed that they could have as much or as little of any European war as they wanted (until two world wars shattered the illusion), for 175 years after independence Americans supposed that they could have as much or as little of the international system as they wanted. World War II and the Cold War seemed finally to destroy the American illusion that the United States could drop in and out of the international system at will, but the experience of the last five years calls that conclusion into question.

Of course, law within civil society and international law are not the same. French officers broke French law in the Dreyfus Affair, while basic US actions in Iraq seem not to have broken US law (though some administration actions, like empowering the National Security Agency to conduct domestic surveillance, may have). Yet whatever the differences, American policy for well more than a century has invested great energy in the practical benefits of international law, and, make no mistake, current Bush administration policies and doctrines contradict and undercut that investment.

Again there is a notable analogue with the Dreyfus Affair. The founding principle of the Third Republic, born of the French Revolution, was liberty and equality for all citizens under the same law. True, during both the Revolution and the first two republics (1792–99 and 1848–51) things were done that undermined and discredited that principle, but it remained the Third Republic's essential foundation, and the Army's stance in the Dreyfus case clearly (though in secret) contradicted and undercut it. Once the United States entered World War II, it based sixty years of policy and world leadership on the principle that international relations must be conducted fundamentally on a basis of rules and international law equally applicable to all. It did not always act on that principle and sometimes violated it, but it never repudiated and often defended it, and it reaped great benefits from so doing. The Bush administration's doctrine and practice on preventive war and indefinite preventive detention fundamentally reject and undermine that principle, claiming in effect a higher law for the United States and thus negating any general rule of law in the international arena. Even if this is not how administration principals see what they have done, it is how virtually all the rest of the world sees it. And in regard to this fundamental principle of law it apparently still enjoys the support of a substantial majority of the American people and encounters relatively little domestic political opposition. Put bluntly, most Americans still seem to believe that anything done at home or abroad supposedly to make them safer from terrorists is fine regardless of legal niceties.

Indeed, though it is not a matter of law, it is a frustrating sign of insularity and self-preoccupation that the American people should, now years later, still think that the only serious charge to be made against the administration with respect to the Iraq War is that it (perhaps inadvertently at the outset) misled the American people and Congress. This ignores the fact that the administration misled the international community, too, and defied its collective judgment in a case that directly involves other countries' vital interests as much and, in many cases, more than it does American interests. It is almost maddening to hear Americans denounce other countries for not supporting the United States in a war that these countries rightly considered premature and unjustified by the available evidence. Even now, long after the judgment of most Europeans and others has been vindicated by events, American commentators still speak of European leaders (e.g., German Chancellor Angela Merkel) feeling the need to mend fences with the United States for opposing the war—when it is the United States that ought to be seeking to mend fences with them for waging it.

And it is an equally telling sign of America's blithely acting as a law unto itself that President Bush still justifies the American occupation of Iraq as a way to fight terrorists in their new center and breeding ground, thus keeping them away from American shores. This ignores both the fact that Iraq was not a center for Islamist terrorism until the United States invaded it, and that fighting terrorism by an American occupation there promotes its spread throughout the Muslim world and adjoining areas, making Spaniards, British, Indonesians, Jordanians, Egyptians, Moroccans, and very conceivably Israelis, too, pay a price for the current level of American security from direct attack.

What Next?

Such a state of affairs reveals the current national deficit in intellectual and moral integrity in stark terms. The deficit is still not equivalent to bankruptcy, however, and is not necessarily headed toward it. The Dreyfus case, after all, did get resolved, though messily and incompletely, and led to modest overall gains in civil rights, tolerance, and the rule of law. This was possible because *fin-de-siècle* France, despite its problems, still valued democracy, republican institutions, civil liberties, and respect for law.

The same can still be said, though with less confidence than before, of America today. If certain of its actions and policies violate international law and negate it in principle, the American system does not rest on the negation of law, as many other great power regimes have done and still do. The institutional resources for turning things around exist; evidence points to a turnaround already underway. One cannot expect dramatic changes in hearts and minds from the principals of this administration, but one can hope for more caution and restraint from them and their successors, and more resistance from their opponents.

Nor must the war necessarily lead to disaster. The occupation could end with a gradual withdrawal of American troops, leaving an Iraq very imperfectly pacified, stable, democratic or friendly, but neither a menace to its neighbors nor a serious threat to the United States. Even if that outcome in Iraq complicates other world problems, it need not make them radically worse or insoluble. The United States throughout its history has enjoyed an extraordinary margin for error in international affairs, and probably still has enough to handle this one. In domestic politics, Democrats should gain a short-run electoral advantage, but Republicans will still claim credit for any achievements in Iraq and blame Iraqis, foreign terrorists and liberals at home for any failures—while the public tires of Iraq and moves on.

A common muddling-through outcome, then, is entirely possible—so again, why all this discussion and why drag in the Dreyfus case? There are two reasons. First, only the fact that some persons involved in the Dreyfus case—the best example is Georges Picquart—did not care about its historical consequences but *did* care deeply about justice, truth, and principle made it possible for the Affair to reach even a semi-satisfactory resolution. The same attitude is needed now in regard to Iraq, and it may be developing; Patrick Fitzgerald, the special prosecutor in the Valerie Plame case, might be one of the Georges Picquarts turning American attitudes around. Former State Department chief of staff Lawrence Wilkerson may be another.

The second reason involves the Latin axiom *principiis obstat* ("Resist the beginnings"). The semi-optimistic scenario holds at best only for the near term. The need for a longer-term corrective, again illustrated by the Dreyfus case, is encapsulated in a saying of Jesus: "If they do this when the wood is green, what will happen when it is dry?" (Luke 23:31).

The Dreyfus case ended as well as it did because it happened during the Third Republic's best years (though most Frenchmen did not think so then), when relative prosperity, improved political stability, and a stronger international position helped make a surface resolution possible. But a surface resolution was all it was; French leaders failed to confront and solve the problems that gave the Affair its true character. The real question had never been whether France or the Republic would survive, but whether the Republic would be true to its ideals. The outcome of the Dreyfus affair did not fully answer this question, and after the hellish trials of World War I drained France's reserves of unity and civic virtue, a revived German menace, followed by a catastrophic invasion and defeat, overwhelmed France's democratic institutions and its republican convictions. The highest values and purposes of French civic life after June 1940 became those of saving the government's authority and the Army's honor, preserving national unity and ensuring that most Frenchmen would survive, but at the cost of civil liberties, principles, particular individuals and a whole race—the Jews. Thus did the Vichy regime, with its so-called National Revolution, write the last tragic and shameful chapter of the Dreyfus case. After its fall Charles de Gaulle, Vichy's implacable enemy, said of its leaders, too generously but with deep insight, that they had thought too much about Frenchmen and too little about France. Too little, that is, about what France really stood for.

This is a tragedy Americans would do well to ponder. One can more easily be hopeful about America's chances of escaping the current situation relatively unscathed than about its longer-range future. The main reason is not the danger of heightened terrorism (possible) or more and bigger wars (improbable), but rather that other deficits and problems, too numerous to list, now being allowed to pile up in America's current fat years will present graver challenges both to our standard of living and our way of life than America has ever before faced. Add to this the likelihood of crises abroad and the temptation to use unrivaled American military power to deal with them through preventive war, to unite (and distract) the nation and supposedly solve its problems, and the meaning of the Dreyfus Affair's unsatisfactory ending comes clear. What will an America that took this route when the wood was green (and never rejected it as wrong) do when the wood is dry? And what will we do thereby to what America stands for?

12

Open Fire

2007

I write as an historian, offering no special expertise on current American politics or the military and political situation in Iraq and promising no new facts or ideas. Trying to say something original about the Iraq imbroglio is like trying to invent new letters for the alphabet—impossible and pointless. I propose instead to present familiar facts in another way, believing that sometimes ideas, individually well known and in the mainstream, in different combination suggest an unexpected conclusion.

I also assume that history counts, that the prevalent American historical perspectives on this war are inadequate and misleading, and that a sounder sense of history can not only free us from the tyranny of misleading historical analogies but also suggest different and better ones. While the past does not predict the future, and no historian should pretend to be a prophet, one indispensable way to look into the future is to walk carefully back into the past.

That means starting with recent history, inquiring how six years of global war on terror and five years of regular and counterinsurgency war in Iraq leave the US now facing two apparently unquenchable fires of insurgency, terrorism, and civil war—fires that threaten the entire Middle East and adjacent areas, including Pakistan, as well as South Asia, Central Asia, Europe, and North Africa. While taking note of American intentions, aims, motives, and agendas—declared and undeclared—and the debates over these, I will concentrate, as historians should, more on what the American government actually did in its supposed efforts to prevent and then fight these fires, what its actions objectively constituted within the international system, and what results they produced. In history, especially in international affairs, results count more than intentions, and the most important results are very often the ironic, unintended ones.

Preventing the Fire

Two major facts must be recognized at the outset: the fire in Iraq (though not Afghanistan) could have been prevented, and the American government deliberately decided against doing so. These are not controversial assertions but undeniable facts. Other questions about preventing fires at this time remain debatable—whether the attacks of 9/11 might have been averted or blunted by better intelligence and quicker action, whether the Clinton administration could have weakened al-Qaeda earlier, whether a more determined campaign in Afghanistan could have destroyed al-Qaeda and prevented further terrorism. But this much is certain: first, the Bush administration, supported by most of the Congress and the American people, decided to treat an alleged potential threat of explosion emanating from Iraq as more imminent and dangerous than the actual fire burning in Afghanistan, Pakistan, and elsewhere; and second, it chose against resistance at home and widespread opposition from the international community not to use existing, standard methods of fire prevention.

Much of this—the priority the US gave Iraq over Afghanistan and al-Qaeda and the choice of preventive war—is universally acknowledged. Astonishingly, however, the equally important and undeniable fact that its policy in 2002–03 deliberately rejected international methods for fire prevention in Iraq has still not been squarely faced, much less accepted. This gets ignored or swept aside by disputes over other questions, arguably interesting and important but not central—Saddam Hussein's nature and intentions, Iraq's capabilities, the existence or not of WMD, the motives and aims of America's leaders, the quality and use of American intelligence, the genuine or deceptive character of arguments for military action, and so on.

This shell game, whether it represents a deliberate tactic or not, has led Americans to misunderstand the struggle at the UN that culminated in America's failure to gain a Security Council resolution authorizing the use of force against Iraq and its decision to proceed without one. The American public has been led to believe that the sole, decisive issue was whether Iraq possessed WMD or active programs to develop them. If so, military action would have automatically been justified and needed. This remains the administration's defense of the decision for preventive war: along with other countries and on the basis of reasonable intelligence, it genuinely considered Saddam's weapons a threat to which the only effective response was force.

That completely distorts the debate. It was not simply over whether Saddam possessed WMD and/or active weapons programs, with everyone agreeing that military action was required if he did. The contest was over two distinct questions. The first was about facts and evidence. Had Iraq's weapons and programs already been sufficiently proved (the American position), or should the UN arms inspectors led by Hans Blix be given more time to make sure? The second, even more important from the standpoint of international politics and law, was about the best response. If the threat proved real, should the international community immediately authorize military action or first expand the existing UN-authorized sanctions against Iraq to try to force Saddam to surrender his weapons and submit to international controls?

The choice therefore lay between the American position that the threat was already proved, that other methods would take too long and be ineffective, and that only military action could deal with it, and the arguments of others, led by France, for more time to make sure of the threat and, should it prove real, for using standard methods and instruments of containment, deterrence, and coercive diplomacy before resorting to military action. In other words, it was a choice between starting a fire in the Middle East to counter one allegedly already smoldering and about to break out and trying fire prevention first.

On both scores, the American position proved wrong and its opponents' right—and once again Americans have largely missed the significance of this. The failure to find any evidence of WMD or active programs after conquering and occupying Iraq is not, as is constantly supposed, important chiefly because it undermines the official rationale and justification for the war and shows that the administration manipulated prewar intelligence in order to deceive the American people. Whether or not those charges are true is not the real issue. The inability to locate WMD proved precisely what opponents of war had earlier contended: traditional international methods of containment, deterrence, and coercive diplomacy not only could work in the new age of terror, but in fact had worked. Iraq had no WMD because the previous decade of sanctions and pressure had effectively deterred Saddam from reviving his earlier programs. Thus, by insisting on military action, the US aborted a long-established international protocol for fire prevention that had already succeeded in Iraq. It ignited a fire supposedly to counter another fire that was already effectively extinguished.

Starting the Fire

The US acted in Iraq not as a fire brigade but as an arsonist. This does not describe the administration's aims, but something more fundamental—the objective character of the American decision in the context of international politics. The motives were mixed, but a central reality remains: the Bush administration opted for war because it considered it intrinsically a good idea. No one can seriously doubt this.

The administration has always acknowledged, even boasted of, the war's preemptive (actually, preventive) character. It never seriously claimed that the US had been attacked or immediately threatened by Iraq—a claim too preposterous to believe. The initial military success inspired great celebrations of the war's benefits for America, the Middle East, and the world.

One must therefore consider why this was so, what general mindset lay behind starting the fire, what its particular intent and anticipated effects were. It was supposed to be multi-purpose, first of all preventive, like fires deliberately set by the Forest Service to preempt bigger natural ones—in the famous phrase, to make sure that the smoking gun would not turn into a mushroom cloud. It was also—if one can seriously envision this—supposed to be a surgically precise firestorm. It would kill or drive out the criminal inhabitants of a particular building in a dangerous, unstable, crowded neighborhood without destroying the structure or spreading the fire to the whole city.

The fire-strike, moreover, as launched and executed in spectacular fashion, was unaccompanied by serious planning or preparation for extinguishing it and repairing the building. Indeed, Defense Secretary Donald Rumsfeld flatly prohibited this. The fire-strike was expected to be not only surgical but also purgative and curative, driving tyranny and terrorism from Iraq while also bringing peace, freedom, democracy, ethnic, religious, and national reconciliation, and the blessings of a market economy across the region. It would further be self-limiting, dying out on its own and preventing other fires from breaking out, and would promote new constructive activity. The damaged building would be rebuilt better than before by new owners, with no further American exertion required beyond leadership and advice.

The mindset behind this fire was thus a truly extraordinary, heroic example of a phenomenon all too common in international politics: utopian optimism. This is not the mild verdict it might seem. Utopianism is extremely dangerous in international politics, and this particular kind—reckless, ignorant, arrogant, overconfident, and oblivious to logic, facts, and history—is arguably the worst variety.

Fighting the Fire

After deliberately refusing to plan and provide for extinguishing the fire it had started and doing its best to silence the growing number of calls for doing so, the administration tardily discovered that it had a real insurgency on its hands. The story of how this unanticipated fire started and developed is both too complicated and too familiar to rehearse here, but three general points are important for our purposes.

The first is that the US had chances to dampen the fire it had started, if not entirely extinguish it, and rejected them because doing so would interfere with other goals. The best opportunity to end the fire by simply letting it burn itself out came after the downfall of Saddam's regime and the end of military operations in May 2003, when the first American commander of the occupation, retired Gen. Jay Garner, proposed withdrawing American troops and letting the Iraqis sort things out for themselves. Given the size and character of the American forces and the lack of preparation for an effective occupation, this was logical. But it would have sacrificed the dream of molding Iraq and the entire Middle East according to America's image and the plan to make Iraq the central base for US regional hegemony.

So Garner was replaced by L. Paul Bremer, and a different, more intrusive occupation ensued. Having started the war because it wanted to, the US failed to end it because it did not really want to—that is, it would not pay the price of sacrificing some goals and assuming attendant risks.

The second fact to emphasize is that in fighting the insurgent fire in Iraq, the US has mainly succeeded in feeding it. This conclusion will not surprise anyone with any sense of history—that war tends to feed on war is one of its oldest and most recurrent themes—and is no longer controversial. A huge literature supports it, the most recent National Intelligence Estimate confirms it, and no amount of spin or denial by the president's men will make it go away.

Most Americans have come to accept what many analysts have long seen, but they still discuss the reasons for this phenomenon and the dangers it presents in old, superficial ways. The question remains essentially, "How and where did the occupation go wrong, and who was responsible?" The answers almost invariably blame contingent, tactical factors—the wrong kinds of weapons, training, and military tactics; too few troops on the ground; too little knowledge of Iraq; incompetence, inexperience, and corruption; crimes and scandals; political and administrative blunders; and the like. An interesting variant, more popular today than ever, is to blame the Iraqis themselves—not merely the terrorists and insurgents, of course, but also and especially the Iraqi government for failing to do its job.

The discussion of the dangers of a prolonged insurgency and embattled occupation is just as superficial, concentrating mainly on American casualties, the strain on our Armed Forces, the financial and political costs of the war, and the dangers to the homeland of spreading terrorism. Much less attention centers on the most imminent and important threat. Iraq itself is being destroyed—perhaps has been destroyed—both as a state and as a functioning society. Leaving aside the enormous human tragedy, no stable Middle East is conceivable with Iraq as a political, social, religious, ethnic, and economic black hole, creating problems for world peace and stability that are almost incalculable.

Thus, after five years of counterproductive failure, the dominant American perspective on the Iraq War remains marked by endless vistas of myopia. Concentrating attention on tactical failures enables those who decided on and promoted this war to escape accountability and allows its current defenders to justify the original policy while condemning its execution and continuing the war. It lets Americans scapegoat the Iraqis for results for which they were not primarily responsible. The fact is that the US destroyed the former Iraqi governmental apparatus and created a new government under conditions that virtually guaranteed that it would be dysfunctional. It broke the Iraqis' legs and now complains because they cannot jump the high hurdles. Most importantly, emphasizing the tactical and contingent causes of failure promotes the idea that the war can still be won or further failure averted by changing tactics and adding resources and effort—the rationale behind the current surge. Similarly, concentrating on the immediate costs and dangers of the war for Americans encourages the belief that if these can be reduced to tolerable levels, the problem will basically be solved.

Both views are not merely incredibly shallow but immensely harmful. They ignore the central fact that these tactical and contingent reasons for failure are not accidental. They flow predictably from the nature of the enterprise. The deeper reasons for failure, the fundamental reasons that fighting the war has fed the war, lie in fatal contradictions inherent in the war itself and the policy that led to it and are thus strategic, structural, and irremediable.

First come contradictions in the goals of the war, already noted. One can no more conceive of creating an independent, self-governing, liberal-constitutional democratic Iraq to be America's satellite, ally, and base for the projection of US power in the region through an American conquest and occupation than one can envision dry rain or snowy blackness.

To take just one of many contradictions involved: if miraculously a genuinely independent democratic Iraq did emerge from an American occupation, it would not long remain a dependent

American ally but would act in its own interests, which are far from identical with those of the United States.

This proposition is axiomatic, or ought to be, but it is not at all abstract or theoretical. The attempt by the United States to achieve ends in Iraq that are inherently self-contradictory and therefore impossible has led directly and indirectly to many of the tactical, contingent blunders reinforcing the insurgency.

One example: by common agreement, no one thing has done more to destroy America's image and prestige in Iraq and to feed the fires of insurgency and terrorism there and elsewhere than the revelations about torture and inhumanity at Abu Ghraib. The American response has been either to try to minimize and deflect their impact by blaming and punishing a few low-level offenders while shielding those higher up the chain of command or to demand investigations into who was responsible, all the while denying that this ever represented American policy. This has effectively swept the main fact under the rug (for Americans, not others): this sort of scandal is more or less inescapable in this kind of conflict. Though it was promoted by some shocking decisions by high-ranking military and civilian authorities and should have been foreseen and handled very differently, it also flowed naturally from the war and occupation itself. One cannot expect to conquer a people, overthrowing its government and ruining and humiliating those who supported and benefited from it, without arousing violent resistance, predictably promoting a vicious circle of reprisals and atrocities on both sides.

Equally striking is the mismatch between the goals of the war and the historical means and process supposed to achieve them. In Iraq, military conquest and armed occupation by Western forces were supposed quickly to produce a liberal, constitutional, democratic state with a free-market economy and a strong, stable civil society. Parts of the West, including the United States, have now more or less achieved these goals—but only through an historical process that, ignoring its roots in ancient Greece and Rome, took about a thousand years and involved numerous stages—medieval constitutionalism; the administered police (i.e. social discipline) state; the constitutional *Rechtsstaat*; the parliamentary state, liberal-representative but not democratic; and finally, liberal-constitutional democracy. The evolution involved deep, wrenching social, economic, intellectual, and cultural changes—religious reformation, class struggle, scientific discovery, technological innovation, massive developments in education, literacy, and the growth of a public sphere, industrialization, modernization, urbanization, and so on. It was tortuous, convoluted, and twisted almost beyond belief, full of blind alleys and wrong turns, choked with violence, war, imperialism, and revolution, marked by as many defeats and failures as victories and advances, costly and dangerous, with numerous times when the process seemed hopelessly stalled or defeated. Yet we proposed to bring about this transformation in Iraq through one short easy war. What were we thinking?

This is not to say, as some do, that Iraqis, Arabs, Muslims in general, or other non-Westerners cannot achieve liberal-constitutional representative democratic government because their religion, culture, ideology, values, and history render them unfit. I consider that view profoundly mistaken, if not a lie. Nor does this imply that non-Westerners can learn nothing from the Western experience. It is full of lessons, positive and negative, for West and East alike. I am saying only that if Iraqis and others are to gain the blessings of freedom and democracy, they cannot get them this way.

Even more pertinent, they cannot acquire them at our hands. Americans, especially in this administration, seem oblivious to the disconnect between the characteristics and persona of America as a country and people and the ideals it supposedly pursues in Iraq. The US is Western; it is imperialist in the sense of leading Western expansion into the non-Western world; it is overwhelmingly Christian, strongly pro-Israel, individualistic, and materialist in spirit, culture, and lifestyle; it is capitalist, rich, and extremely powerful. Unlike other American traits like self-preoccupation, provincialism, and widespread ignorance of other peoples' languages, culture, and history, these are basic American characteristics that we will not change, and in many respects should not want to. Collectively, however, they disqualify America from being a direct agent of the fundamental changes we are trying to promote in Iraq or the Arab and Muslim worlds. The United States is an alien presence in that world, and a highly intrusive one, with bases, fleets, capital, and corporations, an invasive and subversive culture, and now an occupying Army. It is not merely the way the United States has conducted itself in Iraq that has fomented resistance and turned it into a breeding ground for more Islamic terrorism. It is the simple fact that being what we are, we are there at all.

This is not to designate the US as the main problem in the region and its exit, bag and baggage, as the answer. The central problems of the Middle East are unquestionably internal and will certainly persist—probably get worse, at least temporarily, when the United States leaves. I am only stating the obvious: that we—being what we are and, in the main, must be and will remain—cannot solve those problems or meet the dangers they pose to our interests by our direct efforts, especially military ones. However executed, these are bound overall to be self-stultifying and counterproductive.

This conclusion seems too obvious to need proof, but let me try to illustrate with an historical example. At one point in the sixteenth century, when Western Christendom was being torn apart by the Protestant Reformation and the attendant struggles and wars, the Ottoman Sultan Suleiman proposed that he be invited to arbitrate the theological disputes and help restore peace in Europe. This may not have been a cynical ploy. He was both a very powerful and fairly enlightened ruler. His favorite wife was a Christian, and Christians in the Ottoman Empire, though discriminated against, were recognized as People of the Book and were not widely persecuted or forcibly converted to Islam. Yet can anyone suppose that European Christians, however divided internally, could seriously consider this offer as a sincere attempt to help them, coming as it did from infidels and historic enemies of Christianity who had just conquered huge sections of southeastern Europe, almost capturing Vienna, and still menaced the whole Mediterranean?

There is an obvious reply to the argument of this essay: even if it is basically true, it is by now outdated and useless—one more pointless discussion of how the US got into its current straits when the only relevant question now is how to get out. The lessons preached here have already been learned. Most Americans recognize that the war has been a failure and want to see the troops brought home. The president is highly unpopular, mainly because of his conduct of the war; his own supporters are abandoning him or threatening to. And the original grandiose war aims have been drastically scaled down even by the administration. Basically both parties and the country are now trying only to escape with a whole skin and avoid worse disasters; the only useful question is how to do so.

That response, for many an obvious ploy to escape accountability, is superficially plausible but nonetheless wrong. Leave aside the consideration that historical truth, honesty, and candid self-appraisal are intrinsically good, and vital for the souls of states as well as individuals. The governing truth is that, in the main, Americans have not learned the most important lessons from this war, and many powerful individuals and groups are doing their best to keep them from doing so. The public senses vaguely that the war has been a failure, but does not genuinely understand how and why it failed. Americans have turned against it and to a lesser degree have come to think that it was inherently a bad idea only because it has turned out badly—lasted too long, cost too many lives and too much money, seems headed toward stalemate or defeat rather than victory, and is making terrorism worse. In other words, most now consider the war something that has gone wrong but not something that was wrong. Public discussion in the media, the literature, and the political arena has therefore overwhelmingly centered on the question "What went wrong with the war?"—not "What is wrong with this war and with us?"

The argument here is that the war never went wrong; it always was wrong, in specific, basic ways. The distinction is fundamental, eminently practical, and involves lessons that the US—its government, elites, and broad public alike—has not yet learned. It accounts for the fact that all of the current plans for getting out of Iraq are not really plans for genuinely getting out, but plans for staying on in one way or another so as to minimize further losses, recoup sunk costs, and protect particular interests. It means that until we squarely face what we have not hitherto faced as a nation—what this war represented, what we have done, and what this says about who and what we are—we will not be willing or able to take the practical steps necessary to contain the fire now burning, dampen and extinguish it as much as possible, and do what is necessary at home and abroad to prevent an even greater fire next time.

The first half of this essay had one central message: the war in Iraq did not go wrong, a spectacular military victory spoiled by a botched occupation, but always was wrong, a delusional attempt to do the impossible. This recognition is still vital for policy because the US seems bent on continuing its efforts to fix the war, thus missing the remaining opportunity to end it and contain the fire we started.

Odd though it seems that this policy persists despite failures, enormous and growing costs, and major shifts in public opinion and politics since 2004, it is easy to explain. The American consensus on the need for change is fairly wide but not profound and includes no consensus on the kind of change needed. Many divergent proposals compete for attention under the rubric of "getting out of Iraq"; none commands general agreement. Beneath this lack of consensus on how to get out lies a deeper reason for the reluctance to leave: one thing military and political experts, politicians, and the public can agree on is that withdrawing will be difficult and delicate and could have grave adverse consequences.

The risks of withdrawing at this juncture are constantly discussed, usually in lurid terms—more ethnic cleansing; all-out civil war and total breakup in Iraq; free rein for al-Qaeda and other jihadists; increased Iranian influence; the spread of conflict and civil war to the rest of the region; more homegrown terrorism in Europe; instability and possible overthrow of important governments; loss of access to Middle Eastern oil and/or use of the oil weapon against the West resulting in economic chaos; and finally (the least important and likely but apparently the most feared by Americans), more direct terrorist attacks on the homeland.

Even if the dangers are often overblown, this fear of unintended consequences is natural, though it regularly leads to wrong conclusions and bad policies. The administration insists that the only answer is to fight on till America prevails—a predictable and contemptible argument. Every threat Bush now cites as a reason to stay the course has either been produced by this war or greatly worsened by it. The arsonist still poses as a firefighter. Other common reactions include a kind of paralysis born of indecision over which is the worse evil, staying or withdrawing, and a Micawberish hope that something will turn up.

A word on the current wave of Micawberism, fed by misleading or mendacious reports that the surge is succeeding; the Iraqi government, police, and security forces could still improve; sectarian violence is declining; and so on. This illustrates how hopes derived from misplaced patriotism and nurtured by clever propaganda can survive unnumbered disappointments, broken promises, and wrong predictions. Gen. David Petraeus, whose views presently command such remarkable credibility, may be an able, honest officer (there are skeptics), but anyone who expects a general handpicked by this president and serving this Defense Department to tell the truth, the whole truth, and nothing but the truth about the results of the strategy he devised and is responsible for executing is naïve. Petraeus's own record shows this. In October 2004, just in time to influence the presidential election, he published a highly optimistic portrait of progress in Iraq in the national press. It proved totally wrong. As for the statistics on casualties and violence, it requires little knowledge of military history to know that governments, war departments, and military officers always cook the books. The Pentagon has been doing this blatantly throughout the war. Above all, everyone knows that this alleged military progress, even if real, cannot be decisive. It rests on a temporary military escalation that cannot be sustained, while the political reconciliation and national unity in Iraq on which durable stability and security depend grow ever more remote.

Less foolish than this Micawberism, but no less futile, are calls for a bipartisan compromise to signal a change in direction, such as Sen. John Warner's proposal to announce a small reduction of forces before Christmas. This is pure tokenism, meaningless and deceptive. Still more troubling, and most likely to represent the fallback position the US will take, are proposals to avoid the unintended consequences of withdrawal by not really withdrawing but staying on in a different way. The suggestions vary, some recycling ideas already tried without success: changing the mission from combat to training, concentrating troops in a few bases, evacuating most of Iraq but remaining in certain areas, moving most or all of the troops out of Iraq but basing them close by ready to intervene to stop civil war or foreign intervention, and so on. Such proposals appeal to moderates in both parties as a way to criticize the war and claim to change course while still looking strong on security and terrorism (which helps explain why Senators Hillary Clinton and Joe Biden each espouse one).

The problem is that they are designed not to get the US out of Iraq but to enable it to stay—thus allowing Br'er Rabbit to stop attacking Tar Baby while remaining firmly stuck to it and continuing to present a target for its foes and a stimulus to Islamists and insurgents. If the US cannot put out the fire it ignited or continue to direct the firefighting effort mainly because its very presence in Iraq and the Middle East by now pours oil on the flames, then compromises between all-out occupation and real withdrawal are worse than useless.

It is of course true that a genuine American withdrawal from Iraq will not be easy or risk-free or solve the problems of Iraq and the region by itself. It is equally true and even more crucial that without one, there is no solution. This seems to create an insoluble dilemma. So long as it stays, the US stokes the fire. If it leaves, it runs the risk of having it grow into a holocaust.

There is an answer, theoretically possible under current international conditions. The basic idea is simple and not original: contain the fire by letting it burn itself out within Iraq, at the same time persuading others to limit its spread by their own counter-fires. The inducement for them to do so will be that only this kind of co-operation, even if limited and grudging, will enable the United States to leave, as most other players want it to.

The first presupposition of this strategy, already discussed, is that the US has no real choice. It must face the hard fact that it must leave Iraq and cannot dictate the terms and conditions of doing so. The question is how to put that recognition and the temporary humiliation and loss of prestige involved to some use.

A second assumption is that this necessity gives the US a chance to avoid further losses and achieve some of its ends indirectly by turning withdrawal from a hard necessity into a useful political and diplomatic tool. Though America has important interests in the Middle East, it is not part of the region geographically, culturally, ethnically, or religiously. This is a reason that it can never be the regional hegemon it has tried to be, but it also means that it can leave, abandoning wreckage in its wake, while Iraq's direct neighbors and other countries in adjacent regions cannot. The US can say to other countries (in diplomatic language), "Sorry—the fire may be partly our fault, but it is now your problem. We know it cannot be handled unless we leave—but unless you give us some minimal cooperation, that cannot happen." A firm American determination to leave Iraq and reduce its direct presence in the Middle East thus becomes a way of inducing other states to participate in making possible the kind of orderly American strategic retreat that they, unlike the terrorists, also desire.

Before discussing more specifically how this strategy might work now, a little history. The object is not to demonstrate that policies of strategic retreat, abandonment of untenable positions, and diplomatic judo to turn defeat into victory sometimes work. European history and even the American experience are so rich in examples that the demonstration should be unnecessary. We are now grudgingly following this path with North Korea, and will eventually have to try it with Iran. The aim is to illustrate what can happen to a country that fails to adopt this strategy when it should, and the example chosen is Austria in Italy in 1848–59.

The story is far too complicated to relate here, but the bottom line can be briefly summarized. After emerging successfully from revolutions and attacks in Italy and elsewhere in 1848–49, the Habsburg monarchy's rulers refused to recognize that Austria's hegemonic position in Italy had become untenable, a strategic and political liability. They insisted instead on maintaining its territories and legal position intact, even expanding its military presence in Italy, and finally touched off a war in 1859, when Austria had a chance to win a temporary diplomatic victory. The result was a severe military and political defeat, the loss of Italy, and the way being paved for still worse defeat in Germany in 1866.

The obvious objection is that given the enormous differences between nineteenth-century Austria and contemporary America and their respective situations, no useful comparison is possible.

The point of comparison here, however, is their analyses and strategies—how these two countries understood the problem that confronted them and chose to meet it in certain ways rather than others. Here there are notable parallels. Both governments envisioned themselves as locked, against their will and without their fault, in a long-term, all-out, zero-sum, life-and-death struggle against ideologically driven foes and forces—global terrorism for the United States, revolutionary democratic nationalism for Austria. Both saw themselves as the special target of these forces and particularly vulnerable to them—the US as leader of the free world with a rich, open society possessing vital interests throughout the world, Austria as a conservative multinational empire in the heart of Europe surrounded by actual and potential foes and forced to defend its historic position and values. Both insisted that their revolutionary enemies and the governments that collaborated with or tolerated them acted not out of ideals or legitimate grievances but greed, nihilistic hatred, and disregard for law and human life. Both insisted that their campaigns were waged for legitimate self-defense and the defense of civilization, peace, and order. Above all, both rejected normal diplomacy, bargaining, and conciliation as worse than useless in dealing with these foes; every concession or retreat would only encourage new demands and more subversion and attacks.

In other words, both took a position basically as rigid and ideologically driven as the one ascribed to their respective enemies. Without going into details, I have to say as an historian that Austria's case against its foes and for its policy was far more reasonable and grounded in evidence than America's today. But that argument has to be left aside. It is irrelevant to the point that Austria committed three crucial strategic errors.

First, it allowed its temporary victories in 1848–49 to blind it to a central, overriding fact clear even before 1848 and glaringly obvious thereafter: control of Italy had ceased to be an asset and become a burden the monarchy could not afford. It could no longer govern its own territories, especially Lombardy, at any sustainable price or by any internationally acceptable means, and it could not even control the other conservative regimes in Italy it was forced to protect. While most Italians active in politics were not revolutionaries or united in their plans and visions for Italy, they were fairly united and passionate in wanting Austria out; even Austria's conservative friends there and elsewhere in Europe could not openly support it in maintaining the status quo.

Second, Austria's leaders were, for understandable reasons, so convinced that defeat and retreat in Italy would be fatal—pushing the empire down the slippery slope of more nationalist revolutions and foreign challenges leading to destruction—that they convinced themselves that the only answer was victory. They much preferred political victory and tried for it through firm maintenance of Austria's rights and the legal status quo, attempts to suppress revolution and terrorism, and diplomacy to gain Austria allies. But when that failed, military victory became essential, and they convinced themselves that with enough resolve and courage and a little help from friends, Austria could gain it. Thus Austrians came finally to rely on military power and victory to solve their Italian problem, despite grave doubts that victory could be achieved and clear evidence that even another military victory like 1848–49 would only make Austria's position in Italy worse in the long run while weakening it elsewhere.

Third, Austria's refusal to face the hard strategic realities of its situation derived from something more than fear of the consequences of defeat and inability to conceive alternatives. Behind the final resolve in 1859 to take arms against a sea of troubles lay a sense of outraged honor and deep moral conviction—sentiments understandable but self-deceiving and ruinous. For Austrians, retreat in the face of revolutionary conspirators like Mazzini or treacherous second-class states like Sardinia-Piedmont would indelibly stain the reputation of the dynasty and army and ruin Austria's standing as a great power. Even more important in promoting the fatal strategic miscalculation of 1859 was the role of moral principle and the belief in Austria's moral superiority over its foes. Austria's leaders were convinced that it was defending not just itself but the rights of all of Europe against international outlaws and that every decent government in Europe, understanding this and appreciating their stand, would support them even if it led to war. This moral hubris, the absolute value they assigned to Austria's just cause, closed their minds not merely to political and strategic realities but also to competing moral values and judgments. Many Europeans understood Austria's grievances but placed a higher value on peace, recognized other rights besides historic and legal ones, and understood the necessity and inevitability of change.

The same three strategic errors—a refusal to recognize when a position has become untenable, a reliance on military victory and power to achieve unattainable ends, and moral hubris leading to political and strategic miscalculation—have also brought the US into its current mess in Iraq. It is so much stronger and less threatened than Austria was that its defeat will not be disastrous like Austria's in 1859 or 1866. The main sufferers from the American adventure are Iraq itself and its neighbors. But the long-term consequences will be serious: the further erosion of America's international position, the wasting of irreplaceable assets at home and abroad, the staining of its honor and good name. No one can prove from history that had Austria chosen a more realistic course of strategic retreat in Italy it would have succeeded in saving important assets and making gains at the negotiating table, though I think this is plausible. Nor can one be sure that similar American efforts would enjoy success today. But one can confidently say for both countries that this represented their only long-range chance and that the one they chose was bound to fail.

Historical comparisons naturally only carry one so far. Why should retreat, indirection, and self-restraint help the US concretely in the Middle East now? First, basic conditions favor it. It is clear that the potential dangers from the spread of war, ethnic-religious conflict, and terrorism beyond Iraq menace its neighbors and adjacent regions more directly and dangerously than they do the United States. While Iran now enjoys more security from and influence in Iraq than before, thanks to the American invasion, it would be seriously endangered by all-out civil war in Iraq, with the Shi'ites appealing to Iran for help and the Sunnis calling on other Sunni states and the US to help stop them. Turkey has a similar problem with regard to the Kurds, shared to a degree by Iran and Syria. The immediate dangers of wider unrest and Islamic radicalism for Saudi Arabia, Kuwait, the UAE, Lebanon, and Jordan need no discussion. Even Israel and Egypt are menaced, along with the wider Arab and Muslim worlds and

Europe. The very dangers that Bush and Co. claim require the US to stay in Iraq could, if used wisely, pave the way for getting out and inducing others to help fight them.

Why should one suppose that they will? Because it is in their interest to do so and because, unlike Americans, they possess both the cultural links, ties, and skills to be effective at it and legitimate standing and authorization for intervening. A major reason that America's appeals to other states in the region to do more to help fight terrorism and pacify Iraq have been ineffective is that the overwhelmingly unpopular American military presence in Iraq negates them. Any actions taken under US control automatically become illegitimate in the eyes of the Arab street and many governments.

Once the US relinquishes control of Iraq or makes clear that that is its real goal, this changes. No one can guarantee that the region's states will co-operate in Iraq or do what we think is needed, but no one can deny their legitimate right to intervene in an affair that directly impacts their security and vital interests as Iraq's neighbors. It is maddening to see the Bush administration defy this obvious truth and stand things on their head, proclaiming America's right to fight terrorism in Iraq (making Iraq a living hell) in order to concentrate terrorist attacks away from the American homeland, and insisting that its 160,000 occupation troops are only defending the legitimate order while Iranian diplomats or businessmen in Iraq are "interfering" as spies, provocateurs, and enemy agents. While many Americans are still fooled by this bogus claim to legitimacy, the rest of the world has long since seen through it, and this has important consequences in ruining the United States' image, credibility, and international influence.

Not only will a clear, credible American decision genuinely to leave Iraq and to abandon its effort to control the region eliminate one major obstacle to useful action by others, it will also make it possible for the US and its natural partners in the Western world and elsewhere to employ the classical tactic of using one danger to balance another. Again, basic conditions for doing this are present. No government in the region, Shi'ite or Sunni, desires the breakup of Iraq and the instability this would inevitably bring. All fear a triumph of al-Qaeda and Islamic jihadism. If they now promote these evils or fail to work actively against them, it is because they see these dangers as acceptable in order to prevent an American triumph or because they dare not appear to their own people to be knuckling under to the United States. A credible American commitment to real withdrawal both removes those incentives and restores traditional rivalries to be balanced against each other—Turk versus Kurd, Shi'ite versus Sunni, Iranian versus Saudi, Iranian nationalism versus Iraqi—while still permitting general co-operation against the Islamic radicalism that threatens them all.

While historians are better at explaining how a strategy worked in the past than how to implement one in the present, certain measures seem obvious. The essential step is to disavow all the goals and commitments that are not really necessary and possible—a liberal-democratic, pro-American Iraq, a market economy, privatization of the oil industry (a goal still being pursued via the oil revenues bill the Iraqi parliament is being pressured to pass), military bases, a secular and pluralist political system, an open field for American investments, and so on. These are at worst illegitimate goals and at best superfluous ones, and in international politics, nothing is more expensive than the superfluous. This also means accepting that a unified Iraq may be desirable, but is increasingly improbable, and a loose confederation is probably the best achievable outcome. It entails redefining America's vital interests in Iraq to include only what is clearly legitimate and necessary: access to the purchase of oil on the same basis as other countries, a non-threatening Iraqi stance toward Israel, retention of the current international borders, and no overt support or toleration for international terrorism.

Next could come concrete initial steps demonstrating the genuineness of the change in policy. Possible examples include an initial reduction and redeployment of troops, cancellation of the grandiose American fortress-embassy in Baghdad, a commitment not to seek military bases in Iraq, and perhaps a proposal for negotiating neutral status for Iraq under international guarantees. One thing these earnest money payments need not include, and probably should not, is a firm date for total evacuation of Iraq or commitment to a particular mode and schedule for doing so. Both eventually would have to be worked out by negotiation, dependent on certain conditions and performances from the Iraqis and other governments, but the key is to make American withdrawal credible and attractive to all except the terrorists.

What their co-payments should be is a further delicate question. The Iraq Study Group and others have suggested that the US convene an international conference of all the regional powers to coordinate policies and actions to stabilize Iraq. The only trouble is that this seems to assume that the US still enjoys the historically coveted ability to summon such a conference, preside over the deliberations, and largely determine the results. To put it mildly, America no longer commands that position in the international community. It now needs to do what many other states facing similar challenges have done: agree in principle to participate in an international conference under other auspices, perhaps the UN, and to go along with reasonable measures it mandates without trying, Bush-fashion, to assert an automatic American right of veto, relying instead on normal instruments of diplomacy and soft power to influence the outcome.

Readers at this point might be asking themselves, "Is this it? The serious answer to the mess in Iraq is to pull out in the hope that it will not blow up and that hostile states like Iran will help us get out more or less unscathed?" The reaction is understandable. The proposal, to repeat, comes with no guarantees of success—only of guaranteed failure if we continue the present course. It is also undeniably vague on just how things would work out once it is launched. That is inherent in the nature of international politics and history. What Napoleon said of battles is even more true of diplomacy: "One engages oneself—and then one sees." Moreover, there are hard political costs it exacts that have to be paid up-front while the payoff, if any, can come only in the longer term and will be less visible. Success depends not only on luck and skill but also on certain assumptions—that the governments with whom we must work can stay in control and act rationally to the extent needed, that even opponents like Iran are capable of seeing their own best interests and acting on them, that the US, despite its follies, retains many friends (meaning states that share our basic interests regardless of whether they like us or not and recognize that disaster for us would mean great harm for them), and that international terrorism really is a common enemy that unites all governments, and open war and revolution are plagues all want to avoid. It also assumes something Americans should be embarrassed to admit, but that represents a current asset nevertheless. Though the recent American recklessness and defiance of international law have made the US a problem debtor state in international politics, as it already is in international finance and commerce, in both spheres, it remains too big and important to be allowed to fail completely and go bankrupt—another major reason it may get grudging help even from countries that dislike it. These assumptions are sound enough to act on, but they are obviously not ironclad.

In theory, therefore, a strategy like this could succeed. Yet I concede that the proposal is unrealistic, for the simple reason that one cannot envision the US, given its political system, leadership, and public, adopting it and carrying it through. The short-term reasons are obvious. Angels speaking from heaven could not make Bush do it, and by the time he leaves office, the opportunity for implementing the strategy may already be lost. Even if the door remains open, and the Democrats win a sweeping victory in 2008, that will not guarantee real change—not when both leading candidates seeking the nomination must prove first of all that they are strong on national security and tough on terrorism. When Rudolph Giuliani has kind words for Barack Obama's foreign-policy ideas and William Kristol praises Hillary Clinton's potential as commander in chief, opponents of the war need to worry.

The problem goes beyond the current and prospective national leadership and politics, however. It extends even beyond the main constitutional barrier to the needed flexibility in American foreign policy, the virtual impossibility of terminating an obviously failed presidency or changing a disastrous policy during a fixed electoral term, or the related political problem posed by endless electoral campaigns during which the most crucial decisions in foreign policy get put on hold. This is no way to run a railroad, much less the foreign policy of a superpower.

The root of the problem goes deeper still, to the American people's level of political education and maturity and the failure of American institutions, politicians, parties, elites, and the media to elevate it—or even try. If one looks at the list presented earlier of wrong reactions to the current mess and looming danger in Iraq—indecision, Micawberism, wishful thinking, self-deception, and stubborn refusal to face facts and accept consequences—one can find plenty of persons and institutions to blame for actively promoting these follies, but one cannot ignore the general public's role in actively endorsing, participating in, or passively tolerating them. True, this administration and its supporters have misled the public on a massive scale. But they could not have done this for so long had not far too many Americans, possibly a majority, preferred comforting lies to unpleasant truths and acted as co-conspirators in their own deception.

Now many, disappointed with the results, would like to see this administration over and the war ended—without holding themselves accountable, accepting responsibility, or being willing to pay a price. Instead, they look for someone else (the president, Congress, the politicians and parties, the generals, whomever) to turn things around and achieve the right results—a different form of the public mindset and outlook dominant in America from the outset. Both the overwhelming response to Bush's initial actions after 9/11 and the original public approval of the war in Iraq reflected the American public's wish to see its leaders do something bold, decisive, and effective to make Americans safe from their enemies, without the general public's having to make real sacrifices to that end or worry overmuch about the legal and moral rights or wrongs of what was done. The current disapproval of Bush and his policy reflects the same desire for a relatively easy and costless fix combined with a loss of confidence that he can produce it. For evidence, look at who has always paid, is paying, and will in the future pay for this war. The grave human costs are borne by a small unrepresentative minority of the population, the service people and their families; the huge fiscal costs are loaded onto the shoulders of our children and grandchildren; the almost incalculable costs in terms of suffering in Iraq and damage to the international system are widely ignored or dismissed. No sacrifices or risks have been asked from the vast majority of present voting Americans, and this fact arouses no revulsion, widespread protests, or serious calls for change, even from Democrats, because this is apparently the way the American people want it.

What I am suggesting is nothing new or revolutionary; it ought to be obvious and banal. In searching for a different outlook and policy on the Iraq War that could both get America out and help contain the fire it has started or helped spread, we cannot look alone to new leaders and a new administration, which will certainly come, or new party control and political alignments, which seem likely. We also need a changed American public, one that in regard to world affairs is both smarter and better (the two qualities go so closely together in international politics as to be almost indistinguishable)—a public better informed, more honest and open to the truth, less self-preoccupied and self-centered and therefore able to discern and willing to follow better leadership and make more exertions for better long-range goals.

This is not a hate-America rant by a scholar angered that the American public fails to meet his ivory-tower expectations. Historians are rightly reluctant to explain political developments by such broad categories as "the American character and experience," preferring to assign more precise and demonstrable causes. Only the conviction in certain cases that these are not sufficient prompts the conclusion that the reigning mindset of particular peoples also makes a crucial difference. I suggest that this applies here—that a serious examination of the sources of our current mess and the possible remedy require a hard look not merely at the policies and actions of the administration and the workings of the American political system but also at the level of political maturity of the American people, especially in regard to foreign policy.

Nor is this a verdict delivered from above by a dispassionate observer confident he has all the answers. It is a painful, disillusioned reflection from someone long convinced that the American public was by and large growing up and changing for the better also in international politics, who now, near the end of his career and life, grows less confident of that progress toward maturity. Worse still, he knows that even if some of his ideas about particular foreign-policy problems are worthwhile, he has no clue what to do about this basic one other than to pen Cassandra cries.

13

Leave or Lose

2008

The question "What if we win?" seems to involve three core assumptions. The first is that America is currently winning in Iraq by making significant progress in defeating the insurgency, and that the present strategy and tactics, resolutely pursued, could lead to actual victory in the sense of restoring reasonable security and effecting economic recovery and political stability there. The second assumption is that Iraq would then be capable of governing and defending itself, cooperating in the general struggle against terrorism, and affording the United States and others access to its oil, freeing America to turn its main attention and resources elsewhere. The third assumption is that now is the time for Americans to begin thinking about how to exploit this opportunity.

The Bush administration, along with the Republican Party and virtually all its presidential candidates, support the first two assumptions; most Democrats and other critics reject them. My views are that the first assumption may prove true after a fashion, that the second and more important one almost certainly will not, and that, therefore, the opportunity offered by "victory" will be quite different from the one currently envisioned.

As evidence of progress toward victory, the war's supporters point to fewer incidents of violence in certain areas and fewer Iraqi and American casualties overall; signs of increased cooperation and better relations between the American occupiers and some Iraqis; improved security and more normal living conditions in particular areas; and some signs of economic recovery. Other, less tangible indications of progress are sometimes claimed—improvements in Iraqi security forces, less interference from outside forces and governments, more divisions and quarrels among the insurgents.

Critics deny or disparage these signs of alleged progress as far too fragile, spotty and superficial to prove a sustainable trend. Meanwhile, more important indicators are missing or remain negative: no political progress toward national reconciliation and unity, supposedly the main point of the military surge and the key to victory; unsolved and increasingly insoluble constitutional, ethnic, sectional and religious dilemmas; continued strain on the American armed forces, making the surge in its present form unsustainable; worsening problems and dangers in the region (Afghanistan, Pakistan, Waziristan, and the Turkish-Kurdish frontier); the survival and growth of al-Qaeda and the spread of Islamic radicalism; the rise in Iranian influence; the persistent Israeli-Palestinian struggle; and growing strains in America's relations with its erstwhile regional and Atlanticist allies. When one adds to this the collateral damage done by the war—its enormous ongoing and future costs, the damage to America's prestige and credibility, the critical domestic and world problems left unaddressed, and the divisions and deadlock produced in the country—it becomes senseless even to talk about "winning" in Iraq.

The critics' case seems stronger, yet it is not currently gaining ground. The war, though not becoming popular, may be becoming marginalized, half forgotten. While various factors may explain this—among them the very limited public sacrifice the war has demanded and the persistence of patriotic ideas about supporting the troops and trusting battlefield generals—one important reason is that supporters of the war, even as they deny, minimize, or ignore most of the critics' arguments, appropriate some of them as reasons for pressing on to victory. Yes, many concede, the outlook is uncertain and the road to victory long and hard. But because so much rides on defeating the insurgency—because it could allow a stable, self-governing, secure and pro-US Iraq to emerge; because an American success now, after many setbacks and predictions of disaster, would strengthen us in the face of other threats and problems; and because all the efforts, sacrifices and gains made will likely be lost if America loses heart now—we must carry on.

This shows why critics of the Iraq War (as I have been, even in anticipation of it, since day one, i.e., 9/11) need to separate these two assumptions, emphasizing that success against the insurgency will not entail victory in the larger so-called war. The defeat or decline of the insurgency may be happening; given the enormous disparity between the two sides in weapons and resources, that would hardly be surprising. Historically, most insurgencies have ultimately died out on their own or been crushed by military force, especially if they are not supported by some organized outside forces. One should hope that it is happening, for the sake of the American forces and, even more, the suffering Iraqi people. The real question, however, is whether a US military victory over the insurgency can be expected to promote a durable, worthwhile American victory in the Middle East and the wider Muslim world. The answer is that it cannot.

Assume for the sake of argument that the insurgency does continue to subside before military deployments have to be cut back (say, by the time George W. Bush leaves office). Will we know with confidence what caused this, or what the development means? No doubt the surge and changed tactics will have been one factor, but what of other plausible ones? The ethnic cleansing involved in most of the violence in Iraq—4 to 5 million internally displaced persons, 1.2 million refugees abroad—may simply have largely run its course and exhausted its targets (though key trouble spots like Kirkuk and Mosul remain). How much of the decline in violence is due to simple exhaustion, despair, local battles, struggles for power and opportunistic shifts in alignments—all commonplace in insurgent struggles? How much is due to American bribes and concessions? How much to typical guerrilla/insurgent tactics of lying low under pressure, only to resume the struggle after the pressure abates?

These points are not cited for purposes of scholarly explanation, or to illustrate the logical flaws in the Administration's arguments (arguing *post hoc ergo propter hoc* and analyzing on the basis of a single dependent variable), or to make political points for the coming US presidential elections. They concern the central practical issue: What defeating the insurgency (i.e., reducing violent resistance to the American occupation to low levels) will actually be worth, and what wider effects it will have. If we assume, plausibly, that a large US armed presence and active anti-insurgent operations helped bring this about, but that many other factors—known and unknown, most of them subject to change, beyond our control and impossible to measure accurately—undoubtedly also contributed vitally to it, then we cannot ensure that the victory will "stick." We will therefore be unable to end the occupation or cut back seriously on it. Thus "victory" over the insurgency will serve to tie America down indefinitely from a military standpoint, making it a permanent target for enemies vowing to destroy foreign occupiers, and politically setting up the United States to be exploited by rival factions within Iraq and attacked by radical Islamic propagandists for as long as we remain there. As any competent historian will tell you, this is a common result from the suppression of insurgencies (take for example Britain in Iraq, Palestine, and Egypt; France in Syria and Algeria).

If current US military strategy thus promises to promote an American victory of the sort won by Br'er Rabbit over Tar Baby, the same conclusions hold even more for its political implications. The central premise has been and remains that a decline in violence and an improvement in essential services will provide Iraq's leaders the space, time, and incentive required for necessary political compromises and conciliation. This premise now epitomizes the triumph of blind faith and hope over logic and experience. All the efforts and gains made to date have promoted precisely the opposite outcome—to encourage contenders for particular power and advantage to continue fighting, without having to fear either complete destruction for themselves or the total collapse of the country, because the United States will intervene to prevent it and maintain a modicum of order. The same holds for training and equipping Iraqi armed forces and police to provide Iraq's external and internal security. Even assuming that Americans are capable of success in this endeavor despite formidable cultural obstacles, there is no way that US and allied trainers can predict or ensure whom the trainees will be loyal to in a pinch. Thus, the more we train and equip Iraqis to defend and govern themselves, the more we will have to remain in charge in sufficient force to ensure that they do not ultimately defect to some enemy. Again, history is full of examples. Britain's experience in India, especially after 1857, offers one.

The long-range, wider implications are worse still. It boggles the mind how anyone could think that military victory over a relatively minor insurgency, a "victory" that results in keeping American forces in Iraq over many future years, would win more support for the American position and policy in the Middle East from other once-friendly regimes; how it could gain more cooperation from Iran and Syria, or restore the confidence of Turkey and other NATO allies; how it could palliate the Arab street or undercut the propaganda and recruiting efforts of al-Qaeda and other Islamic jihadists; how it could overcome the disastrous heritage of five years of scandal, crime, humiliation, and destruction in Iraq, and the legacy of neglect of the Palestinians and other issues; or how it could re-knit our frayed alliances and restore our blackened reputation in the world.

All this has been said many times. It is disheartening to repeat it, knowing that it will have no more effect than before. One senses a ghastly inevitability about this American adventure—half tragedy, half farce, and all folly. But there is one important purpose that military victory over the insurgency could serve. If relative quiet does settle over Iraq, and if the United States recognizes this development for what it is—a merely tactical success in a secondary theater that affords us an opportunity to retreat without further loss and concentrate on the wider contest, using a different strategy with better hope of genuine success—then that would constitute at least a step toward a real victory.

14

From Hegemony to Empire: The Fatal Leap

2009

Most people consider the United States still the leading power in the world, and most of its citizens believe that it should exercise world leadership.* The question is mainly what kind of leadership and how to exercise it. In this chapter, I draw on the history of international politics to argue that the United States, even if its position as leader is shaky, still faces a choice between two modes of political leadership, empire and hegemony, that seem similar and are often identified or discussed as synonymous, but differ fundamentally in their nature and effects. The lure of achieving world order and peace through empire is a treacherous mirage, while hegemony presents a path open to these goals. In today's global international system, moreover, it is impossible to pursue policies of empire and of hegemony simultaneously or keep them separate but compatible, as was possible in previous eras, because they now lead in opposite directions and contradict each other. This means that US policy in recent years, especially in Iraq, which I will argue has constituted a bid for empire, has already undermined and continues to undermine the possibility of a useful US hegemony. It has contributed instead to a growth of Hobbesian disorder in the Middle East and the world that the pursuit of a sane hegemony could have avoided.

Asserting this is one thing, proving it quite another, requiring a detailed theoretical argument and extensive historical exposition impossible here. This chapter can only attempt to

---

* An earlier version of this chapter appeared as "The Mirage of Empire Versus the Promise of Hegemony," in Paul W. Schroeder, *Systems, Stability, and Statecraft: Essays on the International History of Modern Europe*, ed. David Wetzel, Robert Jervis, and Jack S. Levy (New York, 2004), 297–305.

state the case in bare outline and illustrate it at crucial points with historical evidence and examples. I start by explaining why the distinction between empire and hegemony is not merely a device for formal definition and analysis but reflects a concrete set of choices or alternatives in history leading to different outcomes. I further try to show why the pursuit of empire within the current international system has proved counterproductive and destructive, whereas hegemony remains compatible with that system and is often needed for it to function and endure.

Any such argument from history, however, whether it is extensively developed or cursory and fragmentary as it will be here, is unlikely to be considered seriously by the advocates of the current US policy. They instead continue to dismiss historical arguments as irrelevant for policy today because history itself has changed drastically since September 11, 2001. According to this view, the most serious threats to the United States and the so-called free world today, consisting of international terrorist organizations, radical ideologies and movements subject to no law or moral restraints, rogue regimes, and the danger of weapons of mass destruction coming into the hands of rogue states and terrorist organizations and movements, are so different from those confronted by the old international system that they cannot be met by its traditional diplomatic and military measures, rules, and procedures. The main current dangers arise not from sovereign states with regular governments, but can come from anywhere and must be fought everywhere and nowhere in particular, necessarily by proactive and preventive means and weapons. The old international system, with its emphasis on state actors and its legalistic rules, simply obstructs the appropriate response and has to be circumvented, discarded, or replaced with something better. In addition, the military power and margin of superiority held by the United States today is so much greater than any other power's has ever been; the ability of the United States to project that power globally with great speed and devastating effect is so unprecedented; and the economic global reach and soft power given the United States by its attractive material culture and widely envied political and social institutions and values are so effective in penetrating other countries and societies that limits placed on US action by the old rules no longer apply.[1]

My response is that this argument has already been refuted by events. The US bid to win the so-called global war on terror and promote world order and peace by creating a Pax Americana kind of empire, a project proclaimed with the Bush Doctrine in 2002 and launched with the invasion of Iraq in 2003, is not merely fated to fail ultimately, as some observers, including me, predicted before the project was begun.[2] It has already failed; a majority of Americans have recognized this long after it had become apparent to the rest of the world. The Obama administration is not likely to continue this failed venture and redouble the reckless gamble of its predecessor, further undermining stability in the Middle East, the position the United States holds in the world, and world peace. It is also unlikely to acknowledge failure and abandon the venture, choosing instead to redirect US goals, strategy, and tactics. Meanwhile, there is one surprising and hopeful aspect to this melancholy story: the old international system, attacked from opposite sides by the Bush administration and its neoconservative allies in the United States and by revolutionary forces of various kinds, radical Islamist and other, has so far survived the onslaught and proved itself more resilient, resourceful, and valuable in the crisis than even ardent proponents like me expected.

---

[1] Some examples of arguments for unipolar US world supremacy are Charles Krauthammer, "The Unipolar Moment Revisited," *National Interest* 70, no. 1 (1990–91): 23–33; William Kristal and L. F. Kaplan, *The War over Iraq: Saddam's Tyranny and America's Mission* (New York, 2003); and Robert Kagan, *Of Paradise and Power: America vs Europe in the New World Order* (New York, 2004). A much more ambitious and outwardly impressive attempt to ground both the US world military and political supremacy and the emergence of what the author calls a "market state" in history is P. Bobbitt, *The Shield of Achilles: War, Peace and the Course of History* (New York, 2002). For a critique of the work as history, see Paul W. Schroeder, "A Papier-Maché Fortress," Chapter 5 of this volume.

[2] Paul W. Schroeder, "The Risks of Victory: An Historian's Provocation," Chapter 3 of this volume; "Iraq: The Case against Preemptive War," Chapter 4 of this volume.

The Empire/Hegemony Dichotomy as Concept and in History

Now to try to put a little historical flesh on these assertions. For reasons of space, the argument must be sketchy, apodictic, and apparently dogmatic. Qualifiers like "It seems to me" or "In my opinion" should therefore be assumed in much of what follows.

Both empire and hegemony are slippery terms, often defined in misleading or vague, excessively broad ways blurring or obliterating the difference between them. That is especially true with "empire" and "imperialism." A central, essential element of empire, however, can be identified: the ability of one organized community to exercise political control over another organized community different from and separate from it, making the former the final locus of decision and authority in central political decisions for the community under its rule. Obviously, many elements can go into the acquisition and exercise of that kind of imperial authority—military and economic power, scientific and technological prowess, culture, religion, ideology, ethnicity, and so on. Nonetheless, the essence of empire lies in the possession and exercise of political control over a foreign community.

Less obvious but equally important is the fact that empire need not involve *direct* political control and administration by one unit over another, and historically has not for the most part. Most empires, ancient and modern, have existed as *informal* or indirect empires (i.e., indirect control exercised by the imperial power through local authorities in a particular region without having to govern it directly, based on and derived from its recognized paramountcy).[3] This kind of informal and indirect control,

---

3 This was clearly the case with the second British Empire in the late eighteenth, nineteenth, and early twentieth centuries, for example. The famous "imperialism of free trade" thesis of Ronald Robinson and John Gallagher in *Africa and the Victorians* (1961) was and remains controversial at many points, but the recognition that British ascendancy in Africa, India, and elsewhere at its height was mainly a matter of informal but recognized dominance, and that the empire actually passed its peak when international competition compelled the British to change to formal rule, has not been overturned. For an excellent

of which there are many ancient and modern examples, still constitutes genuine empire because (and so long as) final authority and decision-making power in critical political matters rests with the imperial authorities.[4]

The term "hegemony" is also slippery and problematic as currently used in international politics. One difficulty is that the revisionist Marxist sociologist Antonio Gramsci's definition of hegemony as cultural dominance functioning as an instrument of class rule has become standard in sociology and other social sciences and has come to dominate popular usage, thus contributing to the common identification of empire and hegemony.[5] Both the theory and the history of international politics, however, require a different understanding of the term. Hegemony in international history and politics does not mean, like empire, the possession of final political authority over another community. It means the possession and exercise of clear, acknowledged

---

analysis and survey of the controversy, see W. R. Louis, ed., *The Robinson and Gallagher Controversy* (New York, 1976). For the best introduction to the massive subject and its literature, see W. R. Louis, ed., *The Oxford History of the British Empire* (5 vols.); on "informal empire" see especially vol. 3, *The Nineteenth Century*, ed. Andrew Porter, 8–9, 170–97. For the relative decline of the British Empire in the era of new imperialism as informal empire gave way to more formal rule, see M. Beloff, *Imperial Sunset*, vol. 1, *Britain's Liberal Empire, 1897–1921* (New York, 1970); Ronald Hyam, *Britain's Imperial Century, 1815–1914* (New York, 1976).

4 To illustrate: Yugoslavia was part of the Soviet satellite empire in Eastern Europe until 1948, when under Marshal Tito it successfully resisted Soviet authority and broke free. Hungary remained part of the empire; its attempt at independence was crushed in 1956. So long as the British were able to keep their chosen ruler of Afghanistan in power in the First Afghan War (1839–42), Afghanistan was part of the British Empire, as was much of India. When the British were expelled, Afghanistan remained loosely within the British sphere as a buffer against Russia but was no longer under British imperial control.

5 For example, see N. J. Smelser and P. B. Baltes, eds., *International Encyclopedia of the Social and Behavioral Sciences*, 6642–50; A. G. Johnson, ed., *The Blackwell Dictionary of Sociology*, 141–2. C. J. Nolan, *The Greenwood Encyclopedia of International Relations*, is not very helpful on hegemony (vol. 2, 699–700) but rightly stresses political control as the essence of imperialism. So does the famous authority on the structure of empires Shmuel N. Eisenstadt, "Empires," in D. L. Sills, ed., *International Encyclopedia of the Social Sciences*, vol. 5, 41–9.

leadership and superior influence by one unit within a community of units *not* under a single authority.[6]

Thus a hegemon is in principle first among equals. An imperial power rules over subordinates. A hegemonic power is one without whom no final decision on crucial issues can be reached within the system, whose task and responsibility it is to see that necessary decisions are reached. An imperial power can finally impose its decision if it chooses, and must do if seriously challenged or it will cease to be an empire.

True, this distinction, like most such distinctions in social and political life, is not airtight but one of degree, like the differences between warm, hot, and boiling. As will be argued later, hegemonic powers can become empires and are regularly tempted to do so. There are also instances in which empires devolve or attempt to devolve into hegemonic structures (the British Empire into the Commonwealth, the French Empire into the Union Française, the Soviet Union into the Commonwealth of Independent States, the US informal empire in Latin America into the good neighbor policy and the Organization of American States, etc.). But the very fact that each can evolve into the other shows that the distinction is more than merely verbal or a matter of degree, and has important implications for the international system.

In systemic terms, hegemony as here defined is compatible in theory and practice with the workings of the modern international system (usually called, somewhat misleadingly, the Westphalian system), one made up of autonomous coordinate units (mainly states) regarded as juridically equal in status, rights, and obligations, though vastly unequal in size and power.

---

6 The best discussions of hegemony within the modern international system have gained little attention in the Anglo-American literature, perhaps because they come from German historians (Heinrich Triepel, E. R. Huber, and Rudolf Stadelmann) in the Nazi and immediate postwar era, though the basic ideas they present are much older. For a good brief discussion of the relation between hegemony and balance (*Gleichgewicht*), see O. Brunner, W. Conze, and R. Koselleck, eds., *Geschichtliche Grundbegriffe*, vol. 2, 968–9. For the importance and value of hegemony in political economy, see Robert Gilpin, *The Political Economy of International Relations* (Princeton, NJ, 1987), and Charles Kindleberger, *The World in Depression, 1929–39*, rev. ed. (Berkeley, CA, 1986).

Empire is not compatible with such a system. Whatever the leaders of empires may claim, empires cancel that essential juridical equality between all the units and the autonomy that goes with it.[7] The fundamental principles of empire and of a genuine international system of independent states mix like oil and water.

The difference extends to functions. Empires function to rule, to establish the final locus of authority in one center. Hegemony functions essentially to manage, to maintain some degree of order and decision-making capacity within a system of dispersed authority. Empire means the negation of balance within the system, both that of a sustainable balance of power and a balance in other elements equally important for a stable international system, namely, a desirable or at least tolerable balance in the distribution of rights, status, privileges, duties, responsibilities, and honor. Hegemony, in contrast, is fully compatible with equilibrium in both areas and is often necessary to achieve and maintain it.[8] Empire tends by nature toward exclusive, final

---

7 Two examples: Following the British conquest and occupation of Egypt in 1882, Egypt remained technically an autonomous province of the Ottoman Empire with certain residual rights of suzerainty belonging to the sultan. Officially, the British were there only to advise the Egyptian government, and the British government even used the Egyptian government's claims to ownership of the Sudan to carry out a conquest of the Sudan in 1898 with the aid of Egyptian forces and resources (though subsequently denying the Egyptians any control over the Sudan). No one was fooled as to who really ruled Egypt under this arrangement, which also applied in various ways to other parts of the British Empire. Similarly, the Soviet Empire after 1945 included not merely ostensibly sovereign and independent communist states behind the Iron Curtain, but supposedly independent republics within the Soviet Union itself, some of whom had seats in the United Nations. Once again, no one was fooled. Nor were many outside the United States deceived by the absence of formal US rule in Latin America, especially the Caribbean, into denying the reality of US empire through much of the nineteenth and twentieth centuries.

8 R. Stadelmann's definition of hegemony as "guided balance" (*gelenktes Gleichgewicht*—see note 6, above) often applies in history. For example, the relative stability and peace of the Bismarckian era in Europe (1871–90), frequently attributed simply to the operation of the balance of power, actually would have been impossible without what Andreas Hillgruber aptly described as a labile German half-hegemony and Otto von Bismarck's skillful use of that half-hegemony to devise and impose expedients for managing European crises (Andreas Hillgruber, *Bismarcks Ausenpolitik* [Freiburg, 1972]). Two excellent

control and cannot be shared or exercised in partnership or in common. To be sure, colonial territory can be parceled out and divided up among imperial powers, but only if the respective parcels are clearly marked, each controls one, and each honors the agreement.[9] Hegemony, however, can readily be shared and exercised in common, and often works better when so shared and exercised in either equal or unequal partnership. One can sensibly speak about hegemonies shared between two, three, or even more members (e.g., the hegemony of the great power Concert of Europe in the nineteenth century, Franco-German hegemony in the Common Market, NATO hegemony after 1985, etc.).[10]

This distinction between empire and hegemony, far from being abstract or academic, reflects lived and perceived reality and practice in history since the beginnings of the modern international system in the sixteenth century. The difference between policies of empire and hegemony has repeatedly made a critical

---

accounts of this are Klaus Hildebrand, *Das vergangene Reich: Deutsche Aussenpolitik von Bismarck bis Hitler* (Stuttgart, 1995), and G. F. Kennan, *The Decline of Bismarck's European Order: Franco-Prussian Relations, 1875–1890* (Princeton, NJ, 1979).

9   Again, examples are easy to find: the breakdown of Anglo-French dual control in Egypt (1875–82), leading to heightened tension and imperial competition in Africa and elsewhere and a serious crisis in 1898, only healed by a clear delimitation of spheres in 1904; or the Anglo-Russian partition of Persia into spheres of influence in 1907, which worked badly and was breaking down by 1914 despite the two powers' shared interest in excluding and blocking Germany, because each side believed the other was interfering in its exclusive sphere and the intervening neutral zone or illegitimately expanding its control. For the Anglo-French contest, see G. N. Sanderson, *England, Europe, and the Upper Nile, 1882–1899* (Edinburgh, 1965). For the Anglo-Russian one, F. Kazemzadeh, *Russia and Britain in Persia, 1864–1914* (New Haven, CT, 1964).

10   For an example of how dual and shared hegemony can work, I argue in my book *The Transformation of European Politics, 1763–1848* (Oxford, 1994), that peace and stability in the Vienna era (1815–48) is best explained by the existence and operation of an overall Anglo-Russian shared hegemony in Europe (Britain's in Western Europe and Russia's in Eastern Europe), complemented by the subhegemonies in Central Europe and Italy enjoyed by Austria and Prussia. France, the great power that felt excluded from its legitimate share of influence in Spain, Italy, and Germany, felt injured and threatened by this even though no serious territorial question, economic stake, or concrete military threat was involved.

difference in outcomes. Empires, both traditional and modern, can work for a considerable time, prove stable, and produce and maintain order—but only in premodern, non-international settings outside or alongside an international order. They produce such order essentially by imposing stable governance and law on areas either too little governed and organized or too mired in chronic, uncontrolled violence and war to enjoy peace and stability. However, once stable autonomous polities have evolved and been organized within an international system such as the one that has developed from its Western European origins to the global system of today, attempts to create order within that system or impose a new order upon it through empire regularly produce disorder, instability, and war. Hegemony, however, can promote peace and systemic stability and has often done so. In fact, the absence of a hegemonic power or the failure of actual or potential hegemons to exercise hegemonic leadership where and when it is needed can be and frequently has been an important cause of systemic breakdown and war.

I do not mean that the effects of hegemony are automatically beneficial or those of empire always and everywhere harmful. Austrian hegemony in Germany and Italy after 1815, for example, arguably was harmful on balance, its repressive and regressive political effects too high a price to pay for the international stability and peace it promoted. Napoleon's military-colonial empire, in contrast, had major stimulating and progressive aspects in parts of Western Europe, though overall it led to escalating tyranny, exploitation, and war. Other examples could be cited. The central point is simply that hegemony can exist and operate within an international system of independent states and help sustain it, and empire cannot.

These sweeping generalizations can only be illustrated here by a few leading instances. First, one can cite crucial points in history at which leaders of states that already enjoyed potential or actual hegemony within the existing international system or could have tried for it chose (consciously or subconsciously, willingly or under perceived necessity) to seek empire rather than hegemony. These bids for empire, one should note, did not usually or necessarily involve attempts to gain direct rule over their opponents by annexation or conquest; as noted earlier, most empire historically has not required that. What they did involve were various efforts to secure and exercise that power earlier defined as the essence of empire: the power to make and enforce decisions in other countries on issues regarded by other authorities and peoples as under their jurisdiction, critical to their autonomy and rights within the prevailing order. There could be many diverse reasons and motives behind these bids for empire, ranging from momentary impulse and personal predilection to perceived strategic or political necessity or religious and ideological commitment. Yet the imperial ventures shared two things in common. They all ultimately failed, thereby ruining whatever chances the empire seekers and their governments had to sustain a durable hegemony within the system, and they promoted instability, wars, and in some instances the breakdown of the entire system.

What follows is a list of some major historical instances in which hegemonic leaders who arguably were in a position to preserve and enjoy hegemony for a substantial period of time instead chose to make bids for empire. The brief and incomplete list is intended only to show how their policies involved a choice between empire and hegemony, as defined here, and led to the kinds of results I have indicated.

Charles V, the Holy Roman Emperor, and German Lutheran Princes and Cities, 1521–1552. In this case, the bid for empire grew out of Charles's view of his political and religious duties and prerogatives as emperor and his determination to defend Christian unity and orthodoxy in the German empire against Lutheran heresy.[11] The German princes and free cities joined in the Smalcald League did not challenge the emperor's constitutional suzerainty and hegemony as their elected overlord, but regarded this policy as an attack on their historical rights to control public worship and religion within their own domains—in short, as empire rather than hegemony. The result was that after two minor wars, Charles was compelled to accept failure in his attempts to suppress heresy or prevent a schism in the church. Rather than sanction this himself, he abdicated as emperor, and the religious divisions in Germany, though kept within bounds

---

11 A. Kohler, *Karl V: 1500–1558. Eine Biographie* (Munich, 1999).

for about sixty years through a political and religious truce between the parties, subsequently led to war again in 1618.

Philip II of Spain and the Magnates of the Netherlands, 1560s. Here the issue, though similar, involved Philip's determination to exercise direct and full political and religious authority over subjects who, though initially loyal to his authority, believed that he was usurping long-standing political and religious rights and privileges guaranteed to them by the king's oath of office.[12] Once again, Philip's choice was one essentially between empire and hegemony and resulted in a revolt and series of wars lasting off and on for eighty years. It ended in Spain's concession of independence to the northern Netherlands (the United Provinces) and helped undermine Spain's position as a world power.

Ferdinand II as Holy Roman Emperor and the German Estates in the Thirty Years' War, 1618–1635. Here the decisive issue was Ferdinand's determination to respond to a Protestant, mainly Calvinist revolt in Bohemia by not merely suppressing the political revolt against his rule as king of Bohemia but also wiping out Protestant heresy entirely, or at a minimum reducing it to harmless dimensions and ultimate extinction.[13] It was part of his attempt, supported by some other Catholic princes and by Spain, to apply to the entire Holy Roman Empire of which Ferdinand was only the elected suzerain the religious policy he had followed in his Austrian Habsburg hereditary lands—this despite the fact that most German Lutheran princes had not supported the Bohemian-Palatine revolt, remained loyal to the existing imperial constitution, and were willing to accept a political-religious settlement that would recognize traditional imperial authority, stabilize the religious status quo in Germany, and thus end the fighting. This choice by Ferdinand of empire over hegemony, urged by some of his religious and political advisers, resulted eventually, despite initial Habsburg-Catholic victories, in alienating even some Catholic princes worried about their autonomy, calling new outside forces (Lutheran Denmark and Sweden and

---

12   G. Parker, *The Grand Strategy of Philip II* (New Haven, CT, 1998).

13   R. Bireley, *Religion and Politics in the Age of the Counterreformation* (Chapel Hill, NC, 1981); J. Burkhardt, *Der Dreißigjährige Krieg* (Frankfurt am Main, 1992).

Catholic France) into the fray against the emperor, and prolonging a war that ravaged Central Europe and ultimately undermined the emperor's authority.

Louis XIV of France and His Bid for "Universal Monarchy," 1665–1715. Louis's quest for empire defies any brief summary. Suffice it to say that during his long reign (1660–1715), Louis had many opportunities to consolidate France's natural hegemonic position in Western Europe through alliances, subsidies, and judicious territorial acquisitions and fortifications.[14] Some of his political and military advisers repeatedly urged him to exploit them. Instead, his actions convinced even would-be allies that his policy was one of endless conquest and political and religious despotism (the latter illustrated by the revocation of the Edict of Nantes) that threatened the "liberties of Europe" (i.e., the independence of other states). The resulting series of European wars ended in partial French defeat, the exhaustion of France, and Louis's own admission at the end of his reign that he had gone too far in pursuit of military glory and unchallenged European supremacy.

Charles XII of Sweden in the Baltic after 1702. Again, no summary of the story is possible here.[15] The central point is that a war that began as a struggle by Charles to defend the existing Swedish empire in the Baltic and surrounding region against a coalition organized by Czar Peter of Russia turned into an aggressive imperialist effort by Charles to defeat and subjugate all his enemies, ending in his defeat and death, the exhaustion of Sweden, the end of the Swedish empire, and the rise of a new imperial threat in the Baltic from czarist Russia. Whether Charles could have established a peaceful hegemony after his initial victories is unclear (though his predecessor Charles XI had enjoyed one); what is certain is that he did not try for it.

These choices of empire over hegemony in early modern Europe, as well as others that could be mentioned, are admittedly not as clear-cut as one might wish. The lines between empire and

---

14 F. Bosbach, *Monarchia Universalis: Ein politischer Leitbegriff der frühen Neuzeit* (Göttingen, 1988); A. Lossky, *Louis XIV and the French Monarchy* (New Brunswick, NJ, 1994).

15 M. Roberts, *The Swedish Imperial Experience, 1560–1718* (New York, 1979).

hegemony were then blurred by the undeveloped condition of the early modern states system, in which the locus and extent of authority were often unclear and instances of mixed sovereignty and overlapping jurisdictions were commonplace. Still, they illustrate how bids for empire even then clashed with the development of the international system and promoted instability and war. Modern bids for empire have been more obvious and deliberate, and prove the point with little need for elaboration or demonstration.

Napoleon, for example, had many chances between 1801 and 1814 to convert his conquests in Europe into durable French hegemony over western and central Europe. Certain of his supporters, most notably his foreign minister Prince Talleyrand in late 1805, repeatedly suggested plans for achieving it. Many of the satellite states he created or enlarged in Germany and Italy had leaders loyal to him, ready to accept French leadership for their own purposes. Even countries unfriendly toward France, such as Spain or the Dutch Republic, contained important leaders and groups who wanted to accept French hegemony for the sake of the peace, security, and modernization it could bring. Most important, all the other great powers in Europe who fought against Napoleonic France, including Britain, were at various times ready to recognize Napoleon's military invincibility on the Continent and live with French hegemony.[16] What essentially kept France from consolidating its victories into durable hegemony was Napoleon's character—his refusal to renounce conquest and exploitation, his insistence on an ever-expanding military-colonial empire.

The same thing is even more obvious with Adolf Hitler, who had a program for empire far more explicit, deliberately chosen, and brutal than Napoleon's. After the Munich agreement in 1938, Germany was clearly hegemonic in continental Europe; no power including the other great powers wanted at that point to challenge German hegemony. Germany's eastern neighbors from Finland to Greece were not only afraid to oppose Germany but in many instances looked to it for economic recovery and

---

16   I make the case for this in Schroeder, *The Transformation of European Politics*.

protection against the Soviet Union. Britain and France had accepted German leadership in Central and Eastern Europe. Joseph Stalin, as ever most concerned about defending his personal dictatorship against possible internal enemies, dreaded another war and defeat like 1914–18 that would overthrow his regime. Nothing stood in the way of durable German hegemony save Hitler and the ideology, regime, and movement he led. He explicitly and totally rejected mere hegemony in Europe as useless; only the worst and most brutal form of empire would do.

In the latter stages of World War II, Stalin had ample opportunity and considerable incentive to try to build a durable Soviet hegemony over the greater part of Europe. The Western allies took for granted that the Soviet Union's enormous wartime sacrifices and the power it had displayed in breaking the back of the German army and liberating most of Europe entitled it to an extensive security zone and dominant sphere of influence in all of Eastern and much of Central Europe. Even states within that security zone historically hostile to Russia, such as Poland and Hungary, accepted this reality so far as international politics was concerned and only hoped to preserve their internal independence. Some states, like Czechoslovakia and Bulgaria, welcomed the idea of close relations with the Soviet Union under its protection. Marshal Tito in Yugoslavia not only accepted Stalin's general leadership of the world communist movement but pursued a domestic agenda and ideology more Stalinist than Stalin himself. By the end of the war, there were some in the United States and Western Europe calling for resistance to a possible Soviet threat, but there was no organized movement or capacity for one. The West was far too divided, exhausted, and (save for the United States) weak to pose any challenge to Soviet leadership in its sphere. The obstacle to Soviet hegemony, as everyone knows, was Stalin himself—his inability to be satisfied and secure merely through having friendly, dependent countries as allies on Russia's western frontier (the kind of glacis policy that czarist Russia had pursued for centuries). Stalin could only consider a neighbor as friendly if it was tightly under his control (i.e., he had to have empire).

Everyone knows what choosing empire over hegemony led to in these cases. In 1814–15, it caused Napoleon's ultimate downfall and put an end not only to his French empire in Europe but to any real chances for durable French hegemony in Europe for the rest of the century.[17] Hitler's bid for a Thousand Years' Reich lasted a scant twelve; the unprecedented devastation and atrocities it caused ended Germany's history as a great independent military power once and for all. Stalin's empire proved more durable, sustained mainly by military power and the ruthless suppression of opposition and dissent, but the Soviet Union never became really stable, either at home or in its satellite territories, or overcame the fatal flaws in its original conception that led to its collapse in the 1980s.

Many realist international relations theorists, especially so-called structural and offensive realists, have a simple explanation for all this. They ascribe it to international anarchy and the competitive search for security—proof that weaker states threatened by hegemonic powers normally and of necessity balance for security against them and usually defeat them in the long run. But even these thumbnail historical accounts show that this interpretation is historically untenable. In all the above cases, with the possible exception of that of Charles XII of Sweden, what caused these imperialist ventures to fail was not the resistance of various smaller states to hegemony by greater ones, but their rejection of empire. They usually accepted and often welcomed leadership and protection from a hegemonic power, only to resist, often late and reluctantly, when the hegemonic power was perceived (in most cases correctly) as no longer content with exercising acknowledged leadership and superior influence within a community of autonomous equals but clearly seeking imperial control over them.

The central point that hegemony, unlike empire, is compatible with an international system is reinforced by numerous cases in which, when a particular leader or government decided to seek hegemony rather than empire (even if that choice was forced on

---

17 The attempt by Napoleon's nephew Napoleon III in the 1850s and 1860s to revive French leadership in Europe was nothing like the military imperialism of his uncle. It consisted instead of a series of ill-conceived and badly coordinated initiatives that ended in creating new rivals for France (Italy and Prussia-Germany), alienating possible allies (Britain and Austria), and bringing both Napoleon III and his empire down in disastrous defeat in 1870.

them by necessity or appeared the only rational policy available), their choice helped them stabilize their position and promoted peace. Following are some examples.

Charles V's successors as Holy Roman Emperor, especially Ferdinand I and Matthias, were able to maintain their imperial positions and leadership under difficult circumstances even while religious wars were raging in other parts of Europe, especially France and the Low Countries, by accepting a religious truce and not pushing religious issues to a confrontation.[18]

Cardinal de Richelieu and Jules Mazarin, as prime ministers in France from 1624 to 1660, achieved an impressive leading position for France in Europe through war and diplomacy.[19] Yet even as they pushed French prerogatives and claims very far, they carefully avoided laying claims to empire, presenting France instead as the champion of religious and political liberties in other countries (e.g., the estates of the German empire). Doing so gave France the commanding position in Europe inherited by Louis XIV that his brand of imperialism ultimately undermined.

As ruler of Habsburg Austria and Holy Roman Emperor (1658–1705), Leopold I adopted a policy of carefully managing the German estates in the Reichstag rather than trying to dominate or control them. Thereby he succeeded both in restoring much of the prestige and authority of the emperor in Germany lost in the Thirty Years' War and in enlisting German help for Habsburg causes (notably in the second Ottoman Turk siege of Vienna in 1683), thus helping Austria to emerge as a European great power in its own right during his reign.[20]

Britain and France after the Peace of Utrecht in 1713 deliberately cooperated as leading powers in compelling restive states aggrieved at the peace settlement, principally Spain and Austria, to accept their terms and thereby to maintain a fragile peace and

---

18   A. Kohler, *Das Reich im Kampf um die Hegemonie in Europa, 1521–1648* (Munich, 1990).

19   K. Malettke, *Frankreich, Deutschland, und Europa im 17 und 18 Jahrhundert* (Marburg, 1994); P. Goubert, *Mazarin* (Paris, 1990).

20   H. Duchhardt, *Altes Reich und Europäische Staatenwelt, 1648–1806* (Munich, 1988); A. Schindling, *Die Anfänge des Immerwährenden Reichstags zu Regensburg* (Mainz, 1991); K. O. von Aretin, *Das alte Reich*, vol. 1, *1648–1684* (Stuttgart, 1993).

the so-called balance of power. This was shared hegemony, not empire.[21]

As first minister of France in the 1730s, Cardinal Claude Fleury rejected the urging of other bellicose French leaders to take advantage of opportunities they saw for France to destroy its hereditary enemy and rival Austria, thereby giving France unchallenged supremacy in Western Europe.[22] Fleury opted instead for sparing Austria and making it a kind of junior partner in a French-led program of peace and hegemony. When Fleury's rivals led France into an aggressive imperialist course of attempting to break up Austria in 1741, it not only expanded a local Austro-Prussian war into a great European one, but quickly led to French defeat and the abandonment of this plan in favor of pursuing another version of French hegemony under the Marquis d'Argenson.

If these instances of choosing hegemony over empire are unfamiliar to nonspecialists, more recent history contains instances both better known and more compelling. The victorious allies who defeated Napoleon in 1814 and again in 1815 deliberately chose in the Vienna Settlement to establish a peace based on various kinds and spheres of hegemony rather than empire.[23] After Prussia's brilliant victories in 1864, 1866, and 1870–71, Prince Bismarck deliberately chose to found Germany's security from 1871 to 1890 on a labile, carefully restrained, and managed half-hegemony in Europe rather than further conquest and military supremacy.[24] The most obvious and impressive example is also the most recent: the US option for hegemony in Europe and the West during the Cold War, in contrast to the Soviet choice of

---

21 D. McKay and H. M. Scott, *The Rise of the Great Powers, 1648–1815* (London, 1983); J. H. Plumb, *Sir Robert Walpole*, 2 vols. (Boston, 1956–61); J. Black, *British Foreign Policy in the Age of Walpole* (Edinburgh, 1985); J. Black, *Natural and Necessary Enemies: Anglo-French Relations in the Eighteenth Century* (London, 1986).

22 P. Vaucher, *Robert Walpole et la politique de Fleury* (Paris, 1924).

23 Paul W. Schroeder, "Did the Vienna Settlement Rest on a Balance of Power?," *American History Review* 97, no. 2 (June 1992): 683–706, 733–5.

24 There are many excellent treatments of this, but the best short analysis remains Andreas Hillgruber's *Bismarcks Ausenpolitik*.

empire in its sphere, made a critical difference in the ultimate results.

This argument is further strengthened by important instances in which the absence or failure of hegemony (i.e., the refusal or inability of actual or potential hegemonic powers to exercise leadership and fulfill the needed hegemonic managerial functions in critical situations) promoted the breakdown of the system and resultant disorder and war. Two illustrations will have to suffice. In the era following the Seven Years' War (1756–63), the fact that one hegemon, Great Britain, withdrew from most European affairs to concentrate on reorganizing its empire, while the other, Russia, ruthlessly exploited its dominant position in Eastern Europe for territorial expansion against Poland and the Ottoman Empire, contributed greatly to promoting the wars, international crimes (the partitions of Poland), and revolutionary instability that led to a generation of general systemic war from 1787 to 1815.[25] More obvious still, in the interwar era of 1919-33, the victors in World War I, the United States, Britain, and France, either declined to fill the hegemonic roles required to ensure general security throughout the system or in trying to do so contradicted and frustrated each other's efforts. The same picture holds for Britain and the United States in the vital arena of international economics and is one major explanation for the disaster of the Great Depression.[26]

Even if some of these individual historical instances can be debated, the overall conclusion is clear. Empire can conceivably work reasonably well for purposes of governance and stable order outside the modern international system, even alongside it, but not within it. It is incompatible with a genuine international system composed of autonomous units. The pursuit of empire attacks and undermines any such system, creates disorder, instability, and conflict within it, and ruins the chances for the empire-seeking power or powers to enjoy a durable and tolerable hegemony within the system.

---

25 H. M. Scott, *British Foreign Policy in the Age of the American Revolution* (Oxford, 1990); Isabel de Madariaga, *Russia in the Age of Catherine the Great* (New Haven, CT, 1982); M. G. Müller, *Die Teilungen Polens: 1772, 1793, 1795* (Munich, 1984).

26 S. Marks, *Illusion of Peace: International Relations in Europe* (London, 1976); Kindleberger, *The World in Depression*.

Why Is This Distinction Relevant Today?

It is possible, of course, to accept the distinction between empire and hegemony as a historical generalization and deny its relevance for the current world situation and US foreign policy today. Many do; at least four different sets of reasons are commonly given for deeming it irrelevant. Briefly summarized, they are: (1) Both the world and the position of the United States in it have changed so radically that the old international system, its rules, and historical examples and generalizations like this are obsolete. (2) The United States did not seek empire, in Iraq or anywhere else; the war was and still is a war of liberation, waged to end tyranny; defend against international terrorism and other threats; spread liberty, democracy, and a market economy; and help to peacefully transform the Middle East and other parts of the world. (3) Whatever the motives and character of the US initiative originally were, subsequent events and developments have drastically changed them; the bid for empire (if there ever was one) is effectively over. Now that even the administration basically hopes only to get out of Iraq with some dignity and honor and to leave behind a country that can govern and defend itself, it is irrelevant and distracting to worry about whether the original motives and aims were imperialist or not. (4) The overriding concern now should not be whether the war was justified or its motives aggressive-imperialist or what caused the present difficulties, but the fact that the war has now become an integral part of the struggle against Islamic radicalism and jihadism, the most dangerous element in the general terrorist threat to the United States and the world. This makes the Iraq War one that the United States cannot escape, abandon, or afford to lose and renders irrelevant the debate over what led the United States into it. The only serious question is how to prevail in Iraq as the current central battleground in a wider conflict.

Plainly these four lines of argument do not fit together very well, either as a defense of the original US policy or as a prescription for the current one. They all reject the empire-versus-hegemony case made here as irrelevant, for different, partly contradictory reasons. The first says it is irrelevant because all previous history is; the second, because US policy and the war in Iraq were never imperialist; the third, because whether they were or not, the United States is now only trying to get out; and the fourth, because why the United States got in makes no difference now—it must stay and win. I am reminded of the lawyer who defended a client being sued because his dog attacked a neighbor, who argued in his defense that (1) the attack never happened; (2) the dog was provoked and acted in self-defense; (3) the neighbor's injuries were trifling; and (4) his client did not own a dog. Nonetheless, each deserves some answer on the issue of relevance.

The best one to start with is (2), the denial that US policy in Iraq constituted a bid for empire, and the best response is not to try to prove by historical comparisons and analogies that it really was. However plausible a case might be made (and it would be easy to refute the president's assertion that the whole world knows that the United States never fights wars of conquest), historical arguments of this sort can always be denied, dismissed, or shunted aside, and the effort to make it would be distracting. Nor is the best response, at least for me, another argument that other, real motives for going to war were hidden under the justifying rhetoric of self-defense, liberation, and democracy. If existing arguments along this line made by real experts in current politics in Washington and the Middle East have not convinced people, I as a historian surely cannot. Instead I would like to point out an elemental fact of international politics. The decisive criterion for judging the real character of policies and of wars that result from them is not the reasons given by those who launch them or even the aims and motives they might subjectively feel and more or less genuinely profess, but rather what the actions involved in the policy leading to war objectively mean within the system of international politics (i.e., what they actually represent as moves within an ongoing game of action and response, and how they concretely affect the international system and the other players within it). Intentions and motives are important in interpreting history, but for judging the fundamental nature of a policy or decision, its actual systemic impacts and results, immediate and longer-range, are decisive.[27]

---

27 A historical illustration: Napoleon, in engineering the overthrow of the Bourbon dynasty in Spain, installing his own puppet ruler, and sending in his

For the United States in this instance, it means that when one country, without having been attacked or overtly threatened by another, chooses to invade and conquer that country for the purpose of overthrowing and replacing its government and then occupies it for an indefinite period with the aim of determining the kind of government, social system, and economic system that conquered country will have, who will govern it, who will control its natural resources, and what alignments and positions that foreign government will take in regard to vital regional and international questions; when in addition that invading country rejects international supervision of its actions and essentially insists on controlling the process and the outcome unilaterally, that course of action ipso facto constitutes a bid for empire—informal rather than formal empire, perhaps, but empire all the same.

On this score, it also does not matter whether the advocates of war were sincere or insincere in professing noble aims and disinterested purposes, or how the policy was publicly justified and how the public responded to that justification. None of this is decisive in determining whether a policy was imperialist; the question of the sincerity and genuineness of reasons and motives is often impossible to answer and relatively unimportant. Historically, most imperial ventures and acquisitions have not arisen simply either from deliberate design or from accident and contingency, but usually out of policies and actions chosen for a mix of reasons; the critical point is that the objective became that of acquiring empire. It happened in this instance with the United States, both the government and the people. As often in history,

---

army to occupy Spain in 1808, may genuinely have believed that he was conferring great benefits on Spain and the Spanish people—an end to a feeble, corrupt regime and ruling house; modernization; efficient government; economic revival; liberation from superstition, clericalism, and backwardness; and the like. Though Napoleon's real motives are almost impossible to determine, some Spaniards at the time undoubtedly saw French leadership as a source of enlightenment and reform and were willing to collaborate with a pro-French regime. None of this makes any difference in deciding on the character of this Napoleonic venture. It was by definition imperialist, as the whole Napoleonic adventure in Europe was, and Spanish resistance to it turned the venture into a savage colonial-imperialist war.

it is probably less important and enlightening to ask what motives and aims drove the United States forward and why they did so, and more important to inquire what restraints should have held it back and why they failed to do so; to concentrate, in other words, not on what caused the United States to choose the course of empire, but on what failed to stop it. But in any case, it is essential for Americans to recognize once and for all that it did choose empire.

The other three arguments—(1) that the argument over empire versus hegemony, like lessons from earlier generally, does not apply to the post-9/11 world; (3) that whether or not the war was a bid for empire, the bid has failed and the effort has been tacitly abandoned, making the warnings against empire outdated and irrelevant; and (4) that debating the war's origins and initial character and purposes is futile and debilitating now that it has merged into a wider struggle that the United States and its allies must fight and win—can be addressed more or less together, even though they diverge and in some ways contradict each other.

Here too the best response is to point out important facts about international politics, historical and current, that they miss. No historian should expect historical evidence, analysis, and analogies to convince people that their strongly held views about recent and current events and future prospects are wrong, especially on so heated an issue as the war in Iraq. History is not suited for that. It cannot offer a single unified and unchallengeable interpretation of the past, much less predict the future. But where history can make a vital contribution to public policy is by performing another task, triage. Armed with some serious knowledge and a sound sense of history, things arguably missing in Americans in general and this administration in particular, one can separate out of the welter of opinions, analyses, and policy options proffered in the public sphere the relatively few that are within the bounds of historical possibility, and by this triage help concentrate attention on those relatively few policy analyses and choices that are rationally defensible.

I hope—probably with the incurable optimism of the incorrigible rationalist—to do such a useful job of triage here, showing that certain premises in arguments (1) and (4) and in a different, lesser way in (3) can be shown to exceed the bounds of historical possibility and that conclusions and policy recommendations based on them should be discarded.

Both arguments (1) and (4) say essentially the same thing: the world has changed so drastically since the late twentieth century and the threats obvious since 9/11 have grown to such dimensions that the United States cannot afford either to be inhibited in its responses by the cumbersome legalistic rules and procedures of the old international system or to accept failure and defeat in Iraq. In short, the United States must prevail in Iraq and in the global war on terror regardless of the rules and whatever the cost. Leave aside here the arguments made by current analysts that these supposedly apocalyptic threats have been exaggerated for partisan purposes,[28] or that US policy has already failed in Iraq, so that continuing it will only make things worse.[29] Let me instead try to draw on history for an answer.

The historical argument here, though it involves comparison and analogy, accepts—indeed, insists—that there have been profound changes in the world's international order and even deeper ones in its economic, social, ideological, and political orders over recent decades. But it cites these changes along with earlier ones in the mid-twentieth century as precisely the main factors that make the Bush Doctrine delusional and unworkable and the US invasion and occupation of Iraq doomed from the outset to long-run failure. It agrees that the global scene has been altered drastically by terrorism and other factors, but claims that these changes are just what make the Bush administration's attempt to revive late nineteenth- to early twentieth-century imperialist assumptions and act upon them futile and counterproductive, while at the same time they make a rapid return to the late-twentieth-century international order more imperative than ever.

The way to show this, as often holds for historical analysis, is to pose the basic question differently. Instead of debating, as virtually all the current discussion does, just where, when, and

---

28 John Mueller, *Overblown: How Politicians and the Terrorism Industry Inflate National Security Threats, and Why We Believe Them* (New York, 2006).

29 For example, Thomas E. Ricks, *Fiasco: The American Military Adventure in Iraq* (New York, 2006).

why the US venture in Iraq went wrong and what better decisions and measures might have made it succeed or could still enable it to do so, let us ask, "Have any similar ventures in the Middle East succeeded in the past, and if so, what made their success possible?" That question might enable us to escape the endless and futile search for particular decisive errors or turning points and fix on certain general, minimal requirements for success.

Here is where history ought to be useful. If it cannot show exactly why this current venture failed or even prove decisively that it has, it could conceivably provide analogous instances of durable success in the past and analyze what made that success possible and whether those conditions are replicable today. Hence, the particular questions to ask are: "Are there historical examples that indicate the general conditions under which the United States might, starting in 2003, have succeeded in conquering Iraq, restoring order, setting up a government it approved, and then leaving the country to be governed by local administrators, retaining only a small military presence to keep the new government from falling into dangerous hands and to protect US strategic interests? Are there historical examples of prevailing conditions and circumstances in international politics that might have enabled the United States to persuade or compel other members of the international community to accept this outcome of US victory and dominance in Iraq and the region as permanent and legitimate, so that some of them would even help the United States maintain that dominant position? Can history further indicate under what conditions this durable US success in Iraq could help transform the region politically, ideologically, and economically in ways favorable to US interests and acceptable to other major actors in the world? In other words, are there historical instances in which the sort of project the United States undertook in Iraq and still pursues today has enjoyed durable success, indicating what basic conditions might have led or might still lead to US success in this one?"

There certainly are. The two best examples are the successful British suppression of an Arab revolt in Iraq in 1919–21 and subsequent control of the country, and (my favorite choice here) the British success in occupying and controlling Egypt from 1882 to 1936.[30] The basic story, greatly oversimplified, can be sketched as follows: The British military intervention in Egypt and occupation in 1882 that turned Egypt into a de facto British colony until 1936, developed in a far more hesitant, bumbling fashion, with much less deliberate intent at military conquest and occupation, than that of the United States in Iraq. But analogous motives and fears lay behind it. The chief British concern was strategic (control of the eastern Mediterranean Sea and the route to India through the Suez Canal), but with it also went broader ones—Islamic jihadism already raising its ugly head in the Sudan, dislike of French and other European interference and competition in Egypt and the rest of Africa, and fears for British prestige and the security of the empire, especially in India with its large Muslim territories, should Muslim Egyptians succeed in resisting British pressure.

In any case, when the British government finally decided to go in to restore order in Egypt for the benefit of British strategic security and European bondholders, Prime Minister William Gladstone (like George W. Bush) needed to believe that he had good moral reasons for acting. He found them principally in the menace posed by the leader of the Egyptian resistance, Colonel Ahmed Urabi of the Egyptian army, whom the British denounced as a potential tyrant and terrorist and falsely blamed for atrocities committed against Europeans and Egyptians. Though many in the British government understood that the real reasons were strategic and imperial, the official justification for the venture was to liberate Egypt and restore law and order. Gladstone's long-standing and subjectively genuine slogan of "Egypt for the Egyptians" remained the ostensible British goal.

As with the US experience in Iraq, military victory over the Egyptian forces proved swift and easy, and superficial order was restored in Egypt relatively readily and quickly (unlike in Iraq) because the British enjoyed the aid of a subservient head of state

---

30 The reason for preferring the latter is that although the Iraq case looks more similar to the present one, it is harder to describe British policy in the Middle East then as a durable success. The occupation of Iraq and especially the connected British administration of its mandate in Palestine were always a burden for Britain rather than an overall asset, and became increasingly troublesome in the 1930s when other strategic concerns grew more urgent.

and a Europeanized professional and commercial class willing to serve their new masters. The man placed in charge of Egyptian affairs, Evelyn Baring (later Lord Cromer) was experienced and efficient, the Egyptian authorities for whom British officials served as advisers proved mostly compliant, the Egyptian masses turned out to be inert and apolitical rather than nationalist as feared, and the financial burdens of the British occupation and of protecting British and European financial interests in Egypt and British imperial and strategic interests in the Suez Canal and East Africa were borne by a wretched but powerless Egyptian peasantry.

Thus the internal problems in taking over Egypt were successfully managed. International complications proved more difficult, but ultimately through showing sufficient resolve, the British triumphed—first ignoring France's pressure to regain its former role in the so-called dual control of Egypt, then ignoring and violating Britain's own repeated promises to evacuate Egypt, next using Egyptian forces and treasure to help conquer the Sudan in 1898, then facing down the French in a confrontation in the Sudan immediately thereafter, and finally making a favorable deal with France in 1904 over Morocco and Egypt. All that enabled Britain to shake off the remaining international restrictions on its financial control of Egypt imposed by European bondholders and the international Treasury of the Ottoman Debt that supervised Egypt's debt payments. Thus Britain, despite signs of growing Egyptian restiveness, which were especially evident in 1907, remained in control of Egypt before World War I at little or no cost to itself, and used that control to help it bring most of East Africa from the Cape of Good Hope to Cairo into the British Empire, making friends with France against Germany in the process.

These great successes were possible without provoking an international conflict only because of Britain's especially favorable position within the international system, which at the time maintained general world peace. In the 1880s, Prince Bismarck, Germany's chancellor and the most powerful statesman in Europe, used the Egyptian question for his balance-of-power purposes but would not allow a European war to develop over it or other colonial questions. After his fall in 1890 the continental great powers became locked in a great competition for world power and continental security that Britain was able to exploit for its imperial purposes. This special British advantage, however, was either ignored by British leaders and the public or, if noted, accepted as the natural order of things. The imperial success was ascribed to Britain's power and wealth, the special, universally admired virtues of British imperial authorities and of the British people and their political system, and Britain's indispensable role as leader of the international system. Thus Britain's imperial venture in Egypt proved a great success, outlasting even World War I and promoting a further major expansion of the empire in the Middle East in its aftermath.

This British experience, then, provides us with a good historical recipe for achieving a durable, successful US informal empire in Iraq and the Middle East. The secret is simple: restore the general conditions prevailing in the Middle East and the world during the late nineteenth and early twentieth centuries. That is, eliminate nationalism among Iraqis and Arabs, or at least reduce it to an inchoate, unorganized proto-nationalism; eliminate militant radical Islamist movements and regimes (as the British destroyed the Sudanese one with a British-led Egyptian army in 1898); abolish Iraq and other independent Arab states in the Middle East, returning them to their pre-1914 status as loosely governed backward territories and parts of decaying regimes (the Ottoman Empire and Persia) offering easy prey for Western imperialism; eliminate Israel as a powerful Jewish state established in the midst of Arab lands and perceived as their common enemy and a tool of the United States; eliminate the United Nations, the North Atlantic Treaty Organization, the European Union, and all the other international and transnational institutions and organizations that now interfere with empire building; eliminate the existence and influence of radio, TV, the Internet, and other means of mass communications; eliminate the educated middle and professional classes in the region; reverse the globalization of industry, commerce, science and technology, and culture that has occurred throughout the twentieth century; and finally, restore the general international competition in alliances, arms, and imperialism prevalent in pre–World War I Europe, so that the United States would now find intense rivalries between other great powers it could exploit for its purposes—do these small things, and a similar US venture today might well succeed.

Those who believe that the US strategy toward Iraq and the Middle East could have succeeded with better planning and execution or can still succeed by these means, and those who dismiss the constraints of the existing international system as quaint and obsolete in the face of recent global threats, thus are guilty of precisely what they accuse opponents of doing: living in the past. Out of their reckless ignorance both of the actual conditions in the region and of the historical preconditions for success in any such venture, and their arrogant confidence that US power, resolve, and virtue would sweep away every obstacle, the Bush administration and its followers have led the United States in Iraq and the Middle East not into a bold, forward-looking effort to create a brave new democratic world, but into an attempted revival of late nineteenth-century imperialism—an imperialism that could succeed for a time then (with ultimately devastating consequences) only because of conditions special to that era, long since vanished and now impossible to imagine reproducing.

Those who defend position (3) are in one respect more realistic. They recognize that the Iraq venture has failed and want it ended with whatever damage limitation is feasible. They conclude, however, that this failure makes further discussion of whether the venture was a bid for empire a useless distraction from the important task, that of getting the United States out of Iraq with a whole skin. That argument, however, is also problematic on practical and historical grounds. It ignores or at least fails to answer the claim made by many that the United States cannot get out of Iraq with a whole skin without a victory and dare not try to do so, since Iraq has now become an inseparable part of a bigger, more fateful struggle that would become much worse and more dangerous if the United States withdrew from Iraq before achieving a satisfactory settlement.

This claim, though it is obviously an attempt by those responsible for the war to escape blame for its consequences and is often made in exaggerated and alarmist fashion, cannot simply be dismissed as empty or foolish. A US withdrawal at a time when the Iraqi government and society are threatened by dissolution and civil war would undoubtedly risk making sectarian violence worse. It could further increase Iran's influence in Iraq and the region, might lead to full-scale civil war, and could possibly promote international conflict and war (e.g., through Turkish armed intervention in northern Iraq, pro-Sunni interventions by Saudi Arabia and others, a Saudi-Iranian conflict, or Sunni-Shiite conflict in other countries). Other ripple effects on terrorism, oil supplies, the world economy, and Muslim-Western relations in general are possible—all this besides at least temporary damage to what remaining prestige and credibility the United States possesses.

This makes the impasse seem complete and hopeless. The United States cannot stay in Iraq with any hope of real success, not only because the occupation has been fatally compromised by manifold failures in planning and execution but even more because the whole enterprise was a bid for nineteenth-century-style empire structurally impossible and unthinkable in the twenty-first century. Every effort to achieve success in it therefore must make things worse in the long run. The United States cannot get out of Iraq, however, because the immediate side effects of withdrawing would be worse than the current problems of staying on and would not extricate it from the wider struggle but drag it further in.

Here, at this point of impasse, the other half of the "empire versus hegemony" argument kicks in. This chapter has focused so far on the "mirage of empire," emphasizing the futility, destructiveness, and structural impossibility of the US bid for it. The other side, the promise and necessity of hegemony, now offers an answer—not a clear, bright, confident one, but the only one available—to the impasse that bid has created. The way out lies in changing the main objective away from either (1) getting out of Iraq and stopping the ongoing loss of US and Iraqi lives and treasure and other collateral damage, or (2) staying on and somehow, anyhow, managing to win the global war on terror by more of the same methods used thus far. Neither of these courses is possible; both are self-stultifying. Instead, the United States needs deliberately to focus its aim on a third alternative: regaining its former position of hegemony in the international community, now gravely compromised and damaged, because recovering that position, necessary and valuable per se both for the United States and the international system, is also the only means likely to help it escape from the morass in Iraq and achieve a sanely defined success (not military victory) in the global war on terror.

Are there historical examples that illustrate and support the notion that a country involved in a war or prolonged struggle that it was not losing but that offered no way to victory or a negotiated exit on tolerable terms, might be able to solve the dilemma by changing its central goal and priority away from the simple alternatives of victory or abandonment of the war to hegemony—that is, to achieving leadership in a coalition genuinely dedicated to reaching joint goals based on consensus?

Yes, there are: the United States did so at certain junctures during the Cold War, and Britain did so vis-à-vis the United States in 1940–41 before the US entry into World War II. The clearest example, which I will briefly discuss, is the policy Britain followed in the latter stages of the Napoleonic wars, especially in 1811–14.

As noted, the dilemma the United States faces now is that it can neither win the Iraq War nor get out of it by negotiation. It faces no immediate danger of defeat, but the war's political and economic burdens and costs at home and abroad continue to grow exponentially, at the same time as the consequences of quitting or accepting failure appear intolerable. It was the dilemma that confronted Britain in a vastly more dangerous form from June 1807 on. Its situation was in some respects even worse than in June 1940. Napoleon had just defeated France's last remaining continental foe, Russia, and had drawn Russia over to France's side in the Peace of Tilsit, leaving Britain completely isolated. The British still controlled the seas and could capture colonial prizes and at least hold their own in the economic war waged between Britain and France and its continental empire. But they could make no serious dent on that French empire even after Spanish and Portuguese resistance to Napoleon's takeover in Spain and Portugal gave the British a toehold there. The popular view is that Britain only needed to hold on until a new coalition against Napoleon arose on the continent, provoked by his insatiable ambition, aggression, and exploitation. This view is highly misleading. Austria did rise in 1809, was crushed again, lost all strength and heart for another contest, and joined Napoleon's camp. Prussia was firmly under the French heel, as was all of Western Europe. Even Russia, though it grew restive and broke with Napoleon, feared taking Napoleon on alone, and when its attempts to recruit allies for defense against France failed badly in 1811, the Russian government tried hard to avoid war with France. By 1811, war-weariness was spreading in Britain; the burdens of wartime debt, popular unrest, and industrial and economic problems were growing more serious; further triumphs at sea and overseas seemed pointless; and no real ally was in sight. Even when Napoleon attacked Russia against the advice of almost all his civilian and military advisers, Britons could not be confident that Russia would win or survive. The United States, in contrast to 1940, posed an additional threat, exploiting Britain's difficulties to wring concessions from it and make its own territorial gains, and in 1812, in one of the supreme acts of folly in US history, actually joining the war on the side of Britain's enemies.

How then did Britain finally manage to win? Grit, staying power, determination, economic and naval strength, and some good generalship were all important, without doubt. It also profited from great good luck in the form of Napoleon's fatal strategy in Russia, the ensuing destruction of the Grand Army, and a subsequent unexpected rising that brought Prussia back into the war and enabled Russia to pursue the war into central Europe. Yet all this would not have been enough for final victory had not the British also changed their own strategy. Slowly and painfully, they learned lessons from their first three failed coalitions against the French Republic and Napoleonic empire in 1793–1807 and changed the basic character and style of their war effort. Until 1807 Britain had fought this war against France, as it had others, in the usual British way of war in Europe: using diplomacy, alliances, loans, and subsidies to build continental coalitions that would fight France on the continent with their armies as Britain's proxies, while Britain concentrated on defeating France and its allies at sea, destroying its commerce, and picking up colonies, trade, and strategic strong points round the world. This strategy generally paid off for the British, giving them major naval victories and colonial prizes that cemented their control of all the world's sea lanes, but on the Continent the strategy failed disastrously and created bitter resentment and distrust among Britain's erstwhile allies in Europe.

From 1807 on, Britain's war strategy and tactics changed gradually from those of empire (i.e., exploiting the strategic vulnerability of France's continental neighbors and compelling them to fight and lose while Britain profited) toward hegemony. That meant British leadership based on a genuine British commitment to a common cause with war aims and a strategy jointly defined, as well as British readiness to make an all-out effort and great sacrifices in Europe itself: not simply to win the war for victory's sake, but also to meet the particular war aims and security requirements of its allies in the coalition, regardless of whether these aims benefited Britain or not. Put too simply but accurately enough, British strategy in the final victorious coalition switched gradually from empire building (waging war simply to defeat France and expand the British Empire) to hegemony (leading a wartime coalition that would found a lasting European general peace). The story is far too complicated to relate here, but every aspect of British policy in the final coalition—military, fiscal, economic, and above all political and diplomatic—reflects this fundamental change and helps account for the coalition's success in war and peace.

How this model applies to the US situation in Iraq should be fairly obvious. The basic point has been made by political and military analysts over and over: the United States cannot succeed in Iraq, Afghanistan, and the region until it ceases to go simply for military victory—as if that alone would solve everything—and becomes leader of a genuine coalition, military and political, working for common goals jointly debated and agreed on. The Baker-Hamilton Iraq Study Group's recommendations, assiduously ignored by President Bush, stressed above all the critical necessity of enrolling more Iraqis and all of Iraq's neighbors, including Iran and Syria, in the attempt to stabilize and unite Iraq, and to do so by reconciling all the legitimate needs and requirements of the different groups and countries. Such advice and much more like it simply calls for benign, sensible US hegemony—leadership in a coalition of (this time) the genuinely willing—willing not because they have been pressured or bribed into participating, but because they are persuaded and pulled into cooperation by the prospect of really being heard on the goals and purposes of the coalition, and actually advancing their particular interests as part of a general solution.

It is impossible here to discuss in detail how this goal of recovering US hegemony could be pursued, either in Iraq and the Middle East or the world. One can point to certain prerequisites. The United States would have to disavow frankly and clearly the attitude of "My way or the highway" that has pervaded its approach from the outset. It would have to admit, without groveling about it, that the venture has failed and promise it will not be repeated. It will have to stop using stupid, insulting arguments to justify continuing the war, such as the claim that the war in Iraq is worth it because so long as the terrorists are being fought there they will not come to the United States. What that argument, factually false and foolish per se, clearly implies is that Americans do not care if this war makes life hell for Iraqis, destabilizes the whole Middle East, threatens the regimes of Iraq's neighbors, some of them US allies, and heightens Arab-Muslim outrage and alienation from the West, increasing the danger of terrorism in Europe and elsewhere—just so long as it makes Americans feel safer for now at home. The United States, in sum, will have to get over its remarkable self-absorption and start seeing itself more as others see it, to have any chance of recovering its former leadership.

It is also impossible to predict confidently that even such a good faith effort under new leadership (an obvious prerequisite) would succeed. In more pessimistic moments I fear that the US potential for a beneficial leadership in international affairs has already been fatally compromised by this venture and other follies; at others I feel there is a reasonable chance it could be restored over time and work tolerably well. What one can say with assurance is that a quest for recovery of its former kind of hegemony is the only way to go. For that belief there is striking evidence, astonishingly neglected, in the story of the Iraq venture itself. Almost everyone looks to that story to find what went wrong, leading to failure and disaster, and who was responsible. Few examine the story to see who had it right, whose judgment and recommendations now stand vindicated by events, whose actions, individual and institutional, pointed in the right direction and should have been followed. Everyone, for example, now concedes that the US claim that Iraq had weapons of mass destruction was wrong and argues about why the mistake or deception occurred and who was responsible. No one seems to recall that at that time US allies at the UN, along with Hans Blix and the other UN arms inspectors, had it right. Their judgment was that Iraq might possess some such weapons and might be trying to get more, but that since they did not know for certain and needed more time to find out, the international community should exhaust all other means of finding out and dealing with the problem before using military force. That was sound policy. The United States rejected it.

Similarly, most Americans have now learned that the use of military power to effect regime change, even when that power is overwhelming, technically sophisticated, brilliantly applied, and apparently successful, cannot in itself solve basic political problems but can easily create new ones and make existing ones worse. No one now notices or recalls that many Europeans and others knew this all along and said so, but were brushed aside. These same people also knew and said further that conventional deterrence and containment could work and was actually working in Iraq. Here too they were right and the US government was wrong.

What all this means is that had the United States acted in 2003 as a genuine hegemon in the international community, willing to consult its allies and other vitally interested parties, to listen to their counsel, and to consider their interests in order to achieve a real consensus, this whole tragedy might have been avoided. Cleaning it up now will be very difficult and messy, if it is possible at all, but sane hegemonic leadership within the international community is the only possible road for the United States to follow. A good initial step would be recognizing the empire-versus-hegemony distinction, abjuring further attempts at empire, and acknowledging frankly that the United States failed to act as a responsible hegemon in this instance.

PART III

15

Europe's Progress and America's Success, 1760–1850

2012

This essay must start with some disclaimers serving as truth in advertising. It discusses a vast subject very briefly, making broad generalizations without sufficient nuance, qualification, and citation of evidence, so that many assertions may seem arbitrary and dogmatic. It also covers familiar ground, recounting things many readers already know, in the hope that looking at well-known facts and conclusions from a different perspective can lead to different, possibly unexpected insights.[1] Finally, I can claim expertise only on the European international history of this period, not the American side to which I am a relative newcomer. Since it would be tedious and time-wasting constantly to insert phrases like "in my opinion" or "so far as I know," they should be taken as understood in much of what follows, especially on the American side.

As the title indicates, the aim is to look at America's independence, expansion, and rise to greatness in this era in the context and through the prism of European international history. Its thesis is that America owed its success in international politics in certain important ways to progress that Europe made in this arena before and during this period.

Part of the thesis is uncontroversial: the history of the US in international politics is a success story. Not everyone applauded

---

1 These admissions should include a comment on the footnotes. Each of the many questions the essay touches on has its own huge literature, impossible to survey adequately here, and most involve controversies impossible to discuss. I will therefore cite sources only for statements I think especially need grounding, and even there will be selective, in some instances merely suggesting further reading.

that success at the time, of course, or applauds it now, yet judged in terms of the master narrative that tends to dominate international politics and the ethics of success that often characterizes it, embodied in a narrative of the rise and fall of competing powers, America's success is incontestable—all rise and no fall. A comparative European perspective only serves to emphasize how remarkable America's rise was—its speed and extent, and especially the ease with which it happened. No other state's path to independence, expansion, and greatness has been remotely so free overall from serious challenge, opposition, and external threat and smoothed by so many favorable external circumstances as that of the US.

Rather than attempt to present concrete evidence to undergird that sweeping statement, which is only the prelude to my main theme, I will ask readers to accept some further broad, baldly stated propositions at least provisionally for the sake of argument. None of them seem to me open to serious dispute. First, while American expansion across the North American continent was only one part of a great European land rush in the world and has been compared to other cases (Russian, Boer, Canadian, Australian, and Spanish),[2] America's expansion was unique in the combination of its vast scope, continuity, value of the acquisitions, ease of acquisition, and absence of formidable obstacles and opposition to it.

Second, though many of the factors that favored American expansion did not involve international politics, one vital factor was firmly rooted in it. The essential ground for American expansion was laid by seventeenth- to eighteenth-century international wars fought mainly in Europe, with the North American continent and adjacent waters as secondary theaters. These wars by 1760 had largely eliminated or neutralized resistance to British-American expansion by their European rivals—Dutch, Swedish, Spanish, and above all French—paving the way for full occupation and settlement of the continent by British-Americans, naturally at the expense of the indigenous peoples. These wars, especially the French and Indian War (Seven Years' War) of

---

2   John C. Weaver, *The Great Land Rush and the Making of the Modern World, 1650–1900* (Montreal, 2003).

1754–63, fought and won mostly by British sailors, soldiers, and taxpayers, laid the basis also for the American War of Independence and America's further expansion.[3]

Though these facts are well known and the conclusion not at all controversial, many Americans and even some historians may not appreciate how extraordinary a development in international history this was and what an amazing boon it gave the infant American Republic. To illustrate, let me offer a counterfactual alternative history supposedly relating the emergence and rise of Russia, which, as it happens, became a great power and leading member of the European system at about the same time the US entered the international system in the eighteenth century, between the reigns of Peter the Great (1689–1730) and Catherine the Great (1762–96).

Instead of the actual story,[4] imagine instead that the Kingdom of Poland-Lithuania, which was a major European power in the early seventeenth century, had established flourishing colonies of Poles in much of what is now European Russia, defeating or pushing aside in the process various rivals and competitors for control of this area—Mongol khanates, Cossacks, Ukrainians, Swedes, Muscovite Russians, and Ottoman Turks. Imagine then that after the Kingdom of Poland had achieved this historic triumph at considerable sacrifice and expense, the Polish colonies in Russia had rebelled against being ruled from Warsaw. Securing major military aid from the Turks and Swedes, the Russian-Polish colonies had succeeded in gaining their independence from the Kingdom of Poland and declared themselves a republic, naming themselves the United States of Russia (USR). Suppose further that in the ensuing peace settlement this new

---

3   For the North American side, see Fred Anderson, *Crucible of War: The Seven Years' War and the Fate of Empire in British North America* (New York, 2000); on the European conflict, Frank A. J. Szabo, *The Seven Years' War in Europe, 1756–1763* (London, 2008).

4   For an excellent overview, see Geoffrey Hosking, *Russia: Empire and People, 1552–1917* (Cambridge, MA, 1997); for Peter the Great's reign, Lindsey Hughes, *Russia in the Age of Peter the Great* (New Haven, CT, 1998); for Catherine's, Isabel de Madariaga, *Russia in the Age of Catherine the Great* (New Haven, CT, 1991); for the international history of Russia's emergence, H. M. Scott, *The Emergence of the Eastern Powers, 1756–1775* (Cambridge, UK, 2001).

USR was quickly recognized as an independent, sovereign nation not only by its allies in the struggle against Poland but also by the Kingdom of Poland itself, which readily ceded all the territory of western Russia outright to it, and that then these two recent enemies, Poland and the USR, soon became commercial partners and quasi-allies, so that the USR could continue to expand across Eurasia to the Pacific Ocean without serious foreign interference, doing so under the protecting arm of the original territorial possessor of the USR, the Kingdom of Poland.

One cannot of course imagine such an impossible, absurd scenario within the European international context. Like every other power, Russia rose to become a fully recognized European great power at this time in 1763 only after two centuries of struggle, surviving numerous critical threats and fighting hard for every gain and conquest at enormous costs in lives, treasure, and freedom. Yet the inconceivable scenario just presented, so amazingly contrary to the international norm, represents America's story.

As this hypothetical counterfactual analogy indicates, another feature of the American experience, the comparative ease with which the US gained recognition and acceptance as a member of the international community and acquired its attendant political and economic advantages, also represented a striking departure from the international norm. Throughout modern European history, most struggles for national independence have either failed or succeeded only after repeated failures. Even countries and peoples that finally won their struggles for independence usually faced years or decades of efforts to gain full recognition and membership in the international community, a process often accompanied by periods of international supervision and sometimes by attempts to overthrow their independence. One might suppose that widespread popular sympathy in Europe for the American Revolution and support for its ideals helped the American republic quickly gain full member status in the international system, but this would be mistaken. Leaving aside questions of whether 1776 was part of a wider Atlantic Revolution[5] and of

---

5 R. R. Palmer, *The Age of the Democratic Revolution*, 2 vols. (Princeton, NJ, 1959–64).

how much long-range impact the American Revolution and the Declaration of Independence had on revolutionary ideas and movements then and since,[6] regardless of whatever role America may have played in promoting revolutionary ideas in the 1780s and 1790s, that role clearly does not help account for its rapid recognition and acceptance in the international community. Quite the contrary; in this era the tides of international history ran strongly against attempts by particular territories or peoples within various empires or composite monarchies to win independence and be recognized as part of the European family of nations—witness Ireland, Hungary, the Dutch Republic, Belgium, Poland, various parts of Italy and Germany, Norway, Switzerland, and Serbia.

Furthermore, the radical course that was soon taken by the French Revolution quickly gave the overall cause of revolution, popular sovereignty, and national self-determination a bad name throughout the continent and served to set the cause of democracy there back by a couple of generations. As for the continued existence and independence of the states and other independent and autonomous units in Europe at the time of the American Revolution, the wars that started in eastern Europe in 1787 and spread to France and western and central Europe in 1792 came quickly to constitute a great assault on their independence, with smaller states being initially the main target of more or less all the great powers, and France from the late 1790's through the Napoleonic era becoming the main threat to the independence of all the major powers as well. The decades from 1776 to 1814 in Europe are noteworthy for how many states and units *lost* their independence—Poland, the Venetian Republic, various principalities in Italy, dozens of German ecclesiastical principalities and free cities, the Crimea and Georgia, and the Holy Roman Empire, which though never a state had been for centuries a functioning entity of great value for the international system, above all for protecting the autonomy of its many components. The only revolutionary independence movements that did eventually win out arose outside Europe in Latin America

---

6 David Armitage, *The Declaration of Independence: A Global History* (Cambridge, MA, 2007).

and the Caribbean, and even these movements were partly caused by assaults on independent states in Europe—in this case, Napoleon's attempt to take control of Spain and Portugal. These independent countries, moreover, had far greater difficulty gaining recognition and membership in the international community than did the US. The United States was the only country in this era able to gain its independence and to retain it without serious external challenge.

Perhaps the most remarkable thing about America's comparatively easy acquisition of independence and subsequent expansion is that it required, comparatively speaking, only a modest military exertion and mediocre military performance. This applies not just to America's early years but to its whole history. Every other state that has attained great power or world power status over the last 500 years—Spain, the Dutch Republic, France, Great Britain, Sweden, Russia, Prussia, Austria, the Ottoman Empire, Imperial Germany, the Moghul Empire, Japan, and China—has had to fight much harder, endure greater wars, survive more defeats, win greater victories, face more formidable foes and challenges, and suffer more loss and devastation in war by a large margin than has the US. The US has never fought a major external enemy, as it did in the Revolutionary War, the War of 1812, World War I, and World War II in Europe, without powerful allies whose help proved decisive for American success. The only major power the US has ever defeated mainly by its own efforts was Imperial Japan, which in 1941 had about half America's population, one-tenth its industry and natural resources, and less than that in national territory. Most of America's wars have been waged against small, disorganized states or forces and resemble colonial expeditions more than serious military contests.[7] No war against a foreign enemy has ever directly and immediately threatened America's national existence, or caused the American standard of living to go down, or led to the occupation and devastation of major portions of American soil.

These assertions about America's remarkable good fortune should be cause neither for outrage nor excuses or apology, but

---

7 Bruce Vandervort, *Indian Wars of Mexico, Canada and the United States, 1812–1900* (London, 2006).

gratitude. A mediocre military record is normally a blessing for states and their peoples, a glorious one a curse. Historically peoples have usually become happier and countries better off once they ceased to pursue military glory. But along with being thankful that America has been largely spared having to pursue this, Americans and others might feel surprised to see how far it has come without it.

A different response to this discussion of the US's remarkable good fortune in international politics, however, might be that this is all very old news. The fact of America's good fortune is familiar, well understood, and readily explained. Americans have not only always known about their good luck but often celebrated it—hence the prominence of exceptionalism, manifest destiny, providential history, and triumphalism in many American historical narratives—and also often felt guilty about it—witness the recurrent criticisms of American imperialism, greed, waste, exploitation, materialism, aggression, violence, and racism. America's success in the international arena, though remarkable, is well known and not at all puzzling. There are plenty of well-known, fully adequate ways to explain it.

The response is natural and to a large extent correct. The reigning explanations for America's easy international success are obvious and familiar and do account for it in the main; the question is whether they are complete and adequate, and especially whether they overlook elements particularly important in regard to international relations. The usual factors cited to explain American expansion include the natural material conditions with which Americans had to work (geography, demographics, climate, disease, communications, soil, technology, etc.), all of which were on balance and in different ways favorable to it, and the human factors driving the restless and ceaseless process of expansion westward—the culture, religion, political ideas and organization, and especially economic motives and incentives of the colonists and their descendants. I have nothing to contribute or contest on these internal or endogenous factors and concede that they constitute the prime driving forces behind the process of expansion and explain much about it. But there was another exogenous factor in American success, involved not as a driving force but as a catalyst, capable of influencing it either as a major obstacle or as an important facilitator. That element was the developing and changing structure of international politics and the European international system.

This is not to imply that historians, especially American ones, have overlooked or neglected the role of international politics and the international system in America's rise to greatness. To the contrary—no one denies that European international politics and the European states system facilitated America's rise in important ways as an exogenous factor. The roles that Anglo-French rivalry and the outcome of the Seven Years' War played in the origins of the American Revolution, that the French alliance and the French-Spanish Bourbon Compact played in the diplomacy and military outcome of the Revolutionary War, and that the Revolutionary and Napoleonic wars in Europe played in the survival and growth of the American Republic have been thoroughly analyzed in many good, detailed, well-researched, archivally based histories of early American diplomacy and foreign policy. In general these take the European international scene seriously into account, and currently the non-European, Muslim, and Asian aspects of the story are gaining increased attention, which is as it should be.

Nonetheless, there is one significant way in which scholars have missed or misunderstood the role of international politics. Its impact on America's success is still perceived as essentially passive or negative. According to it, international politics and the reigning international system are important for their role in allowing America to rise or failing to prevent it, not presenting as great an obstacle to it as they might have. The reigning explanations can be summed up in two axioms, the first one used by Americans at the time, the second later coined by historians. The first, "Europe's distress is America's success," points to the European conflicts, rivalries, and wars in 1760–1815 that helped first the rebellious colonies and then the infant republic to play the European powers off against each other and thus achieve their goals. The second is a variation on the same theme: "Europe's distraction is America's success": It says that even when Europe enjoyed peace and relative stability in the Vienna era (1815–50), the powers were still too distracted by their conflicting individual interests and aims to devote much attention or resources to checking the US in the Western Hemisphere. As so often with conventional interpretations, both axioms make considerable sense, but both, especially the latter, overlook certain things and thereby mislead.

Another slogan supplies what is missing: "Europe's progress was America's success." It does not merely fill gaps and answer minor questions left by the others, but significantly alters the overall interpretation. The first two maxims portray the European states system's contribution to America's good fortune in the world scene as a by-product of that system's inherent defects, vices, and limitations. The incurable competition, rivalry and conflict in which history, geography, and culture kept Europe imprisoned helped free America to take a different path, pursuing its own independent way of nation-building and international relations. This path, many have argued, represented real progress in international politics, a proof that peaceful, democratic domestic development could be combined with fruitful coexistence in international affairs.

"Europe's progress as America's success" indicates a different master narrative. It suggests that the US succeeded so spectacularly internationally in part precisely because it inherited, benefited from, and exploited major advances in international relations achieved by others, in particular Europeans. Thus in the field of international politics the United States was a net consumer and beneficiary of progress in international relations, not a producer or contributor to it.

Before attempting to make a prima facie case (nothing more is possible in this essay) for this thesis, I need at least to mention two principial objections to key terms I will use in the argument, not so as to refute them, but only to comment briefly on them. The first objection denies that the notion of progress can legitimately be applied to international politics or the international system at all. While there has been change and development in international politics as everywhere in history, it is said, to speak of "progress" in a pursuit or practice that is and remains so inherently anarchical, competitive, and conflict-ridden makes no sense. The very notion is Whiggish, teleological, determinist, and therefore unhistorical. I know the arguments for this view and think I know the answers, but it would take too long and be distracting to take them up here, and so will pass on,[8] merely observing that in practice I cannot make sense of the history of international politics and the international system without using the notion of progress in it, and do not understand how anyone else can. The rest of this lecture should give some concrete indications why.

A similar objection can be lodged against using such terms as "international community" and "international system" or cognates like "the European community," "the European family of states," or "the European states system" in ways that suggest that these were active forces in international politics producing tangible results. Unless carefully qualified and restricted, this usage, it is claimed, promotes the fallacy of reification—attributing real existence to an abstract concept. In terms of international politics, Europe was only a geographical expression, a diverse collection of individual actors pursuing their individual interests, not an actor or force on its own.[9] Again I note this objection without trying to refute it here, except to remark that I cannot see how the history of European international politics can be understood without recognizing the vital, active role that the

---

[8] I should at least define what I mean by progress in international politics, however, and hope that this may make the notion more comprehensible. By "progress" I understand simply change and development that enhances the ability of the participants in a particular form of human endeavor or institutional practice to solve or manage problems in that endeavor or practice in one era that were impossible to solve or manage before. This kind of progress seems to me as clear and demonstrable in the practice of international politics as it is in those of, say, market capitalism or liberal representative government or medicine and public health. Nor do I see why this concept of progress in international politics need represent Whig history or be teleological and determinist. It is entirely open-ended, points toward the future not the present, and predicts no final outcome. Plainly progress of this sort cannot prevent new problems and dangers from arising; it could conceivably engender these and promote new disasters in the process of averting older ones. This happens with progress in many practices; it does not make the progress unreal.

[9] This objection has sometimes been voiced by famous practitioners as well as students of international politics. Bismarck, for example, famously insisted, "Whoever speaks of Europe is wrong"—"*Qui parle l'Europe a tort.*" But Bismarck had practical, self-interested purposes for saying this, and so may some scholars.

idea and perception of a European community of states has always played in it, still less without employing the concept of an international system.[10]

Now to the real task: making plausible the notion that Europe in this era made real, tangible progress in international politics, and that this progress contributed materially to America's spectacular success within the international system. The conventional view, as noted, attributes this to America's special ability to exploit inherent systemic defects that imposed restraints and limitations on others while America remained largely free from these restraints itself. This analysis is true enough up to a point; it merely fails to ask the more fundamental question: Why was there was a states system at all in the latter eighteenth century? The European system that the new-born United States asked, or rather demanded, to be allowed to join in 1776 was not an accident or a gift of nature. It was an historical achievement, the product of European progress over the two previous centuries in meeting the central problem of international relations: that of creating enough order in international relations that a permanent community of independent units could exist and endure.

To expand a bit on this basic problem, one familiar and repeatedly analyzed, yet often ignored or underrated: constructing an international or states system requires solving (i.e., rendering manageable, getting a handle on) a daunting task. The task is that of establishing practices, rules, norms, principles, procedures, conventions and institutions that will enable a sizeable number of territorially contiguous, autonomous political units diverse in their nature, aims, and interests to co-exist as separate entities; that will treat them as coordinate in status and law even though they are highly unequal in size, power, and wealth; and that will enable them to interact with tolerable regularity and predictability and without intolerable violence and coercion in the many, various vital relations, communications, activities and transactions engaged in by and among them—all this in the absence of any recognized supreme lawgiving and law-enforcing authority. A genuine interstate or international

---

10 For a recent discussion and account of its importance, see Peter Krüger, *Das unberechenbare Europa* (Münster, 2006).

system, in short, must somehow do what theoretically cannot be done: provide governance without governing authority, establish international order under conditions of legal anarchy. The problem itself constitutes a prescription for unmanageable chaos, constant conflict, and a Hobbesian war of all against all. The theoretical solution to the problem, often attempted in practice, would apply Hobbes's solution to anarchy within the state also to the international arena—i.e., to erect Leviathan, make individual units surrender their autonomy to an overriding authority, and thus abolish international politics and establish empire.

The same problem in a slightly different form confronted Europe in the realm of the international economy: how to enable the changing and dynamic economic and commercial activity of Europe, rapidly expanding since the late fifteenth century into the rest of the world, to continue and to flourish under similar conditions of anarchy without producing a similar Hobbesian war of all against all.

These problems were not theoretical, but intensely practical. When as an historian I view the sixteenth and seventeenth centuries and ask whether it could ever have appeared to contemporary actors likely or even possible that the welter of religious, political, and economic wars and lawless behavior of every kind then prevailing could ever lead to a sustainable, manageable system of international political and economic order, the answer is "No." Many yearned for order and peace, of course; some dreamed and made schemes of it—but these remained Utopian, reserved for another better world to come. In this one, the practical problems and obstacles to the emergence of international order and system were simply too great.

Yet by the mid- or late eighteenth century these twin, seemingly insoluble problems had been met in the sense of being rendered manageable and tolerable. The practices of European international politics and international economics, though naturally still full of competition, conflict, and war, had become to some extent rational enterprises involving rules and norms and subject to a measure of rational calculation and decision-making. In other words, by the time the USA was born there was an international system to join.

Once again there is no room here to begin to describe the long, painful, and extremely costly process by which this change came about—a change that in Heinz Duchhardt's estimation makes eighteenth century international politics more like the nineteenth and twentieth centuries than the seventeenth, while seventeenth-century politics were more like the fourteenth than the eighteenth,[11] and that H.M. Scott depicts as constituting the birth of a modern states system.[12] In any case, this represented a breakthrough, real progress. On the political side, it involved first of all the general acceptance of individual state sovereignty and coordinate status as the legal basis for international politics (no empire or universal monarchy). This was achieved despite the fact that this fundamental concept of state sovereignty and coordinate status was and remained in many respects a legal fiction. Most European unit-actors did not fit the standard definition of a state, meaning a clearly defined territory with a central government that exercised authority over all its parts and could successfully claim a legitimate monopoly on the use of force within its boundaries. Instead, many, including the most powerful, were composite monarchies with varying and limited control over their different territories. Others were loose confederations of provinces, or free cities, or ecclesiastical principalities, i.e., half church and half state: Even in the latter eighteenth century the bulk of Europe, especially Central and Eastern Europe, was riddled with instances of mixed sovereignty, overlapping jurisdictions, and competing "sovereign" rights and claims. Yet a system based upon these principles had nonetheless emerged, and it more or less worked.[13] It required developing institutions and practices of negotiation and diplomacy—diplomatic immunity,[14] permanent foreign offices and professional trained

---

11 Heinz Duchhardt, *Balance of Power und Pentarchie 1700–1785* (Paderborn, 1997).

12 H. M. Scott, *The Birth of a Great Power System 1740–1815* (London, 2006).

13 M. S. Anderson, *The Rise of Modern Diplomacy 1450–1919* (London, 1993).

14 Linda and Marsha Frey, *The History of Diplomatic Immunity* (Columbus, OH, 1999).

diplomats, developments in the laws of war and peace,[15] permanent representation of countries abroad, and consular services. Along with this went practical developments in ideas and means for pursuing individual state goals while managing conflict and limiting war. Some were unsavory but useful, e.g., advanced methods of espionage and intercepting and deciphering mail.[16] Most were more respectable—peace conferences and congresses, changes in the form and purpose of alliances, agreements for neutralization or spheres of influence, better organized efforts at mediation.[17] A major, indispensable change lay in the role of religion in international politics—not the separation of religion and politics, impossible and probably undesirable in that era, but the cessation of wars fought mainly for particular religious or confessional purposes.[18] Equally important was a gradual, incomplete shift in political culture and the concept of the state, from the state being the monarch's patrimony and princes being God's representatives to the state as an impersonal institution, politics as including a public sphere, and monarchs as rational rulers.[19]

---

15 Richard C. Tuck, *The Rights of War and Peace: Political Thought and International Order from Grotius to Kant* (Oxford, 1999); Hedley Bull, Benedict Kingsbury, and Adam Bull, eds., *Hugo Grotius and International Relations* (Oxford, 1992).

16 Lucien Bély, *Espions et ambassadeurs au temps de Louis XIV* (Paris, 1990); Lucien Bély, ed., *L'invention de la Diplomatie: Mayen Age-Temps modernes* (Paris, 1998).

17 See especially works by Heinz Duchhardt, above all his *Gleichgewicht der Kräfte, Convenance, europäisches Konzert: Friedenskongresse und Friedensschlüsse vom Zeitalter Ludwigs XIV bis zum Wiener Kongress* (Darmstadt, 1976); his *Studien zur Friedensvermittlung in der frühen Neuzeit* (Wiesbaden, 1979); and his edited work *Zwischenstaatliche Friedenswahrung in Mittelalter und Früher Neuzeit* (Cologne, 1993).

18 Johannes Burkhardt, *Abschied vom Religionskrieg: Der Siebenjährige Krieg und die päpstliche Diplomatie* (Tübingen, 1985); Heinz Schilling, *Religion, Political Culture, and the Emergence of Early Modern Society: Essays in German and Dutch History* (Leiden, 1992).

19 Tim Blanning, *The Culture of Power and the Power of Culture: Old Regime Europe, 1660–1789* (Oxford, 2002); Hamish Scott and Brendan Simms, eds., *Cultures of Power in Europe during the Long Eighteenth Century* (Cambridge, UK, 2007); Paul Kléber Monod, *The Power of Kings: Monarchy and Religion in Europe, 1589–1715* (New Haven, CT, 1999).

Similar change and progress can be seen in international economics—a great expansion of commercial and maritime law and institutions to support it; advances in both the law of the sea and suppression of piracy; better-regulated markets and rules for monetary and commercial transactions; and somewhat better control by governments of the commercial activities of their subjects and of chartered companies abroad.[20]

The picture should not be idealized or the progress made by the eighteenth century exaggerated.[21] It remained in its infancy or adolescence, vulnerable to setback and reversal. Wars were still frequent and long and the system was still full of structural defects that directly promoted them.[22] The dominant economic and commercial policies of all important states remained a fairly predatory version of beggar-my-neighbor mercantilism; military expense still dominated state budgets, military glory was still prized and pursued by rulers and elites. Yet the point remains that by the mid- to late eighteenth century, viable, manageable systems of international order had emerged that made war at least more humane, especially for civilian populations, trade more extensive and secure, and durable, relatively peaceful and predictable relations more possible. This was a huge European achievement.

What connection does this have with American success? In the Declaration of Independence, the Revolutionary War, and subsequent American foreign policy, the Founding Fathers sought two basic goals: recognition as an independent, sovereign country with full membership in the European community of states, and the right to participate fully and equally in world trade under the

---

20 John Braithwaite and Peter Drahos, *Global Business Regulation* (Cambridge, UK, 2000) offers good compact historical surveys of these developments in various areas—e.g., 88–111, 175–93, and 418–24. Classic studies by Richard Pares, *War and Trade in the West Indies, 1739–1763* (London, 1963) and *Yankees and Creoles: The Trade between North America and the West Indies before the American Revolution* (Cambridge, MA, 1956) show among other things how the development of maritime law aided the American colonies.

21 For an excellent portrait of the age and a fascinating read, see Tim Blanning, *The Pursuit of Glory: Europe 1648–1815* (London, 2007).

22 Johannes Kunisch, *Staatsverfassung und Mächtepolitik: Zur Genese von Staatenkonflikten im Zeitalter des Absolutismus* (Berlin, 1979).

existing rules. They requested this, or better, demanded it, on American terms, without admitting any obligation on America's part to take any part in European quarrels, disputes, or questions that did not concern them. It remains striking how easily and quickly the US succeeded in getting this bold claim accepted, but (as is well known) geography and historical developments ideally suited it for a position of profitable neutrality, reaping the advantages of membership in the European states system without bearing its risks and costs. Another striking feature of this picture is regularly overlooked, however: without the great European efforts and struggles in previous centuries, no viable, manageable systems of international political and economic order would have been in existence for the US to join and exploit.

This sounds like a charge of ingratitude against Americans, both the original founders and citizens of the Republic and their successors, for ignoring or refusing to acknowledge what they owed to their historical predecessors. As a general accusation this would clearly not be true. American historians and the educated public have instead known and readily acknowledged the major contributions made to the American heritage and experience by past generations, celebrating what they inherited from Greece and Rome, the Judea-Christian tradition, the Protestant Reformation, the Enlightenment, civic republicanism and individualist liberalism, Magna Carta and the tradition of British civil liberties and parliamentary representative government, and the like. They have even sometimes acknowledged doubtful or spurious debts, to things like Teutonic concepts of liberty supposedly spawned in the ancient forests of Germany. But one thing not recognized or acknowledged is the boon conferred upon America in the form of automatic membership in a working international political and economic order forged out of centuries of struggle, coming to fruition just as the US emerged on the international scene. Here a gibe that Senator Tom Harkin (D-Iowa) somewhat unfairly directed in 1988 at then-Republican candidate for President George H.W. Bush, that Bush was born on third base and thought he had hit a triple, applies to America in regard to international politics and the international system. In this arena, America was born on third base, and many Americans have ever since loudly proclaimed that it had hit a triple.

This is not to say that Europeans deliberately did America any favors. The European creation of a working international system in the seventeenth and eighteenth centuries was entirely self-centered and driven by necessity, the product of a ruthlessly competitive power game waged for survival and gain. The fact that Americans could turn this to their advantage in 1776–83 can be seen as simply fortuitous and serendipitous. But this was not exactly true of further contributions the European international system made to America's success in the revolutionary and Napoleonic era of 1787–1815 and the succeeding Vienna era. This was an era in which even the great events and developments of America's formative years—the Constitution, the formation of a viable national government, the Louisiana Purchase, Indian wars and boundary disputes, diplomatic contests and confrontations with Britain, France and Spain, party and sectional clashes, the War of 1812, and expansion to the Pacific—pale in comparison alongside those in Europe. These were the decades of Europe's greatest and most destructive revolutions and wars since 1648; the gravest threat to the survival of the European states system until 1939–45; the most durable peace settlement Europe has ever achieved; and the most important advances in the conduct, rules, practices and institutions of international politics ever made at a particular time. And it was not coincidence that these colossal events and developments contributed importantly to America's survival and consolidation as an independent state and its expansion then and later.

As earlier noted, while no one denies a connection between the course and outcome of the Revolutionary and Napoleonic wars and America's fate, the link seems adequately explained in the slogans mentioned earlier. Europe's distress, so long as it was locked in great wars from 1787 to 1815, promoted America's success. The US could maneuver between the warring parties, exploit its neutral position, expand its trade, push settlers across the Appalachians and drive the natives back or out, gain the Louisiana territory in a corrupt bargain with Napoleon, threaten, harass, and finally invade Spanish West and East Florida, and assert and defend its neutral rights at sea against both Britain and France. The policy involved risks and included some serious gambles and missteps, to be sure, but overall it worked successfully at least until the War of 1812. Even that war, after some anxious moments, turned out well, becoming a second War of Independence that freed Americans to turn westward, ignoring Europe and its bloody quarrels. Even after 1815 when peace and conservative monarchical order returned to Europe, exhaustion and distraction aided America's success. Plagued by internal difficulties and persistent rivalries and conflicts of interest, the European powers could offer no serious or united opposition to American expansion. As American historians pretty much agree, the feared and alleged European threats to Latin America, Florida, Texas, Mexico, Oregon, and California proved wildly exaggerated or wholly imaginary.

What this plausible narrative omits is the big story in Europe—the great crisis, survival, and transformation of the European states system in this era. When this is taken seriously, it not only changes the European narrative from one of distress and distraction to one of progress, but shows how international progress in this era contributed substantially to America's success, and it strongly suggest a reappraisal of America's policy and actions and their potential and actual impact on the international system.

Three specific European achievements in international politics in 1787–1815 contributed significantly to America's success. The first achievement is well known and the connection to American history is fairly obvious; the second is almost equally well known but not as readily linked to America's success; while the third, known to American historians but not the wider public, is never connected to America's success or, for that matter, considered a European achievement or a sign of its progress.

The first such contributor was the nineteenth-century Pax Britannica. This is presented in the historical literature in two versions. The main one (at least in Anglophone historiography) makes the Pax Britannica, i.e., the European and worldwide hegemony Britain had supposedly attained by 1815, the key factor in creating and maintaining general peace in Europe and much of the world after 1815. According to this version, British maritime, commercial, and industrial supremacy in combination with Britain's insular security enabled Britain to hold and manipulate the balance of power in Europe, exploiting rivalries between the other European powers to preserve peace, prevent aggression or dangerous gains in power by any one power or group of powers, and promote peaceful trade and political reform in place of war.[23] As an account of nineteenth-century European international politics that attributes the long nineteenth-century peace in continental Europe to British hegemony in European affairs, this version of the Pax Britannica is simply wrong and helps to perpetuate a myth. I cannot go into the argument here, but will get to what really preserved peace in continental Europe later.[24]

Another account of the Pax Britannica, however, long sound and important and deepened and strengthened by recent scholarship, rightly credits the Pax Britannica with a leading role in establishing and maintaining peace and stability in much of the wider extra-European world—and at the same time in aiding and protecting America's independence and expansion. This version stresses the importance of changes during and after the American Revolution in the direction, purpose and character of British imperial policy in its great contest with France in the eighteenth and early nineteenth centuries. Where earlier Britain had focused on contesting the North Atlantic sea lanes with France and Spain and gaining territories mainly in the New World for purposes of settlement, rule, and commercial exploitation, in this latter phase, especially after the recognition by 1782 that its main American colonies were lost, British leaders consciously switched to a strategy of gaining control of sea lanes, bases, and certain territorial settlements throughout the rest of the world, especially India, deemed necessary for purposes of trade rather than settlement. Moreover, its imperial trade policy switched gradually from destroying the trade and seizing the

---

23 A classic statement of this thesis is in Robert Gilpin's *War and Change in World Politics* (Cambridge, UK, 1981); for a recent version, see Patrick K. O'Brien, "The Pax Britannica and American Hegemony: Precedent, Antecedent or Just Another History?," in Patrick K. O'Brien and Armand Clesse, eds., *Two Hegemonies: Britain 1846–1914 and the United States 1941–2000* (Aldershot, 2000), 3–64.

24 John M. Hobson discusses some of the flaws in this interpretation—"Two Hegemonies or One? A Historical-Sociological Critique of Hegemonic Stability Theory," in O'Brien and Clesse, *Two Hegemonies*, 305–25.

assets of rivals to one of gaining control over an expanded world commerce so as to create a world-wide empire of freer trade founded on British maritime, commercial, and industrial supremacy, a commercial world in which Britain would set the rules and conditions for world commerce but include others. A combination of British exploration and discovery, the establishment of bases and outposts, and various wars and strategic territorial conquests overseas, sealed by the final victory over Napoleon's France won mainly by Britain's European allies, made this British empire of freer trade a reality, laying the foundation for Britain's nineteenth-century hegemony.

This shift in British imperial strategy had decisive importance for America's success. Once Britain's leaders put the humiliation of defeat and surrender in the American Revolutionary War behind them and eliminated the temporary threats to Britain of isolation in Europe and loss of naval supremacy in the Atlantic, both of which happened quickly in 1782–83, they recognized that an independent, growing America did not necessarily represent a loss to Britain or a threat to its imperial aspirations and could actually be turned to their advantage. Its former colonies, now independent, were valuable to Britain for trade, not territory or power, and British commerce could continue and expand with an independent US on even better conditions for Britain than before. Under certain minimal conditions (provisions for a military-naval balance in North America to defend Canada, some protection for British interests in regard to the North American fur trade and the Indians, and the maintenance of Britain's position in the Caribbean and Latin America) it was better for Britain that Americans should expand westward across the continent than that French, Spaniards, or Russians should do so. And once Britain gained control of the sea lanes around South America, which it did during the Revolutionary and Napoleonic wars, it had no reason to fear American interference or competition in trade there or in the Pacific.[25]

---

25 Some valuable recent additions to the literature include P. J. Marshall, *The Making and Unmaking of Empires: Britain, India and America c. 1750–1783* (Oxford, 2005); Steven Sarson, *British America, 1500–1800: Creating Colonies, Imagining an Empire* (London, 2005); and Alan Frost, *The Global*

This conscious British imperial strategy is essential for understanding various factors in America's success: why Britain was generally so eager to conciliate the US and avoid war from 1783 to 1812;[26] why the War of 1812 ended with the surprisingly favorable Treaty of Ghent; why Britain took the stance it did on Latin America and the Monroe Doctrine; why various Anglo-American boundary and other disputes ended in amicable compromises; and why neither the British nor other Europeans interfered seriously in American expansion. A good deal of nineteenth-century international history can be summed up, oversimplified, in a couple of generalizations. Between 1783 and 1870, the two powers that mattered most to Britain politically and commercially were France and the United States. First, from 1815 on, every French government, with one brief exception in 1824–30 (the reign of Charles X), was anxious to avoid war or serious confrontation with Britain, and almost all of them tried for an alliance with it. This was a major asset for British policy generally, and redounded also to America's benefit. One important influence helping to keep French intervention in Texas, Mexico, and the American Civil War restrained and ineffective was France's determination to stay on reasonable terms with Britain.[27] Second, after 1783 every British government wanted to remain on good terms with the United States, an even greater

---

Reach of Empire: Britain's Maritime Expansion in the Indian and Pacific Oceans, 1764–1815 (Carlton, Victoria, 2003). The standard history of the British Empire is now William Roger Louis, editor-in-chief, *The Oxford History of the British Empire*, 5 vols. (Oxford, 1998–99); important here is vol. 2, *The Eighteenth Century*, ed. P. J Marshall. On Britain's maritime expansion, see most recently Jeremy Black, *The British Seaborne Empire* (New Haven, CT, 2004).

26 Charles R. Ritcheson, *Aftermath of Revolution: British Policy toward the United States, 1783–1795* (Dallas, 1969); Bradford Perkins, *The First Rapprochement: England and the United States, 1795–1805* (Philadelphia, 1955); Bradford Perkins, *Prologue to War: England and the United States, 1805–1812* (Berkeley, CA, 1963).

27 Nancy N. Barker, *The French Experience in Mexico, 1821–1861: A History of Constant Misunderstanding* (Chapel Hill, NC, 1979); Lynn M. Case and Warren F. Spencer, *The United States and France: Civil War Diplomacy* (Philadelphia, 1970); David M. Pletcher, *The Diplomacy of Annexation: Texas, Oregon and the Mexican War, 1835–1850* (Columbia, MO, 1973).

asset for America in terms of security, commerce, and foreign policy generally. A pathbreaking study by Lance Davis and Robert A. Huttenback analyzing who bore the costs of the nineteenth-century British Empire and who profited from it concludes among other things that the main territorial beneficiaries were the white settler colonies, Canada, Australia, New Zealand, and South Africa, who gained security and a share in the benefits of imperial trade and prosperity at low cost.[28] It could be argued that a former British white settler colony, the United States of America, was an even greater beneficiary.

This resulted not from British charity or indulgence, but prudent policy based on mutual advantage. Imperial historians teach us to view the early nineteenth-century British Empire not as a single entity, but as a combination of four different areas and kinds of imperial control: the large white settler colonies; India; a collection of bases and small strategic settlements scattered around the globe; and general British naval supremacy and control of the sea lanes world-wide. America's independence and territorial expansion in North America threatened none of these four categories of empire, so long as Canada remained reasonably secure, an end secured by a combination of British naval power and amicable compromises over boundary issues.[29] Meanwhile, all these elements of the British Empire potentially benefited from good relations with the US, particularly since America represented a vital market for British manufactures, raw materials, trade, investment, and emigration. If one accepts Roger Kennedy's argument, there was a further category of British indirect imperialism, a textile empire which tied the British textile industry closely to the American Southern plantocracy and promoted the expansion of cotton cultivation and American slavery. This putative form of British "empire" actually required that America remain as it was, internationally independent, internally divided, and territorially expansionist,

---

28 Lance E. Davis and Robert A. Huttenback, *Mammon and the Pursuit of Empire: The Economics of British Imperialism*, abridged ed. (Cambridge, UK, 1988).

29 Kenneth Bourne, *Britain and the Balance of Power in North America, 1815–1908* (Berkeley, CA, 1967).

in order that the antebellum South could continue to supply the British mills.[30]

The second major European contribution to America's international success, the Vienna Settlement, promoted that success in ways less obvious but no less important. It did so not merely by establishing a solid basis for European peace in the form of treaties, alliances, and institutions, especially the Concert of Europe that for decades served to preserve peace, maintain the legal status quo, and promote respect for treaties, legal rights and obligations, and international norms and rules. Of more direct importance to the US, the settlement was consciously intended and designed to fence Europe off from the rest of the world and insulate it from extra-European quarrels.[31] It outlawed territorial expansion or aggression within Europe, encouraged European governments to concentrate on preventing revolution, avoiding war, and promoting peaceful internal development, and discouraged imperialism outside Europe wherever it would cause European complications.

If one cannot prove a direct connection between all this and the easy success of American expansion (at least not here), one can show a strong indirect one by pointing out how differently Europe and the US respectively played the game of international politics from 1815 to 1850. An older American patriotic view still sometimes encountered contrasts a militarist and bellicose Europe with a peace-loving America that only sought peaceful trade and tried to avoid quarrels that did not concern it, merely asking the same from Europe (e.g., in the Monroe Doctrine.) Granted, the US did not engage in many important international wars in the nineteenth century—in this era only the Mexican War would count—while Europe experienced many more serious crises, threats of war, and persistent rivalries, and its states remained more heavily armed and militarist in culture and spirit. But one cannot judge whether countries are bellicose or peaceful simply by the number and extent of their wars, militarized

---

30 Roger G. Kennedy, *Mr. Jefferson's Lost Cause: Land Farmers, Slavery and the Louisiana Purchase* (Oxford, 2003).

31 G. A. Rein, "Über die Bedeutung der Überseeischen Ausdehnung für das Europäische Staaten-System," *Historische Zeitschrift* 137 (1927): 28–90.

crises, rivalries, and military exertions. That is far too crude a standard. Statistically speaking, wars are rare—that is, the ratio between the number of armed conflicts that actually occur and those theoretically possible among all the dyads of autonomous units in the world is quite small, for the obvious reason that the overwhelming majority of those dyads have no occasion, reason, or possible means to fight each other. No one considers Mexico and Thailand, for example, more peaceful simply because they have never fought each other. The basis of judgment must be how countries conduct themselves in the presence of serious occasions, reasons, causes, and possibilities for war. When that standard is applied to Europe and America in the Vienna era, the picture looks very different.

The Vienna Settlement, though easily the most thorough, comprehensive, and durable in European history, certainly did not eliminate potential occasions, motives, and causes for war. After 1815 all of Europe suffered the pains and stresses of postwar depression and serious economic dislocation (including the last subsistence crisis in European history), early industrialization, and widespread poverty and social unrest. It was shaken by three successive waves of revolution (1820–23, 1830–32, and 1848–49), each deeper and more extensive than the one before. The last wave was the most widespread ever in European history; all carried in them the seeds of international conflict. The era also witnessed the rise of dangerous social and political movements—liberalism, socialism, communism, and above all nationalism, all of which threatened the reigning governments and ruling elites and represented potential and actual causes for international conflict. The peace settlement of 1814–15, prudent and moderate though it was, could not prevent the emergence of revisionist territorial ambitions and grievances. Therefore crises and threats of war did arise and some armed conflicts occurred which, though minor and limited by European standards, involved more real fighting than all those the US fought between 1815 and 1917 put together.

All this makes it possible to think of Europe as still bellicose while America was basically pacific—a plausible but very superficial picture. It is like concluding that because fewer automobile accidents occur on the highways of rural Nevada than the streets of Los Angeles, the Nevadans are safer, more law-abiding drivers. A comparison of the amount of war with all the occasions, causes, and plausible motives for war produces a very different picture. It shows that Europe, in thirty-five years full of dangers and complications, fought no wars at all between major powers and only two minor ones between European states, both of them the result of revolution; committed virtually no violations of treaties; permitted no territorial revisions without international action and consent; organized repeated interventions by the European Concert to settle crises, prevent or end conflicts, and establish and sanction international change; and prevented virtually all attempts at territorial aggrandizement.

Meanwhile, the US, which never faced a serious foreign threat throughout this era, carried out an unprecedently rapid and extensive course of territorial expansion marked by aggressive war, treaty violations, ethnic cleansing, coercive diplomacy, and widespread organized and spontaneous violence. One oversimplifies but does not seriously exaggerate in drawing this conclusion: while in the Vienna era the powers of Europe had many occasions and serious reasons for war, territorial aggrandizement, and organized violence, but used almost none of them, America exploited almost every occasion and reason for these activities it had.

These contrasting phenomena are connected. An important reason for America's easy and inexpensive success at territorial expansion despite the attendant violence and illegality was the restrained, law-abiding character of European international politics. The Atlantic Ocean and the British navy were not the only things that kept European powers from interfering in the Western Hemisphere. There was also the fact that their governments and elites basically did not want to intervene, were wary of America with its revolutionary ideas, lawlessness, and violence, and were mainly not seeking more territory either in Europe or the New World. This outlook and the resultant conduct on the part of the European powers was more than a temporary product of exhaustion and fear of revolution. It represented progress, showed that some vital lessons had been learned about how to build peace, manage crises, and avoid war. The fact that these lessons were later overthrown or ignored by later generations does not make them unimportant at this time, or annul their contribution to America's success.

The idea that the Pax Britannica and the Vienna Settlement contributed to America's success may seem at least plausible. That a third element in European international politics, the Holy Alliance, also contributed seems absurd on its face. How could an arch-conservative antirevolutionary alliance between three absolutist Eastern monarchies, Russia, Austria, and Prussia, possibly have aided America's success, other than by presenting an ideal bugaboo and target for American patriotic oratory? Yet if one grants part of the main argument of this essay, that the long nineteenth-century peace in Europe (i.e., no war at all between European powers from 1815 to 1854 and no general war between 1815 and 1914) helped America expand territorially and economically, then the Holy Alliance must also be counted a benefactor of the US. For more than anything else it explains that long peace.

This is not the conventional answer. The usual explanations of the long peace stress Europe's general exhaustion from the previous generation of war, a prevailing conservative fear of revolution, British hegemony within the system, and (in that wonderfully useful and protean all-purpose phrase) a stable balance of power overall. None of these pay sufficient attention to a remarkable feature of European international history central to the long peace geographically, politically, strategically, and ideologically. Between 1763 and 1914, three great military monarchies, throughout the period direct neighbors with extensive common frontiers, governed and controlled all of central and eastern Europe containing the majority of Europe's territory and people. These three powers had fundamental conflicts of interest, clashing ambitions, irreconcilable aims and claims, serious dynastic, religious, ideological, and cultural differences, and long histories of ethnic and national rivalries and hatreds. They therefore always remained distrustful rivals more than intimate friends, always posed a potential danger and often an imminent threat to each other, always maintained large standing armies facing each other, and constantly experienced occasions for war. Yet over a span of 150 years (1763–1914) only two of them, Austria and Prussia (just one of the three dyads) ever went to war with each other.[32] They did so twice, first briefly and indecisively in 1778, then briefly but decisively in 1866. Otherwise Austria and Russia, Prussia and Russia, and the three together coexisted in peace and were often close partners and allies.

This side of the record of their relationship, so remarkable in itself, has been given astonishingly little attention, especially in comparison to that paid to the tensions and crises between them. Every historian knows about the two Hundred Years' Wars between England and France in 1337–1453 and 1688–1815, both of which are basically easy to explain. Yet no one speaks of a Hundred-Fifty Years' Peace between Austria, Prussia-Germany, and Imperial Russia, which is a puzzle, hard to explain. Its historic importance, moreover, cannot be doubted. It more than anything else provides the key to the long nineteenth-century European peace. The Revolutionary and Napoleonic wars no doubt made Europe desperately eager for peace; the Vienna Settlement provided the legal framework, ideology, rules, and procedures for establishing and preserving it; but this triangular Holy Alliance relationship provided the heart, muscle, and effective force behind it. So long as this peaceful relationship lasted, it made a general European war impossible. The Crimean War, the wars of Italian and German unification, and all the Eastern crises from 1821 to 1913 were prevented from growing into a general systemic war, sometimes despite serious efforts by various powers to promote one, because the Holy Alliance in one form or another remained intact and survived the onslaught. When it finally broke down irrevocably in 1914, the result was World War I, with all its horrors and the worse ones that followed.

The Holy Alliance's remarkable durability cannot be explained here, but to oversimplify drastically, it rested on two main foundations.[33] First was a shared recognition of mutual

---

32 Technically this is not exactly true. Russia officially was at war with Austria briefly in 1809, and Prussia and Austria were part of Napoleon's coalition against Russia in 1812. But since in both cases without Napoleon's coercion these states would never have gone to war on their own, I consider that these instances do not really count.

33 I have attempted a brief explanation elsewhere—see Paul W. Schroeder, "The Life and Death of a Long Peace, 1763–1914," in Raimo Väyrynen, ed., *The Waning of Major War: Theories and Debates* (London, 2006), 33–63.

interdependence—the realization by all three powers that if any of the others went under, whatever the other two might gain from its downfall would be outweighed by worse and more unmanageable problems its destruction would create. Second was the ability and willingness of the three to sustain and employ their alliance ties in various forms for purposes of mutual restraint and management rather than as an instrument of power and gain. Both of these factors, the grudging recognition of mutual interdependence and the willingness to use alliances as tools of management and mutual restraint, represented real progress in international thought and practice. Needless to say, this does not mean that these powers had good governments or pursued benign ends. By and large for most of this era, their governments, especially Russia's, were absolutist and regressive in character and they often used their partnership for repressive ends at home and abroad. Nevertheless, in helping keep Europe peaceful and self-restrained and the international system working, the Holy Alliance served as an instrument for peace and made a significant contribution to American success.

This all may seem to add up to a denunciation of early American foreign policy for its ignorant disdain of the European states system and ingratitude for its benefits, with an implied criticism of American historians for failing to point this out. That is not the intention. States like individuals get born within a certain environment and a particular set of circumstances, and if these are fortunate they seldom exert themselves to determine the source of their good fortune and the responsibilities this may impose on them. As for American historians, they can hardly be blamed for not detecting supposed virtues and beneficial effects in an international system that many European historians are unaware of and some would dispute. Nor is this an indictment of early American foreign policy, at least up to 1800. The standard interpretation holding that the Founding Fathers were shrewd and sensible in exploiting opportunities the international situation offered them and avoiding unnecessary conflicts seems to me quite sound. I do take a dimmer view of the decades following, especially the War of 1812, a war which though technically justified in international law (the impressment issue constituted a legal *casus belli* for the US against

Britain) meant America's choosing to enter an ongoing world war for the sake of American gains and fighting de facto in that war on the side of Napoleon's empire, which by that time unmistakably represented the worse, more aggressive, militarist, and imperialist side of the world-historical contest. In doing this, moreover, the American government knowingly risked helping the Napoleonic-imperialist side to victory, thereby promoting the destruction of an international system developed over centuries, of which the US had only recently become a new, privileged member and on which its future security and existence would ultimately depend. But this topic, though highly relevant to the themes of this essay, is too big to discuss here.

Yet if criticizing early American attitudes and policy and challenging certain historical interpretations of them is not the real purpose of the essay, what is? Supposing that everything I have argued so far, including the assertions about the War of 1812, is true, what is the point? Should Americans now apologize to Europe for not recognizing its contributions to America's easy success? Sit in sackcloth and ashes for our forebears' failure to appreciate the benefits of the international system? Exhume Jefferson, Madison, and Henry Clay and hang them for getting us into the War of 1812? Resurrect the Federalist party, which was right about the War of 1812, and paid for it by going under shortly thereafter?

Of course not. Debts of gratitude in international politics are seldom recognized and even more seldom honored. Anyway, the nineteenth-century Europe-America relationship was surely not one-sided overall, but rather represented a mutual benefits society. Americans might well claim that greater benefits accrued to Europe from what America offered it in trade, raw materials, industry, and above all opportunities for immigration, without which Europe in the nineteenth and early twentieth century would surely have suffered far more disorder, poverty, social unrest, and revolution than it actually did. If any peoples and states suffered from American expansion and power, it was not the European ones (with the possible exception of Spain) but blacks, Native Americans, and some Latin American ones.[34] In

---

34 For an excellent account of how whites gained almost all of the native Americans' land, showing how the law was always involved but it was always a

any case, it may sometimes be important to recognize historic rights and wrongs and set the story straight, but trying to construct a balance sheet of net historic rights and wrongs over centuries is a mug's game, and trying to set scores right after generations have passed is usually destructive.

The question of what point is being made, however, is a legitimate one. I offer two answers, one academic, the general scholarly conclusion the argument suggests, and the second more personal, the reason for making it now. The historical conclusion is that the US emerged at the beginning as a *rentier* or rent-collecting state within the existing international system and continued to be one throughout most of its history. The concept of rents together with the distinction between rent-collecting and rent-paying are familiar to economic historians and many other European historians, especially students of the Old Regime, but they have to my knowledge not been applied to international politics. Yet, the distinction between rent-collecting and rent-paying states seems to fit international politics and the international system quite well and can with care be applied usefully to them. A rentier lives off rents, income derived from investments, offices, pensions, or favors, as opposed to income derived from the current production and distribution of goods. Typically, *rentiers* never regard their rents, however acquired (by purchase, inheritance, investment, or grants and favors from those in power), as temporary, inferior in status, or revocable, much less illegitimate or parasitical. They are rather regarded as property, entitlements, inalienable rights sanctioned by law and justified by their holders' services to society.

This image, I think, describes America's role in the European/world international community fairly well during its formative years. It was a rent-collecting state living off and profiting from capital accrued from the struggles and achievements of others, confident that this remarkably favorable and profitable position was justified by the contribution its example, values, and ideals were making to the general welfare.

There is nothing unusual or particularly shocking about this rentcollecting conduct in international affairs or the attitudes

---

law of the stronger, see Stuart Banner, *How the Indians Lost Their Land: Law and Power on the Frontier* (Cambridge, MA, 2005).

behind it—certainly not in European history. Many states have practiced it in different forms; all probably would like to if they could; some have succeeded for brief periods, though none so long and successfully as the United States. There is nothing exceptional about this form of American exceptionalism. But an important lesson for the present time is hidden in this conclusion. That earlier age is over. The tide that earlier carried this nation almost irresistibly forward to success and greatness has long been ebbing, and may have turned and be running the other way. The fortunate circumstances that enabled the US to exploit the advantages the international system afforded it without cost or penalty to itself, at that time largely without serious costs to the system, have disappeared. The US cannot count on them any longer. In that respect, as in others, it is no longer exceptional.

16

An Organized Hypocrisy

2016

Two British Liberal Party leaders in the nineteenth century, John Bright in mid-century and David Lloyd George at its end, labeled the Conservative Party "an organized hypocrisy." As an historian, I think their charge largely misses the mark. But it fits better to describe what the current Republican Party has become in the United States.

Party politics, of course, has always involved considerable hypocrisy—particularly in a social-media drenched world, and particularly in a high-stakes election year like this one. The political game itself consists in large part of showbusiness, pretense, and play-acting. As George Burns told aspiring actors in his 1980 memoir, "You've got to be honest. And if you can fake that, you've got it made."

Nevertheless, at first blush, one might object to applying this label to Republicans for any number of reasons. For starters, "organized hypocrisy" seems tame compared to the charges hurled daily against the party and its presidential standard-bearer Donald Trump. Perhaps an even bigger problem is that the label seems too moralistic, too subjective. And finally, as a description of a process, it seems vague. So I need to establish some definitions before we can see why this term is a fitting one for today's GOP.

The word "hypocrisy" comes directly from a word in Greek meaning "stage actor." In Greek theater, the actors wore masks; we all put on different masks for various roles, following rules and conventions we may not believe in but accept and conform to for the sake of various rewards—money, love, friendship, power, and so on. Hypocrisy can be a useful part of the social order.

But there's a big difference between ordinary hypocrisy and *organized* hypocrisy. Ordinary hypocrisy doesn't keep a person from recognizing one's masks and casting them off, if need be. Authenticity can still survive beneath the surface. Organized hypocrisy, however, is designed precisely to keep the mask on regardless of the wearer's efforts to shed it.

Organized hypocrisy arises in many ways—in institutionalized religion, business, and commerce, the law, government, the academy—but everywhere it has certain recognizable features. The group may start out legitimately hewing to the principles it claims to stand for. The people who control the enterprise, however, need the rank and file to believe in the mask, to wear it constantly, to maintain and defend it, and to convince the outside world that it is the group's true image—and they act accordingly. But eventually and often, if not always, these doctrinal enforcement functions increasingly make the mask the point, displacing or distorting the group's original purposes.

Organized hypocrisy varies in degree and kind. Some collective enterprises are less prone to it than others. Some are well protected by internal norms, rules, and safeguards. Political parties and movements, however, are highly vulnerable. Democratic government is no proof against it; indeed, it often provides fertile soil for it.

One more complication: organized hypocrisy varies not only in degree and kind, but also in intensity and internal awareness of the phenomenon. (Similarly, an individual hypocrite need not be a Uriah Heep, consciously bent on deceiving others about his real character and purposes while acting solely for his own advantage. He can and often does believe in his mask, like the Pharisee in Jesus' parable, grateful to God that he was not a sinner like the Publican.) The most effective hypocrisy, individual or organized, includes sincere belief. It is hard to be a perfect cynic. Consider Dostoyevsky's Grand Inquisitor, or, for an historical example, Talleyrand's career from the Old Regime through the French Revolution and the Napoleonic Empire to the restored Bourbons and the Orleans monarchy. For current examples, read Jane Mayer's *Dark Money*, on the current role of the super-rich in American politics.

The essential criterion dividing organized hypocrisy from its ordinary counterpart isn't the dominant motive of the actors, but the distance between the organization's stated purposes and its actions behind the mask. Measuring that distance can sometimes be difficult, but in the case of political parties and regimes it is frequently clear-cut. There are ample historical examples on this score. When a one-party regime puts the maxim "*Arbeit Macht Frei*" over the gates of one of its most notorious death camps; when the slogan "Let a Thousand Flowers Bloom" leads to millions of human heads rolling; when "democratic centralism" means Stalinist dictatorship complete with purges, extinction of classes, show trials, and ethnic cleansing, we see organized hypocrisy at its worst.

These extreme examples aren't the most instructive for our purposes, but many more litter the halls of history. Most revolutions, liberation movements, populist risings, and democratic regimes in modern history have failed; most of these failures resulted in the degradation of the original ideals and goals into a hardened, compulsory mask of organized hypocrisy. Witness the post-Risorgimento Kingdom of Italy; revolutionary France from 1792 on; virtually all the regimes in central and east-central Europe after 1918; the efforts at a union of South Slavs into a single Yugoslavia; the history of most regimes in post-Bolivar Latin America; and other recent and current examples in Africa, Asia, and the Middle East. Political movements set out with vast goals necessary to mobilize political consent if not active support; when some of these goals prove impossible even to pursue, let alone achieve, the regime invariably invents reasons for delay even as it entrenches itself in power. George Orwell understood this syndrome and depicted it well in *Animal Farm*.

Nor does this sort of thing happen only in countries with little experience of constitutional regimes and democratic institutions and practices. In the United States, the oldest and most solid liberal, constitutional, representative democracy in the world, democracy has already broken down twice.

The first failure occurred almost at the very beginning, after 1776, when the new American confederated government proved unable either to support the war adequately or, once independence had been gained largely through foreign arms and incredibly good luck in international politics, to govern its territory and meet its international obligations. This pre-Constitutional Convention breakdown was not due to organized hypocrisy, but it does point to a recurring problem with populist democratic regimes.

The original American government had to be replaced by a stronger federal union with a constitution that was liberal and republican but democratic only to a limited degree. This arrangement in turn broke down in 1860–65, for reasons that did involve organized hypocrisy. The Southern states and the Southern wing of the Democratic Party, having joined the Union and having accepted the Constitution on the basis of the toleration and accommodation of the institution of slavery in some states on the assumption that national problems arising from it would be handled by compromise, came to insist that chattel slavery be recognized as a permanent, untouchable basis for society in much of America, sanctioned and legitimated by the laws of God, nature, science, and the Constitution. They demanded the right to leave the Union whenever, in their view, their inherent right to preserve, develop, and expand this political and social order was threatened. Meanwhile, the interwoven racial, religious, class, economic, and social attitudes, interests, and motives actually driving these Southern political demands—which were understood privately to one degree or another by the slaveholding elite—were hidden or denied.

So with these examples before us, in what specific sense has the Republican Party become an organized hypocrisy? The drastic change that has overtaken the GOP, and that has plunged the American party system into a crisis of dysfunction, can be traced to the overall outcome of the Reagan revolution of the 1980s. Its mantras are familiar: "Morning in America," "a rising tide lifts all boats," government as the problem and not the solution to national problems. That revolution, which seized the GOP, championed less regulation of business, the selective devolution of power from Washington to the states and localities, lower taxes especially on corporations and the wealthy, freer trade and globalization, reliance on rational business decisions and the self-regulating market for growth and stability, increased defense spending and a more unilateralist foreign policy. All these have been tried—and not only by Republicans, of course—and the public perception of the results over the long run has grown increasingly skeptical.

Some explanations of these results, especially in the critical economic sector, involve technical terms experts quarrel over, most of them centering on the financialization of capitalism. The main outcomes, however, are easily seen and sensed: the decline of American industry, a flight of jobs, plants, and industries abroad, bubbles in crucial sectors (savings and loan, housing, banking, the stock market), a Great Recession narrowly kept from turning into a Great Depression by massive government intervention and bailouts mainly of Wall Street banks, major costly wars and foreign interventions now seen as largely unnecessary and counterproductive (though these cannot be tagged a Reagan-era legacy, for the two Reagan Administrations were not particularly interventionist)—and, above all, a growth in inequality unprecedented since the 1870s. All this has produced an economy, society, and government increasingly rigged in favor of the rich and powerful against the middle and lower classes. The so-called populist revolts in both main parties, though different in character and purpose, both stem mainly from this widespread discontent.

This is the kind of situation that in the past led leaders and forces in both parties to re-examine their party's mask, the image and principles it showed to the world, and to attempt repairs, reform, or at least some renovation and adjustment. Both parties have gone through this sort of process in the past, including the GOP—in its formation in the 1850s after the division between Northern and Southern Whigs over slavery, under Teddy Roosevelt before World War I, under Willkie, Dewey, and Eisenhower against isolationism and McCarthyism in the 1940s and 1950s. Were it not for Nixon's personal character problems and their consequences, the historical judgment on the Nixon-Ford presidency now might be that it was one of useful changes and moderate reforms in economic and foreign policy. So why is this not happening now? Why have the GOP elites not re-examined their mask and attempted to change it?

Again the general answer is fairly plain and widely recognized. The same trends and policies that, pollsters tell us, have led a majority of citizens to believe the country is headed in the wrong direction have also proved highly profitable for powerful groups and associations promoting them, with connections to the GOP vital to the party financially and for electoral purposes. At the same time and partly as a consequence, the party itself has moved ideologically sharply to the Right; it is no longer comprised of moderate and conservative camps, but is split even more sharply between older establishment conservatives and newer radicals at odds over major issues of national policy. As a result the Party has fallen into a defensive-aggressive stance that unites it only in opposing whatever the Democrats try to do, while continuing to insist that the GOP's principles and policies have actually worked to set the country on the right course and would succeed again once the rival party and other evil forces are defeated. Dissenters and nonconformists are held in line, disciplined, or purged by various organizational, electoral, and financial means. This has succeeded after a fashion until now, never yielding the GOP full power or control over the national agenda, but keeping it sufficiently in command of enough strategic heights in Congress, the states, and the Supreme Court to obstruct Democratic programs and maintain outward party unity under the mask.

This broadly describes the growth and development of organized hypocrisy. One sees more specific evidence of it in the GOP's responses to the particular national problems and challenges confronted since Reagan. (Not that the Republicans have alone been responsible for the neoliberal globalization story; the Rubin-Summers wing of the Democratic Party played a major role in shaping the disaster that has followed.) These challenges can be divided into two main categories; the first is centered on economics, and the other on a range of issues less directly related to economics and business (foreign policy, guns, violence, and crime, health care, labor unions and right-to-work laws, social welfare programs, race, women's and gender issues, immigration, terrorism and anti-terrorism, education, child care, climate change and environmental issues, the federal government's reach and power versus state and local control, and various constitutional questions among them). The two categories are obviously linked, most of the latter involving powerful economic factors and interests, but still the lists taken together are long and diverse.

What is striking, however, is not only how the GOP's basic policies and proposed solutions have stayed much the same, but also how its responses to attacks and complaints about its policies and actions in most cases of both sets of national problems and issues has also shown a similar unchanged pattern. It consists of a mixture of studied ignorance and indifference toward the alleged problems, direct denial, dismissal of difficulties as minor and temporary or signs of growing pains, denunciation of the complaints as purely partisan and the plaintiffs as unpatriotic, shifting the blame, blaming the victim, scapegoating, distracting public attention with other dangers and threats, and, while professing genuine concern and sympathy for those affected by the problems, proposing the same policies and measures as solutions. Here is organized hypocrisy in action.

Two examples serve to illustrate this. The first is the Republican response to the central socioeconomic issue and primary source of the present discontent: growing inequality, the steep rise in the economic and political power of the 1 percent and the decline of the middle class, promoting the growing influence of unelected wealthy, powerful associations and corporations on national and state government—government of, by, and for the rich and powerful. Though economists date the surge in economic inequality from the late 1970s, the issue did not emerge as a serious public one until after the turn of the century. Reagan's optimism and supply-side economic promises—"a rising tide lifts all boats"—plus the recovery from the stagflation of the Ford-Carter years, the relatively good times under George H. W. Bush, and the spurt in GDP, rise in employment, and budget surpluses achieved during the Clinton years served to veil it. All this changed in George W. Bush's Administration with its tax cuts, business slump, rise in unemployment, deficits, costly wars and occupations fought on credit, and with it the emerging consciousness of a widening gap between the very wealthy and the rest, of Wall Street versus Main Street.

The initial Republican response was to ignore this as a serious political issue, deny that it was happening or significant, and denounce even raising the question as un-American, socialist, or Communist-inspired. Bush repeatedly gave the party's answer in his flat, didactic way: "That's preaching class warfare!"

It soon became impossible even for Republican hardliners to maintain that line. The financial crisis shook even Alan

Greenspan's belief in the self-correcting, self-regulating market, and forced Bush's treasury secretary Henry Paulson, a staunch neoliberal, to seek and gain Democratic support for a massive, unprecedented government intervention and bailouts, mainly of Wall Street banks, to save the global banking system and avert another Great Depression. Neither this, however, nor the relative success of the Federal government's intervention initiated under Bush and continued and expanded under Obama in preventing a national and global descent into another Great Depression made the GOP abandon or alter its belief in the magic of the free, unregulated market and the dangers to prosperity and freedom of government interference in it.

Nor did it matter that under Obama the economy steadily if slowly recovered from the Bush Great Recession. Whatever its private analysis of what had happened, the GOP's public response was to ignore what caused the crisis and its own role in creating it, treat George Bush as an un-person and his administration's policies as non-factors. It laid all the blame for problems of slow recovery and unemployment on Obama and the Democrats, and issued predictions of impending failure and doom, all while carrying on a consistent, organized campaign to obstruct the Obama programs at every stage, even by serious efforts to shut down the federal government. All this was done in order to force through a program of austerity, limited government, tax reduction, and various incentives for businesses. This approach divided the country more deeply and helped reduce the public's regard for Congress to the lowest levels ever, especially for Republicans. That result eventually stimulated a more conciliatory approach, epitomized by Paul Ryan's rise within the GOP establishment, but it left the party's image mixed and the party itself deeply divided.

Every Republican candidate for president during the 2016 campaign season has felt pressure to meet the present discontent with ideas for curing the nation's economic problems and healing its growing inequality and divisions. Yet every such proposal during the primary campaign, even from so-called moderates, included most of the neoliberal nostrums that had promoted inequality in the first place—more tax cuts for everyone, including the extremely wealthy, smaller government, less government spending and regulation of business, abolition of some programs (especially Obamacare), and cutbacks in others as wasteful fiscally and harmful in their effects—all based on the premise that the real solution for America's economic and social malaise lies in vaguely defined efforts to encourage entrepreneurship and risk-taking.

And the vaguest plan of all has been Donald Trump's. What is his view on tax reform, notably corporate tax reform and inheritance taxes? It's not clear. What's his view on collective bargaining? The girth of minimum wage rises? On bilateral as opposed to multilateral trade negotiations? What would having specifics on these kinds of questions matter anyway with a candidate who pulls a stunt like visiting the Mexican President only to return with a speech that casts doubt over one of the main planks of his campaign, that on immigration?

A second example is more striking still: the GOP's response to the death of Supreme Court Justice Antonin Scalia and the need to fill the vacancy created. This question, for all its major consequences and implications, is very different from the issue of how to deal with economic inequality and middle-class insecurity. That problem has multiple causes and aspects, affects almost everyone, and is bound to be contentious. Filling the vacancy is nothing like this; it should be uncomplicated. The procedure for filling a vacancy is settled clearly and concisely in the Constitution, which allows the president to nominate Supreme Court justices, with the advice and consent of the Senate. It fits in perfectly with the Constitution's general principles regarding the separation of powers, an independent judiciary, and checks and balances between the branches of government.

The GOP, however, faced the possibility that replacing the former leading conservative justice might switch the Court from the 5–4 conservative majority it had enjoyed since George W. Bush to a 5–4 liberal one, changing the probable outcome of several major cases now pending and threatening in the future to overthrow earlier decisions vital to Republican interests. Senate Majority Leader Mitch McConnell therefore announced, without any vote or debate by the Senate or even the Republicans in it, that the Senate would not hold hearings on President Obama's nominee, Merrick Garland. He gave as his reason, "Let the people's voice be heard." The "people's voice," he implied, would be silenced were a president in his last year in office permitted to influence the future composition of the Court before the next president and Congress were elected.

This was not even remotely true. McConnell acted for obvious political reasons, having nothing at all to do with "the people's voice." Perhaps he chose this tack because the nominee himself was professionally and ideologically untouchable to any reasonable person. But it amounted to unvarnished hypocrisy. The Founders made the Supreme Court, the ultimate arbiter of the American constitutional order, the least democratically accountable of the three branches of government. Indeed, everyone knows, especially members of Congress, that in a liberal representative constitutional system, democracy means reaching governmental decisions on legislation through open discussion and debate by elected representatives, and the execution of the laws by an administration with a democratically elected chief executive. It does not mean direct expression of the putative people's will by acclamation via a town meeting, mass assembly, plebiscite, mob action, polls, revolutionary seizure of power, or any other similar method. Clearly, the question of how a vacant seat on the Supreme Court should be filled during an election year will not even appear on any ballot on any government level in November, nor will any reference or information relevant to it be forthcoming either in voting booths or outside them. Even Mitch McConnell knows this. His appeal to let the "people's voice" be heard is an echo of the old demagogic principle of *vox populi vox dei*—one that helped undermine the Roman Republic and other republics over the centuries.

In this instance, moreover, McConnell did not even try very hard to preserve his mask. Shortly after President Obama nominated Garland, Wayne LaPierre, the leader of the National Rifle Association, announced that he had looked at Garland's record and had concluded that he would not meet the NRA's standards for interpreting the Second Amendment. McConnell's response was that he could not imagine a Republican-led Senate confirming a nominee unacceptable to the NRA. The Republican watchword became in effect: *vox NRA vox dei*.

This was not surprising coming from McConnell, who had announced in 2008 that his prime goal was to make Obama a one-term President, and after failing in this effort in 2012 devoted himself to obstructing everything Obama and the Democrats were attempting to accomplish. He is the nearest thing possible in a democracy to a Soviet apparatchik, concerned solely with maintaining the party's power and his own—an Andrei Gromyko with a similar amount of charm.

What is more significant is that his strategy met so little Republican opposition in the Senate or elsewhere, despite the widespread public outcry and petitions against it. Only one Republican senator actually broke ranks, Susan Collins of Maine, while another alleged moderate, Mark Kirk of Illinois, hoping to save his seat in a blue state, supported holding hearings but carefully indicated that he would stick with the party on the question of confirmation. The Republicans could of course have opted to hold hearings and then reject Garland, but this would have been embarrassing, forcing Republican senators to explain why a moderate, highly qualified jurist whom they had previously approved for a high judicial post was unacceptable to them now.

If McConnell's stunt represents the most flagrant example of GOP organized hypocrisy, it is far from unique. There are many more examples, on taxation, climate change, environmental degradation, and more. The House of Representatives under GOP control has been as bad or worse: seven House investigations of the Benghazi attack costing taxpayers millions of dollars and countless wasted hours of Congressional and governmental time and yielding nothing beyond denunciations of Hillary Clinton and media attention; sixty-odd House votes to repeal or defund the Affordable Care Act without even indicating what would replace it, knowing these were doomed to failure in advance; Paul Ryan's refusal as House speaker to permit the House even to discuss gun control measures following a terrorist attack in Orlando, his labeling a joint Congressional-Democratic sit-down demonstration trying to force a discussion as a political stunt, and his threat of disciplinary action over it. Ryan may not enjoy orchestrating organized hypocrisy as much as McConnell does. He knows, however, what happens to Republican leaders, however conservative, who fail to fulfill the insatiable demands of Tea Party radicals, and he does the job efficiently.

If the argument thus far makes a case for labelling the current GOP an organized hypocrisy, it still leaves questions and objections unanswered. I merely mention certain of these to indicate that I recognize them and have some notions about replies, in order to concentrate finally on a bigger question to come. First: "If what you say is correct, would it not suggest that Donald Trump's populist challenge to the GOP establishment is useful in shaking the party up, forcing it to lift the mask on some traditional issues and to pay more attention to the alienated lower and middle classes?"

Perhaps, but we will know the answer to that question only if he wins, and some many months after the election. For now, all that can be said is that Trump has pulled off a hostile takeover of the GOP, but from inside. He deviates from the mainstream GOP line on many issues, notably culture war ones, but instead of directly challenging or overthrowing the party's organized hypocrisy, he is outdoing it. He is, in effect, selling essential elements of it to the GOP base in the way an unscrupulous salesman defeats more traditional competitors—through emotional manipulation laid on a certain vulgar charisma, and no shortage of untruths.

Second: "Perhaps so, but is that not the political game both parties play in this era? Isn't the Democratic party likewise an organized hypocrisy, making the only question which one is likely to do more good and less harm?"

Certainly the Democrats have their flaws and their problems. But whereas the Republicans proved too weak from division to resist an insurgency within their midst, the Democrats managed to accommodate an insurgency without being bowled over by it. So rises a certain irony. Will Rogers's famous quip, "I do not belong to any organized political party—I'm a Democrat," still holds true in a sense. The party is not organized enough, has too little party discipline and unified doctrine, is too inclined to compromise and triangulation, and embraces too many diverse interests, causes, and groups to rise or sink into organized hypocrisy. Until the Trump hostile takeover, the GOP's capacity for organization and discipline—and hence the capacity to don masks—rested on the leadership's need to control significant division within its own ranks. The Democratic leadership was able to adapt its views to maintain its position; the Republican leadership resisted change, and failed to maintain its position.

Ordinary hypocrisy, of course, does show up in the usual ways among the Democrats. Democrats are also a part of pay-to-play Washington, and have been known to say things publicly that do not reflect their private understanding. Politics show up, too. Had positions been reversed, could one have imagined a Democratic Senate leader delaying consideration of a Supreme Court nominee in an election year for similar political reasons? The Democrats, after all, have not been above engaging in partisan shenanigans without clear precedent: Take Harry Reid's "nuclear option" as a case in point. That said, I doubt that a Democratic Senate would have acted in a similar way toward a Republican president because GOP obstructionism is rooted in an internal paralysis that leaves a "just say no" approach the only way to keep the party from melting away. The Democrats do not have that kind of problem nearly to the same degree. Their typical failing is that of Stephen Leacock's medieval knight who leaped on his horse and rode madly off in all directions.

This still leaves the decisive question unanswered, however: What is to be done? Rather than present voters with this complex argument, would it not be better to target and fight the main individuals and forces behind the problem—party leaders, dark money, Wall Street, great corporations, various right-wing ideologies, organizations and associations, or some combination of these? I cannot claim that seeing the GOP as an organized hypocrisy somehow offers any quick fix or cure. I do think, however, that it can help define and clarify the goal, strategy, and tactics needed now.

First, the notion of the GOP as an organized hypocrisy underlines what is at stake in the coming election—not just who will win what offices, or where the country will go in the future (to the Right, Left, or middle of the road), but the long-term stability of the two-party system. The government cannot function and meet the problems of a rapidly changing country and world with one party working according to the normal rules of democratic politics (albeit imperfectly) and the other operating as an organized hypocrisy. It thereby clarifies the issue over which the election ought to be fought. It is not simply a contest between Hillary Clinton and Donald Trump for the presidency, or Democrats and Republicans for the control of the houses of Congress and of statehouses and legislatures. More important than these outcomes, more important even than all the issues and concerns in domestic and foreign policy connected with them, the elections are about whether the Republican Party as presently constituted is fit for a constitutional, liberal democratic, representative, federal republic such as the United States.

This in turn defines how the Democratic Party should contest this election. It should have three main goals in mind. The first is to defeat Trump, which seems easy at first blush but may not prove to be so. The second, more difficult, is to wrest control of the Senate and if possible the House from the GOP. The third goal, however, is to help the GOP by means of these defeats to return to its senses and restore it as a normal, sane, reform-minded conservative party.

One can imagine the hoots of derisive scorn and laughter, and the charges of hypocrisy too, that would greet a Democratic announcement that this was one of the party's goals in the campaign. Yet this goal needs to be considered seriously and explained and defended in the campaign. The Democratic Party should not seek to destroy the Republican Party, or even, as some shriller Republicans want to do to the Democratic Party, to reduce it to such size that it could be drowned in the bathtub. Democrats ought to be sensible enough to know that they need a serious Republican Party as a rival if the American political system is to work over the longer term.

The worst mistake Democrats could make in this presidential race is to allow it to become a popularity contest. Of course attacks on Hillary Clinton have to be countered and can be. Yet this defense and counterattack has not only to be conducted with dignity and based on evidence but also integrated into the main Democratic theme: that the Republican Party that offers America Donald Trump as its candidate is as unfit to govern as he is, and needs to be brought to its senses by a massive defeat at all national and state levels of government.

The same holds for the many individual issues and causes each side advocates. These are important; the differences are usually real and significant. But the central question remains the choice of which party should govern—one that is reliable, serious, and that can be counted on at least to try to do what it promises, even if what it promises amounts to small ball in a time of crisis, or one so mired in organized hypocrisy it can only offer fear-mongering, bombastic rhetoric, and empty promises.

The charge of organized hypocrisy may also have some tactical value. A police state can maintain a system based on it indefinitely by controlling communications, information, and the means of coercion (witness North Korea). A working democracy with reasonable civil liberties and regular elections cannot, however—not simply because ultimately the voters decide and because the condition is much harder to conceal, but also because awareness of it can have a powerful effect on the positions of those in power. Hypocrisy uncovered is a particularly repellent trait, even or especially for politicians, evoking an array of reactions that can weaken and chip away at the mask.

There are signs that this may be happening now in Republican ranks—that the mask is crumbling from within. The most obvious evidence lies in the long list of notable Republican leaders and pundits who have left the camp, or intend to sit this campaign out. Whether this rejection will show up among the rank-and-file remains to be seen, but polls increasingly show a widening gap between Republican voters on the whole and the party on many issues. This is something Democrats should highlight, exploit, and tie to the general charge of organized hypocrisy.

Even if somehow this did help, and the 2016 elections did produce a Democratic sweep, the problem of deadlock and dysfunction would not thereby have been solved. The sources of the problem go deeper than party politics, into the fabric of the country and its people, and will be harder to cure. One of the disturbing aspects of the current campaign is the boundless depths of superficiality and trivia it has revealed, and the apparently insatiable public appetite for them.

This, of course, is what Trump feeds on. To call him a demagogue is too mild, even flattering. Demagogues are often people of a certain stature and depth—Hitler, Mussolini, Alcibiades, Shakespeare's Marc Antony, even Silvio Berlusconi; Trump completely lacks these qualities. He is a rabble-rouser, a fear monger conjuring up or exaggerating threats from which he alone can save people, and one cannot account for his success to this point without recognizing that in America there is a considerable rabble to rouse, with a yearning for a savior.

Meanwhile most of the gravest and most difficult issues America faces—the financialization of capitalism, the decline in corporate investment in research and development, climate change and environmental degradation, the lag in education and childcare, and many more—go unnoticed or are denied by his supporters. The Democrats may not have impressive solutions to these problems to propose, but at least they do not dismiss their existence.

Party reform and even broader electoral reform will not solve these kinds of problems. But they represent a first essential step toward addressing them. That could at least give the country a fighting chance.

Sources

CHAPTER

1. ACDIS Occasional Paper, March 1991: 1–15
2. *Washington Quarterly*, April 1994: 25–43
3. *National Interest*, Winter 2001/02: 22–36
4. *American Conservative*, 10/21/2002: 8–20
5. *National Interest*, Winter 2002/03: 125–32
6. *Journal of the Society of Christian Ethics*, Fall/Winter 2004: 193–201
7. *American Conservative*, 6/7/2004: 7–9
8. *American Conservative*, 9/13/2004: 7–10
9. *American Conservative*, 10/25/2004: 14–19
10. *American Conservative*, 10/9/2006: 7–15
11. *American Interest*, 3/1/2006: 41–55
12. *American Conservative*, 9/24: 10–14 and 10/8/2007: 16–21
13. *American Interest*, 3/1/2008: 12–15
14. I. William Zartman, ed., *Imbalance of Power*, Boulder, CO, 2009: 61–87
15. Frederick Schneid, ed., *The Projection and Limitations of Imperial Powers, 1618–1850*, Leiden, 2012: 170–95
16. *American Interest*, 9/19/2016: 36–44

Index

Abu Ghraib prison, xvi, 122, 131, 132, 169, 171, 172, 173, 190
Affordable Care Act (US), 290. *See also* Obamacare
al-Qaeda, 56, 61, 62, 74, 82, 122, 126, 132, 133, 135, 136, 137, 138, 139, 140, 141, 142–3, 168
American Conservative (journal), ixn2, xv
American Interest (journal), ixn2, xviii
American Revolution/American Revolutionary War/American War of Independence, 251, 252, 253, 254, 256, 263, 267, 268
anarchical society, current international system as, 111
The Anarchical Society (Bull), 103
Animal Farm (Orwell), 282
anti-Americanism, 87
anti-Semitism, 87, 166, 171
Arab-Israeli conflict, xxiv, 19, 25, 37, 163. *See also* Israeli-Palestinian question/conflict
Arafat, Yasser, 19, 154
Art, Robert, vii
association-benefits, 36, 43, 44, 45

association-exclusion, 34, 37–8, 40, 41, 44, 45, 46, 113, 115
associations/alliances
formation of, 29, 89–90
to promote durable peace, 112–15
rule of thumb regarding, 30–1
US stand on Iraq as flatly contravening basic requirement for durable alliance, 88
use of sanctions by, 35, 37
Atlantic Revolution, 252

Bacevich, Andrew, vii
Bagram, 173
Baker-Hamilton Iraq Study Group, 243. *See also* Iraq Study Group
Baring, Evelyn (later Lord Cromer), 237
Beard, Charles A., 95–6
Benelux, 29
Berlusconi, Silvio, 295
Berra, Yogi, 150
Betts, Richard, vii
Biden, Joe, xviii, xxiv, 196
Bin Laden, Osama, 55, 56, 60, 67, 133, 135, 136, 137, 138–9, 140, 141, 142, 154

Bismarck, Otto von, 78n2, 103, 118, 163, 218n8, 228, 237, 258n9
Blair, Tony, 80, 108
blind optimism, cautions with, 150
Blix, Hans, 185, 245
Bobbitt, Philip, xiv–xv, 97–108
Boisdeffre, Raoul, 173
Bremer, L. Paul, 188
Bright, John, 280
Bull, Hedley, 103
Burckhardt, Jacob, 73
Burns, George, 280
Bush, George H. W., xi, 130, 264, 286
Bush, George W.
   characterization of administration of, 286
   as compared to John Kerry, 129
   and family-values conservatives, 124
   foreign policy direction under, 130–1, 143, 144
   and Iraq, xviv, 9, 10, 15, 95n4, 120, 123, 145, 159, 168, 171, 172, 175–6, 179, 184, 194–5, 201, 236
   and New World Order (NWO), 21, 23
   popularity of, 192–3
   on preventive war, 178
   re-election campaign (2004), 132, 146, 148
   as rejecting notion of declining utility of war and military force, 116
   on right of self-defense, 177
   and September 11, 2001, 57, 67, 205
   and War on Terror, 137
   on worldwide peace through democracy and free-market capitalism, 117
Bush Doctrine, 116, 131, 176, 214, 234

Carter, Jimmy, 286
Catherine the Great, 251
Chamberlain, Neville, 131
Charles V (Holy Roman Emperor), 221–2
Charles X (King of France), 269
Charles XII (King of Sweden), 223, 226
Cheney, Richard (Dick), 57, 80, 123, 132, 145, 173
Churchill, Winston, 73, 131
Clinton, Bill, xii, 108, 124, 130, 173
Clinton, Hillary, xviii, 146, 196, 204, 290, 293
coercive diplomacy, xxii, 60, 75, 83–4, 185, 186, 273
Cohen, Morris, 87
Cold War, xvi–xvii, xx, xxi, 36, 95, 149, 168, 178, 228, 241
Collins, Susan, 290
community, rise in, 6–7
compellence-deterrence, xi, 22, 23, 31–4, 36, 42, 44
Congress of Berlin (1878), 163
consensus and law, increasing reliance on in international politics, 6–7, 8
constitutional democracy, 114, 190

conventional deterrence, 75, 83–4, 245
Cromwell, Oliver, 124

d'Argenson, Marquis, 228
Dark Money (Mayer), 281
Davis, Lance, 270
de Gaulle, Charles, 181
Deák, István, 39n6
Declaration of Independence (US), 263
democracy
  breakdown of in US, 282–3
  constitutional democracy, 114, 190
  as goal in Middle East, 161
  promotion of in Iraq, 161
Democratic Party (US)
  flaws and problems of, 291–2
  Rubin-Summers wing of, xxiii, 285
Desert Storm, 69
deterrence
  coercion and, 83
  conventional deterrence, 83–4, 245
  successful deterrence, 84
  use of, 185, 186
  See also compellence-deterrence
Dewey, Thomas E., 284
Dimitrijević, Dragutin, 53
diplomatic judo, 12–13, 197
disenchanted loyalty, x, 17–20
Dreyfus, Alfred, 164–6
Dreyfus Affair, xviii–xix, 164–82
Duchhardt, Heinz, 261
Duke of Sully, 113

EC (European Community), 29, 38, 41
economics, preeminence of over politics, 12, 18
Eisenhower, Dwight D., 284
elections (US). *See* United States (US)
empire
  defined, 215–16
  distinction between empire and hegemony, 219–20
  functions of, 218–19
  from hegemony to empire, 212–45
  mirage of, 240
enemy, knowing the enemy, as principle in foreign-policy thinking, 136
epochal wars, 97, 98, 100, 101, 102, 103, 104, 106, 107
Esterházy, Marie-Charles-Ferdinand Walsin, 165
ethnic cleansing, xxii, 40, 41, 42, 43, 108, 194, 209, 273, 282
European Coal and Steel Community, 29
European Community (EC), 29, 38, 41
European Concert, 30n4, 35–6, 59, 61, 63, 113, 219, 273
European Free Trade Area, 29
European Union, 114
"Europe's Progress and America's Success, 1760–1850" (Schroeder), xxi
exceptionalism
  American exceptionalism, xxiii, 255, 279
  existential exceptionalism, 168

exclusion and denial, 35, 43, 44, 45

failed states, xvi, 115, 126, 161
failure
  acceptance of, 151, 157, 159, 234
  acknowledgment of, xvi, 214
  Americans as harvesting success from, 155–7
  in America's counterterrorist system, 125
  examples of, 5, 100, 108, 282. *See also* Iraq War
  "international failure to act," 39n6
  recognition of, 32, 46, 119, 148, 149, 149–50, 151, 156, 159, 161
  Saddam as, 14
  of sanctions, 75
fanaticism, 73
Ferdinand, Franz, 52, 53–4, 78n2
Ferdinand I (Holy Roman Emperor), 227
Ferdinand II (Holy Roman Emperor), 222–3
Fishback, Ian, 173
Fitzgerald, Patrick, 180
Fleury, Claude, 228
force
  declining utility of military force, 116
  Saddam's understanding of, 14
  steep rise in costs attached to use of armed force, 44–5
  use of, 8, 9, 23, 44, 57, 62, 68, 94, 135, 155, 161, 176, 209, 245

Ford, Gerald, 284, 286
"forever" wars, xiv
free-market economy, 117, 190
French Revolution, 97, 106, 178, 253, 281
Freud, Sigmund, 43

Gallagher, John, 215n3
Garland, Merrick, xxiii, 288, 290
Garner, Jay, 187–8
General Agreement on Tariffs and Trade (GATT), 37
Genovese, Kitty, 100
Gentz, Friedrich von, xii, 45
German Confederation, 30n4
Giuliani, Rudolph, 204
Gladstone, William, 236
globalization, xii, xxiii, 84, 98, 114, 117, 238, 283, 285
GOP. *See* Republican Party (US)
Gramsci, Antonio, 216
Greenspan, Alan, 286–7
Gromyko, Andrei, 290
Group of Seven, 37
Guantanamo, 131, 132, 171, 173
guaranteed civil and human rights, 114
Gulf War, ix, xii, 23, 31

Habsburg Monarchy, xiii, 53–4, 59, 63, 68, 106, 197–200, 222, 227
Habsburg-Valois wars, 97, 104
Hamas, 152, 159
Harkin, Tom, 264
hegemony
  and balance, 217n6, 218n8
  defined, 216–17

distinction between empire and hegemony, 219–20
functions of, 218
from hegemony to empire, 212–45
neo-realism on, 67–8
view of American hegemony by people in Middle East, 71–2
Hendrickson, David, vii
Henry, Hubert-Joseph, 165
Hezbollah, 152, 159
hidden agenda, looking for, as principle in foreign-policy thinking, 136
Hillgruber, Andreas, 218n8
Hitler, Adolph, ix, xx, 3, 31, 65, 68, 76n1, 92, 108, 224–5, 226, 295
Hobbes, Thomas, 103, 111, 212, 260
Holy Alliance, 274, 275–6
House, Edward M., 100
Hussein, Saddam
    characterization of, 7, 7n4, 14, 75, 80, 81, 83
    as compared to Mussolini, 7n4
    object of to unbalance and overthrow opponent, 154
    as only understanding force, 14
    and Palestinians, 12, 13
    propaganda advantage of, 12
Huttenback, Robert A., 270
hypocrisy, organized hypocrisy, 280–95

imperialism
    defined, 92, 167n1, 215
    of US to Iraq, 93

international action, meeting international threats and crises with, 60
international integration, rise in, 6–7, 8
International Monetary Fund (IMF), 37
international order, current enemies of, 109–19
international politics
    Americans' difficulty in coming to terms with limits in, 147
    applying long-term thinking and rational calculation to, 72
    Dirty Harry Callahan theory of, 123
    essential values in, 84–5
    history of, 90
    history of US in as success story, 249–79
    "progress" of, 257–8, 259
    role of in America's rise to greatness, 256
    war as easy to understand in, 111
international system
    as anarchical society, 111
    constructing viable one, 4
    current characterization of as anarchical society, 111
    empire and, 220, 226
    future of, 62
    hegemony and, 220, 226
    New World Order (NWO) as, 22
    origin of current one, 5, 27, 89, 112, 219, 265
    principles in evolution of, 77

international system (*continued*)
  role of in America's rise to greatness, 256, 259, 279
  understanding nature of contemporary one, 22
  US as enjoying extraordinarily privileged position within, 177
  US entrance to, 251, 252
international terrorism
  as common enemy uniting all governments, 204
  getting at supposed roots of, 61
  as menace to all decent states and societies, 55
  origin of threat of, 82
  struggle against as real war, 132, 133
  US as not country most menaced by, 141
  victory over, 58
Inter-Services Intelligence Directorate (ISI) (Pakistan), 55
Iraq
  American Embassy in, 162, 202
  British suppression of Arab revolt in (1919–21), 235
  case against preemptive war on, 75–96
  economic blockade of, 11–12
  fire in as preventable, 184
  redefining America's vital interests in, 202
  sanctions against as not working, 13–15
  US as arsonist in, 186, 187, 195, 196, 197
  US as generally supporting of in its war against Iran, 80
  US assault on (2003), xv–xvi, 8–9, 145. *See also* Iraq War
  US damage control strategy in, 120–1
Iraq Study Group, 202, 243
"Iraq: The Case against Preventive War" (Schroeder), 140
Iraq War
  American perspective on as marked by endless vistas of myopia, 189
  Bush administration as misleading American people, Congress, and international community about, 179
  Dreyfus Affair as compared to, 167, 169–82
  as failure, 145, 146, 147, 148, 151, 159, 163, 189, 192, 193, 235, 239, 240
  mismatch between goals of and the historical means and process supposed to achieve them, 190
  as mistake, 152
  origin of, 160
  what if US wins? 207–11
  as wrong, 194
ISI (Inter-Services Intelligence Directorate) (Pakistan), 55
isolationism, objections to, 72
Israel
  as elephant in the room, 163
  security interests of, 77, 95n4
  as supporting American war on Iraq, 74
  US regarded as guardian of, xiii, 139, 191

Israeli-Palestinian question/conflict, xii, xxiv, 13, 19, 37, 65, 66, 69, 139, 163, 208. *See also* Arab-Israeli conflict

judo, use of in international politics, 9, 11, 12–13, 13, 27–8, 154, 159, 197
Just Peacemaking (Stassen), 109, 110
"A Just, Unnecessary War: The Flawed American Strategy in the Persian Gulf" (Schroeder), ix, 3–20

Kant, Immanuel, 86, 113
Kennan, George F., 73
Kennedy, John F., 130
Kennedy, Roger, 270
Kerry, John, 129, 130–1, 146
Kierkegaard, Søren, 124
Kirk, Mark, 290
Kristol, William, 204

LaPierre, Wayne, 289
Layne, Christopher, vii
Leacock, Stephen, 292
League of Nations, 113
Leopold I (Holy Roman Emperor), 227
Lloyd George, David, 280
Long War of 1914–90, 97–8, 107
Lopez, George, 123
Louis XIV (King of France), 68, 223, 227

Mao Zedong, 156
market economy, 114, 187, 202, 230. *See also* free-market economy

Matthias (Holy Roman Emperor), 227
Mayer, Jane, 281
Mazarin, Jules, 227
McCarthy, Joe, 124, 284
McConnell, Mitch, xxiii, 288–90
Mearsheimer, John, vii
Merkel, Angela, 179
Metternich, Klemens von, xii, 45, 155
Meyers, Richard, 123
Micawberism, 195, 205
Middle East. *See also* Arab-Israeli conflict; Iraq; Iraq War; Israeli-Palestinian question/conflict
  America as not part of, 196–7
  central problems of, 191
  democracy as goal in, 161
  domestic critics of US foreign policy in, vii, xiv
  fires as threatening, 183, 185, 196
  need for peace in, 20
  view of American hegemony by people in, 71–2
military judo, 11
military victory, decline in utility of, 5, 8, 18, 19
Monroe Doctrine, 269, 271
Mueller, John, 168n2
Mussolini, Saddam as compared to, 7n4

Namier, Lewis B., 43, 150
Napoleon Bonaparte, 68, 92, 134, 220, 224, 225–6, 228, 231n27, 241–2, 254, 295
Napoleon III, 226n17

Napoleonic Wars, 106
National Interest (journal), ixn2, xiv
National Rifle Association (NRA), 289
NATO (North Atlantic Treaty Organization). *See* North Atlantic Treaty Organization (NATO)
neo-realism, on hegemony, 67–8
New World Order (NWO)
 compellence and deterrence in, 31–4
 and control of "lessons" of history, 43
 cynicism and despair about, 40
 dangers of ruin or repudiation to, 36–7
 "frontal assault" on, xvi
 maintenance of, 38–9
 methods where it is ineffective, 45–6
 origin of phrase, xi, 21, 23
 Persian Gulf War as giving birth to, 31
 promotion of, 35
 as requiring patience, 47
 rethinking of, 29–37
 United Nations as integral part of, 38
 use of term, 21, 22–4, 27, 44
 view of idealists about, 24–5
 view of realists about, 26
"The New World Order: A Historical Perspective" (Schroeder), x–xi, xii, 21–48
9/11. *See* September 11, 2001
9/11 Commission Report, 125–31
Nixon, Richard M., 284

North, Ollie, 123
North Atlantic Treaty Organization (NATO), 29, 38, 88, 108, 114, 219
NRA (National Rifle Association), 289

Obama, Barack, xxiii, xxiv, xxv, 204, 214, 287, 288, 290
Obamacare, 288. *See also* Affordable Care Act (US)
Operation Iraqi Freedom, xviii
Orwell, George, 282

Palestinian-Israeli question/conflict. *See* Arab-Israeli conflict; Israeli-Palestinian question/conflict
Pasic, Nikola, 53
Paulson, Henry, 287
Pax Britannica, 266–7, 274
peace
 as artificial, 111
 growth of/evolution of, 112–13
 as puzzle, 111–12
Peace of Augsburg, 104
Peace of Utrecht, 106, 227
Peace of Westphalia (1648), 89
peacemaking, just peacemaking, 109, 112
Pearl Harbor (December 7, 1941), 51
Persian Gulf
 America's flawed strategy in, 3–20
 Persian Gulf War as giving birth to NWO, 31
Peter the Great, 251
Petraeus, David, 195

Philip II (King of Spain), 222
Picquart, Georges, 165, 180
politics. *See also* international politics
  importance of remaining free, 37
  preeminence of economics over, 12, 18
Posen, Barry, vii
preemptive war
  alternatives to, 94
  case against, 74–96, 177
  pretext of, xv
preventive war, 85, 86, 95, 131, 175, 176, 178, 182, 185
Principl, Gavrilo, 52, 53–4, 55, 57

Reagan, Ronald, 130, 283, 284, 286
regime change, xv, xvii, 83, 161, 245
Reid, Harry, 292
Republican Party (US)
  as organized hypocrisy, 283–95
  Trump's hostile takeover of, 291–2
rewards, use of, 44
Rice, Condoleezza, 121, 123
Richelieu, 227
"The Risks of Victory" (Schroeder), 140
Robinson, Ronald, 215n3
Rogers, Will, 291
Roosevelt, Theodore (Teddy), 284
Rumsfeld, Donald, 120, 121, 123, 127, 173, 187
Ryan, Paul, 287, 290–1

Saddam Hussein. *See* Hussein, Saddam

sanctions
  cooperation regarding, 19
  failures of, 75
  impacts of, 28, 35, 37
  against Iraq as not working, 13–15
  need for, 44
Scalia, Antonin, 288
Schroeder, Paul W., vii–xxiv
Scott, H. M., 261
self-defense, right of, 177
September 11, 2001
  American government's response to, 59
  Bush's initial actions after, 205
  as compared to beginning of Great War (June–July 1914), 51–73
  evidence and probabilities of connection between Hussein or others in Iraqi regime and, 82
  intent of attacks on, 69, 70
  intention of operation on, 137, 138
  invoking memory of, 81
  9/11 Commission Report, 125–31
  as not a national tragedy, 71
  reactions to attack on, 135, 141–2
  real targets of attack on, 142
  requirements for strong action after attacks on, 141
Seven Years' War, xxi, 79n3, 131, 229, 250, 256
The Shield of Achilles (Bobbit), xiv, 97–108

"Shock and Awe," xv
St. Pierre, Abbé de, 113
Stalin, Joseph, 65, 81, 225
Stassen, Glen, 109
Suleiman, 192
Supreme Court (US), 288–9

Taliban, 55, 60, 62, 65, 67, 154
Talleyrand, 224, 281
Terror and Consent (Bobbitt), xiv–xv
terrorism. *See also* international terrorism
  actual and potential danger of, 115
  galvanizing world support in struggle against, 142–3
  Islamist terrorism, 126–7, 179
  as mostly concentrated on particular local and regional aims and directed against particular local enemies, 159
  resentment as feeding, 65
  survival from, 95
  war on, 56, 58, 60, 61, 64, 70, 74, 81, 122–3, 134, 135, 152, 181, 214. *See also* War on Terror
Thirty Years War, 89, 97, 106, 222, 227
Tito, Marshal, 216n4, 225
trading state, rise of, 4–5, 6, 20, 114
The Transformation of European Politics (Schroeder), ix
Treaty of Ghent, 269
Trump, Donald, xxiii, 280, 288, 291, 293, 294
Tucker, Robert, vii

unintended consequences, fear of, 194
United Nations (UN)
  America's failure to gain Security Council resolution authorizing use of force against Iraq, 184
  arms inspections by, 185, 245
  blockade against Iraq as imposed by, 15
  inspectors of in Iraq, 79–80
  as integral part of New World Order (NWO), 38
  and Saddam's invasion of Kuwait, 10–11
  and war and aggression, 113
United States (US)
  acquisition of independence by and subsequent expansion of, 254
  Affordable Care Act, 288, 290
  as alien presence in Middle East, 190–1
  Arab-Muslim reaction to power of, 70
  breakdown of democracy in, 282–3
  damage control strategy in Iraq, 120–1
  Declaration of Independence, 263
  as declared enemy to bin Laden, 138
  on definition of victory, 154–5
  Democratic Party. *See* Democratic Party (US)
  deterioration in world position of, 127

election (2000), 124
election (2004), 132, 195
election (2006), 147, 163
election (2008), 204
election (2016), xxiii, 280, 287–8, 292–3, 294
as engaged in broad global contest, 151–2, 154
as failing to act as responsible hegemon, 245
failure of in Cold War, xvi–xvii, xx, 149
fitness of for world leadership, 16–17
as generally supporting Iraq in its war against Iran, 80
as Great Satan in much of Muslim world, 139
incessant beating of war drum by, 152
indictment of political culture of, 47
and Iraq. *See* Iraq; Iraq War
as needing long-range strategy that recognizes centrality of foreign policy, 127
policy of as representing threat to world order, 116, 117–18
Republican Party. *See* Republican Party (US)
self-absorption of, 244
as self-acclaimed world leader of War on Terror, 140
Supreme Court, 288–9
terrorist leaders and groups as having declared war on, 153
unipolar world supremacy of, 214n1

War of Independence. *See* American Revolution/American Revolutionary War/American War of Independence
Urabi, Ahmed, 236
utopianism, 150, 187

victory
defined, 8–9
risks of, 51–73
Vienna Settlement, 271, 272, 274

Waldeck-Rousseau, René, 165–6, 171
Waldersee (general count), 78n2
Walt, Stephen, vii
war. *See also* epochal wars; *specific wars*
in Bush Doctrine, 116–17
decline in utility of major war as tool of statecraft, 114
as easy to understand in context of international politics, 111
"forever" wars, xiv
military victory in, 5–6
as natural, 111
preemptive war. *See* preemptive war
preventive war. *See* preventive war
problems in dealing with, 4
tension between *carpe diem* and *respice finem* in, 73
on terrorism. *See* terrorism, war on; War on Terror
terrorist leaders and groups as having declared war on US, 153

War of 1812, 17, 154, 265, 266, 269, 276–7
War of the Spanish Succession, 106
War on Terror, xiii, xiv, 122, 125, 132, 137, 138, 140, 143, 150, 154, 160, 168
Warner, John, 195
Washington Quarterly (journal), x
weapons of mass destruction (WMD), xv, 43, 75, 79–80, 81, 82–3, 84, 91, 94, 95, 115, 122, 137, 158, 168, 184, 185–6, 213, 245
Western European Union, 29
Westphalian system, 217
Wilkerson, Lawrence, 180
Wilkie, Wendell, 284
Wilson, Woodrow, 151

Wolfowitz, Paul, 123
World Bank, 37
world order
    impacts of inequities and deformities in, 115–16
    New World Order (NWO). *See* New World Order (NWO)
    US policy as representing general threat to, 116, 117–18
World War I
    causes of, 30, 64, 66, 275
    origins of, xiii, 107
World War II
    Germany's launch of, 148–9
    impact on American illusion that US could drop in and out of international system at will, 177–8
    origins of, 64